# TRIPP/NG
# OVER
# MYSELF

# TRIPPING OVER MYSELF

## A MEMOIR OF A LIFE IN COMEDY

by Shaun Micallef

*Hardie Grant*

BOOKS

Published in 2022 by Hardie Grant Books, an imprint of Hardie Grant Publishing

Hardie Grant Books (Melbourne)
Wurundjeri Country
Building 1, 658 Church Street
Richmond, Victoria 3121

Hardie Grant Books (London)
5th & 6th Floors
52–54 Southwark Street
London SE1 1UN

hardiegrantbooks.com

 A catalogue record for this
book is available from the
National Library of Australia

Tripping Over Myself
ISBN 978 1 7437 9 798 3

10 9 8 7 6 5 4 3 2 1

Design by Reg Abos
Photographs by Brent Lukey
Lyrics from *Rock 'n' Roll Is Where I Hide* © Dave Graney 1995
Excerpt from 'The Meaning of Life' © The Estate of John Clarke
Excerpt from *The Odd Couple* © 1966 by Neil Simon LLC;
copyright renewed 1994 by Neil Simon LLC
Typeset in 13/19 pt Adobe Garamond Pro by Kirbyjones
Printed and bound in Australia by Griffin Press, an Accredited ISO
AS/NZS 14001 Environmental Management System printer.

 The paper this book is printed on is certified against the Forest Stewardship
Council® Standards. Griffin Press holds FSC® chain of custody certification
SGSHK-COC-005088. FSC® promotes environmentally responsible, socially
beneficial and economically viable management of the world's forests.

Hardie Grant acknowledges the Traditional Owners of the country on which
we work, the Wurundjeri people of the Kulin nation and the Gadigal people of the
Eora nation, and recognises their continuing connection to the land, waters and culture.
We pay our respects to their Elders past and present.

# CONTENTS

*If you get into bed with the Devil,*
*he's not going to read you a story.*

# Introduction

I'M NOT SURE this book is such a good idea. No matter what I write or how it's written, the very fact that it's an autobiography is going to make some people think I'm a bit of a knob. After all, who the hell am I to think my life is worth reading about?

It's a good question.

In my nearly thirty-year career as a comedian, I've never thought to write about myself, and even though I've often played a character with my own name, it was never *really* me. Who on earth would pay good money or even flip on the TV to see that? On other planets, sure. But here?

Yet I've always been there somewhere in the roles I've played and the dialogue I've given myself and others. Abstracted, coded, sometimes the inverse of what I think or feel, there I am in full view, concealed.

It's often said that the great thing about being a comedian is you get to misbehave without consequences. If it's funny, that is. If it isn't funny, then you're in big trouble. I'm not sure what the point of laughter is in nature – maybe there isn't one and it's just a noise you make when your expectations are incongruously derailed – but socially it's supposed to be corrective. If you trip or fall or say the wrong thing, that ha-ha noise made by others supposedly chides you into doing or saying the right thing next time. Comedy is essentially just recreating those moments (or the *idea* of those moments) and so my career is really nothing more than an endless series of variations on those trips and falls and sayings of the wrong thing. That's it.

For some reason, our society places a value on the ability to come up with these variations and so I've been able to make a living out of it. Of course, I can do other things as well as trip and fall and say things wrong – and while those other things might be more dignified and perhaps even make for a *better* living, they're nowhere near as much fun.

I've loved comedy since I was a boy. I've loved laughing and I've loved making people laugh. As I grew older, I loved working out the mechanics of what made me laugh and I loved applying those lessons to my own efforts. Everyone who has ever told a joke has done this and, as anyone who has been on the receiving end of a joke knows, some people can do it better than others.

I guess that's what prompted me to write this book. To share with you what made me laugh, why it did and how

2

I learned to do it myself, so that eventually I ended up on TV. On the way, I did other things like grow up and fall in love and have children, and I thought I'd share that with you too. Though hopefully not enough to make you feel nauseous. In truth, I can't really tell you about the funny stuff without letting you in on some of the real-life stuff as well. It's all mixed in together. Being liked, getting rejected, triumph, failure, meeting my heroes, dealing with fools, coping with egos (including my own) – it's as much a day in the life as a day at the office. The real-life stuff has helped when the funny stuff hasn't worked out so well, and vice versa.

When you write a joke, it's perfect – you can hear it in your head; you can imagine how it will play and how it will land – but the only way you can prove it's funny is by having the audience laugh at it, and that means someone's got to get up and perform it. The thing is, though, it's never *exactly* the way you think it will be. Life's far messier than inside your head. Sometimes it's better, sometimes it's worse, sometimes the audience will just shrug and flip over to *Celebrity Bathrooms*. I don't believe in the perfectibility of humankind any more than I believe in delivering the perfect joke, but it should never stop any of us from trying.

See? I sound like a bit of a knob already.

Something else before we begin. I remember once starting to tell my wife what I thought was a very moving story from my childhood when she stopped me a few seconds in to point out it was *her* story. So, be warned that while all my stories

3

will be absolutely true, I can't vouch they didn't happen to somebody else. If at any stage during this book I tell you about the time my *Black Beauty* record got broken by bullies on my way home from Grade 1 show-and-tell, it's my wife you should feel sorry for.

Obviously, the last thing I want to do in these memoirs is recount a whole lot of memories, but I do want to share with you my earliest significant memory – and this one is *definitely* mine – before we get onto some sort of chronological narrative.

Okay, so I'm four years old and I'm playing the prince in a kindergarten production of *Sleeping Beauty*. The role requires me to mount a rocking-horse, ride to an imaginary castle, dismount, and kiss the princess on the cheek to awaken her. It was a lunchtime performance for our parents, and during the morning rehearsal I rode with such fury and dismounted with such gusto that the horse continued rocking through the all-important kiss, causing everyone watching to giggle.

Our teacher, Miss Brooks, told me that when we did the play for real, I was to make sure the horse had stopped rocking or else all the parents would laugh too. This note made no sense to me – *why wouldn't you want the laugh?* During the proper performance, I made the horse rock even longer. It killed and everyone looked at me. What's significant, I think, is that I remember instinctively *knowing* that I should pretend I hadn't noticed that the horse was still rocking as I knelt by the princess; that the laugh would be bigger and better if

I appeared unaware of what had happened. Either that or I wanted plausible deniability if Miss Brooks brought it up after the show.

Anyway, here now follows my life, more or less in the order it happened ...

## CHAPTER ONE

# Have I been a good boy?

IT'S 1962. The Cold War is hotting up with the Cuban Missile Crisis and John Glenn is orbiting the earth. My parents, though, have bigger fish to fry. It goes without saying that I don't remember actually being born, but on all the available evidence so far there is very little reason for me to believe that I wasn't.

I'm told my birth took place in Adelaide, South Australia: specifically, in the Ashford Community Hospital on Anzac Highway, not far from the HMS *Buffalo*, the Old Gum Tree, Glenelg Beach, the school I'd go to, the cinema I'd take my girlfriend to, the hotel with the revolving restaurant both of us would stay at one naughty night, the church we'd get married in, most things. Nothing was ever too far away from anywhere in Adelaide.

When I came into this world, a month earlier than expected, the house wasn't ready. No carpet, no phone, no cot. We didn't even have a car. When my mother went into labour, my father sprinted the three miles to her parents' so he could borrow theirs.

Our brand-new triple-fronted cream-brick house on the corner block of a former almond orchard must have been a paradise to my mother and father even without the carpet (for reasons that will become clear in a few pages' time). Of course, it was all I ever knew, so I had the luxury of thinking it was all a bit dull.

The house was one of many similar houses in a brand-new suburb six miles south-west of the city called Clovelly Park, named after the village in Devon it had so closely resembled before the farmland and vineyards were bulldozed to make way for the building of it. Our street was a fenceless dead-end leading into the back lot of the Chrysler factory. The newly assembled cars would be parked there in rows of a hundred or so for six months of the year, and once they had been shipped out it became a playground of old pipes and bits of wire. As a four-year-old I used to cut across this wasteland on my way to kindy, which was held in an old (it seemed, even back then) scout hall. These days, it's hard to imagine a child of four walking half a mile to kindergarten on his own, but this was 1966 and times were more innocent and the streets a lot safer. Plus, I was a pretty independent kid, although I remember returning home five minutes after being sent off the first time because I had some dust on my shoe and needed it cleaned.

Our house had one of those lightweight hollow-core doors at the back with a big key in it, but it was seldom locked. And even if you found yourself locked out, you could just slide a piece of paper under the door and then poke out the key with a stick. The key would fall onto the piece of paper, which you would then carefully retract with the key on top. Or you could borrow the neighbour's key because everybody had the same back door.

While most of the almond groves had been ploughed under, there was still a big ol' almond tree in our backyard which my sisters – once they came along – and I would shake and hit with a broom every year when the almonds were ripe (if almonds are ever 'ripe'). Next door and to the back of us was a state high school sprawling over several acres. There was a fence of sorts, but it was one of those low cattle ones made from fat wooden posts connected by two lengths of taut wire, so playing in the backyard was pretty much playing on one of the many football ovals that comprised the school's sports fields. My sisters and I weren't allowed to play outside when the students were practising javelin. Even when a taller and more solid corrugated-iron fence was erected in place of our old one, we would often go out into the backyard to find a javelin or two skewered into the lawn and several holes pierced in the new fence.

We weren't poor; at least, I never thought we were. We weren't well off either, by any stretch, but I didn't know that when I was growing up – though it must have been playing on my mind a little when, at the age of twelve, I decided to repaint the second-hand bike I got for my birthday just in case someone in the neighbourhood recognised it. Why I

9

chose sky-blue I don't know. Perhaps it was the most different colour to the original matt teal I could find, or perhaps it just complemented the sparkles in my banana seat. Any way you looked at it, it was a classy set of wheels and I didn't mind being noticed just so long as it wasn't for the wrong reasons.

The first time I became aware that some people 'had money' and others didn't was when I heard my mother use the expression while talking with my father about some friends whose place they had gone to for dinner. I stopped playing with my cars under the radiogram and listened in. What was so remarkable about having money, I wondered. I had money. A sixpence a week in pocket money. It was all in my money box – a tin replica of the Savings Bank of South Australia. I even had a proper coin collection – pennies my grandfather would give me and which I organised in an album in yearly sequence. But no, my mother explained when I asked her later, she meant that these people 'thought they were better' than she and my father. I didn't really understand what that meant either, but I could hear in her voice that it bothered her. I don't think they ever went over there again.

I could always tell when my mother and father were going out. She smelled of perfume and had her wig on. My mother had started turning grey by her early twenties and she had a couple of wigs in the cupboard that she'd alternate. I thought this was normal and maybe it was if you didn't have the money to colour your hair back then. I don't know how convincing the wigs were, but they were certainly fun to play with. Years later they ended up, one on my head and the other fashioned into a beard, in a university revue. In the ultimate of ironies, they'd been spray-painted grey as I was playing an old man.

My father didn't wear a wig but he did speak with an accent. A Maltese one. This didn't seem all that odd even though none of my friends' fathers spoke that way. Had my mother not pretended she couldn't understand him now and then as a joke, I probably wouldn't have noticed.

Not so for the rest of Australia at the time, however. It was quite a big deal back in the 1950s to partner up with a so-called New Australian, but my grandparents were very broadminded and didn't stand in my mother's way. 'If you want to marry a Chinaman, you go right ahead,' my grandmother had told her – and with that blessing, she did.

Two years later, I turned up; but, really, I had existed long before then. In a small country schoolroom up in South Australia's mid-north, my then teenage mother-to-be daydreamed about having a son and practised writing the name 'Shaun' over and over again in the margin of her exercise books. I didn't find it at all odd when my mother told me this story years later and I still don't. I like that I was conceived of before I was conceived; that I was an idea first, the product of some thought and consideration, of writing and rewriting. I was a character with a name waiting to be cast – and, let's face it, it was the role I was born to play.

I was a very neat boy: well turned out in shirts and shorts sewn by my mother and grandmother, both excellent

11

seamstresses. They also knitted, so each winter I would always have a new jumper or cardigan (and once, to my dismay, a football guernsey*). I could always tell who made which item of knitwear because my grandmother smoked like a thurible and it would take a few months for her jumpers and cardigans to be rid of the reek of Marlboro country. Nanna sat in the same corner chair by her lounge-room window for forty years as she smoked and knitted and my grandfather sat opposite her in his corner, reading and watching the television. After they'd both passed away, we took down the curtains and the one on her side weighed ten kilograms more because of the tar.

My favourite Nanna cardigan was an especially soft brown one with a border of golliwogs around the middle. I'd be rightly shunned if I wore it today but times were different back in the 1960s. Casual and Sunday-best racism were as much a part of our national character as drunkenness, swearing, bad teeth, polio and thinking cricket was interesting. For years we had a tin of shoe polish in the cupboard under the laundry sink that featured a grinning black-and-white minstrel, which even as a small child who knew no one of colour I thought was a bit unnecessary, particularly given no one in our family owned any black-and-white shoes.

Sadly, I got to wear my favourite cardigan only a few times. After a hayride I went on, it was always a bit itchy so I had to retire it. I did, however, keep it in my wardrobe so I could

---

* West Torrens. I was forced to wear it to a game they made me go to.

look at it occasionally because it made me feel happy. There is nothing weird about this.

The hayride was in Lochiel, where my mother was born and went to school to doodle my name: not far from Port Wakefield and even closer to South Hummocks, Barunga Gap, Mount Templeton and Lake Bumbunga. If you've never heard of these places, you're not alone. I had to look them up to write this paragraph. Nothing much of interest happened around where my mother grew up, so nowhere there tends to ring any bells today; except for Snowtown, of course. The famous Bodies in Barrels case several decades later would really put the area on the map, but back in the more innocent '40s and '50s, Lochiel was better known for its salt products than its proximity to decomposing murder victims.

My mother's father worked for the Australian Salt Company. During the summer, when Lake Bumbunga went dry, the pink salt left behind was collected, cleaned, sorted, put in sacks and sent to Adelaide, where it found its way into food and eventually arteries all over the country. My grandfather, though, didn't do any of the actual collecting, cleaning, sorting or packing. He worked in the office. Eventually he became manager of the company, inheriting the position from his father-in-law.

My mother would sometimes go back to Lochiel for school reunions or Wicker Man–like harvest festivals and my father and I would go with her; occasionally I'd go there on my own and stay on the farm of some family friends during the school holidays, when my mother's hands were otherwise full with whichever of my baby sisters had come along. These farm visits were a little lonely because there was nothing to do and no one to do it with, so I just played with the sheepdog, a blue heeler with no name (unless it was Get Around). I would build forts with bits of wood, galvanised iron and any other detritus I found strewn about the property that wasn't too heavy to drag to the back of the sheds. There was also an abandoned pigsty, but that was not nearly as much fun as it sounds.

The family friends who ran the farm were the parents of two girls with whom my mother had gone to school. The daughters had grown up, moved out and married and I stayed in one of their rooms, which frankly was a little girly even for a pampered city boy like me. As it would have been unthinkable for someone my age to address an adult by their first name, I was invited to call these family friends Auntie and Uncle, which I did even though I knew they were just pretend ones. Anyway, they were nice people and they looked after me well, although most of the time I was pretty much left to my own devices (of which there were none in those days).

When I wasn't playing with the dog, building forts or hanging around the pigsty, I would occasionally pop down the shops with my pretend auntie to be bought a comic book or sometimes accompany my pretend uncle as he fed the sheep. This was actually quite exciting as he would often leave me in the cabin of the truck while it rolled down the hill and climb into the back to kick slices of hay bale to the sheep following behind. I was probably about seven years old. I was forbidden to touch the steering wheel.

The shearing sheds were fun too. They were full of loud men in filthy singlets and I got to play in the bales of fleece and get covered in lanolin. Most of those shearing used electric shears but there were a few men still using hand-operated ones. I was allowed to hold a pair if I was careful; they were heavier than I thought and rustier. The electric ones were faster but not always safer and I remember a young blood-spattered shearer having to stitch together an enormous gash he'd made in a sheep, to the good-natured jeering of his comrades. My uncle tried to reassure me that the animal was absolutely fine, worried, I suppose, that what I'd witnessed would scar me forever. It certainly did the sheep. Later, I saw the young shearer crying out by the side of the sheds and being comforted by his two older brothers.

I was invited to shear a sheep but declined. I guess they were kidding me, as they did about almost everything. That my name was a homonym for 'shorn' was a great source of amusement to them. 'Shaun a sheep yet?' they would ask. 'Nah, still human,' my uncle would reply and everybody would laugh, including me, even though it wasn't all *that* funny. There was a lot of that. Even things that weren't remotely jokes were greeted with gales of laughter. Asking after each other's wives, someone's ute, a sandwich, an item of clothing, hair colour – all could provoke mirth if delivered with enough bonhomie.

It wasn't the first time I'd experienced laughter in the service of something other than the comic. I'd seen this sort of thing with the local butcher back in Adelaide, but I was more used to jokes and gags; and at least when the butcher chortled 'Hot enough for you?' every time my mother and I walked into his shop, I could tell he was being ironic. With the shearers, there was barely the shape of a joke or gag anywhere, and laughter was being used as a sort of bonding agent for a group of men working long hours together in a hot, noisy, fly-infested shed. It was about having good humour rather than being humorous and, frankly, it did make the day seem a lot less miserable than it probably was.* Because a lot of what was being said wasn't even trying to be funny, though, and they were all laughing uproariously at what seemed to me to be perfectly normal observations, I spent most of my time looking baffled. Of course, they laughed like drains at this as well.

My job was to collect the usually unbloodied fleece and lay it out on the wool table, where I would then push it along the rollers and remove any burrs. Removing the burrs was a bit boring so I usually didn't bother. Once the burrs were not removed, I had to put the wool in a big bag and jump up and down on it to flatten it out. I quite enjoyed this bit.

The shearing sheds were owned by an old friend of my uncle's who would turn up at lunchtime when the farmers' wives arrived with the food. He was an elderly fellow who had lost his thumb years ago in the sort of farm accident usually featured on *Australian Story*. It had been surgically replaced

---

* Freud writes about this in *The Joke and Its Relation to the Unconscious* (1905). It's a lousy book if you're a fifteen-year-old looking for some decent gags to tell your friends. Two hundred jokes and not one of them funny. Also, Freud's delivery is terrible.

with one of his toes. I was regaled with this story as if it was hilarious and, suddenly becoming serious, the man showed me his toe-thumb as a warning to be careful around farming equipment.

From then on, I gave an especially wide berth to anything even remotely resembling a machine, choosing instead to play mainly with the rather safe-looking tap connected to my uncle's rainwater tank (the only source of fresh water on the drought-ravaged property). Sometimes I would stand on the tap in order to try and get high enough to look into the tank and see how full it was, and this was great fun – until the tap broke off and the water started gushing out. I tried to fix it by shoving grass into the pipe but to no avail. Eventually, several hundred litres later (or gallons as they were back then), I summoned enough courage to go and confess to my auntie who, after listening with a rather concerned expression on her face, suggested I'd best wait outside while she went to the next room and told my uncle. I was busy shoving some more grass into the pipe when I heard my uncle yell, 'Bloody kids!' Apart from the word 'bugger', in reference to a cow that had got loose and wandered up to the house one morning while we were having breakfast, I had never heard him swear before. He slammed out of the house with a crossness I'd also never seen in him and immediately set about staunching the flow with tools much more effective than the blades of grass I'd been using.

The highlight of these trips – as it remains to this day regardless of where I'm holidaying – was going home. The long drive from Lochiel was particularly pleasurable because we usually did it in a truck towing a large trailer of sheep to the Royal Adelaide Show, where they would be either sold or admired by other farmers in some sort of ovine beauty contest. I'm not entirely sure which, because once we arrived, my mother would be there to whisk me away so that I might buy a show bag, go on one or two of the less hair-raising rides and, because I was now a seasoned man of the land, look at the cakes made by the Country Women's Association. It is possible, perhaps even likely, that my uncle's sheep participated in the sheepdog trials which were a big part of the show and a real crowd pleaser. Perhaps my uncle's blue heeler, who had watched me so attentively as I built my fort, was competing. If so, I wish I'd been taken to see it because Get Around and I had grown quite close and it would have been nice to have been able to cheer him or her on.

It was years before I went back to Lochiel after the Tap Incident. When I did, I saw that a new tap had been attached to the tank with a thick black piece of pliable rubber. I resisted the urge to see whether it could bear my weight. I'd been worried that if I ever went back my pretend uncle and auntie might mention the tap in passing to my parents as they dropped me off and then I'd be in big trouble, so I kept declining their invitations and instead spent my school holidays doing what every red-blooded Aussie kid did in the 1970s: practising magic tricks alone in my bedroom. And, no, that isn't a euphemism ...

I was sixteen when I returned. I was in a funeral car following my great-grandmother's hearse from Adelaide. Just shy of her one-hundredth birthday when she died, Ellen was my grandfather's mother and had lived in a nursing home for as long as I'd known her, though she'd always been a bit senile so I can't say I really knew her *that* well. Ellen didn't make a lot of sense on our visits to her bedside and my mother explained to me that this was because she had regressed to when she was a child and sometimes lapsed into Gaelic, the language of her youth. Although she was born in Pittsworth in Queensland in 1879, her parents had been born in Tipperary and Carlow so Gaelic had been spoken around the house either out of habit or perhaps as a subversive alternative to the Cursed Tongue. Or perhaps my mother had been joking.

Like a lot of what you're forced to do by your parents when you're a child, these visits to my great-grandmother's nursing home were pretty dull, although when she had her teeth in she'd sometimes break out her jew's harp and play 'Lily of Laguna' for us. That was kind of interesting. She also once told me that she'd been picked up that very morning by a horse and cart and taken to school. Huge if true. I didn't envy her living in a nursing home, though, as it smelt too much of talcum powder and disinfectant. Not that getting old was without its perks. On her ninety-fifth birthday she was allowed out and taken to a big party at a rich cousin's house in the hills, where I met a lot of relatives I'd not seen before or since. I seem to remember Ellen smoking a cigar at one point but I might be mistaken. I'm probably thinking of George Burns, whom she slightly resembled.

About halfway through the three-hour funeral cortège to Lochiel, my mother, who had been gazing out the window solemnly as the blanched pastures of Wild Horse Plains rolled past, turned to my grandfather and said: 'Why don't we just pull over here and leave her in that field.' I'd never seen him laugh so much. His dentures clacked about in his mouth and almost fell out. I only hope my children can make me laugh like that when *my* mother dies – though with a different line obviously, as I've already heard that one.

| | | / ⁄⁓

Ellen's husband had been a man by the name of J.J. Hehir who, according to family legend, hadn't been allowed into the marital home and spent most of his time out the back in a sort of closed-off veranda, drinking beer and reading cowboy novellas. By all accounts he was affable enough, though once got very cross with my mother when he found her and a friend playing around in his veranda room with some kerosene lamps, perhaps worried that if the veranda went up in flames, he'd lose his first-edition Hopalong Cassidys.

J.J.'s folks were born in County Clare in 1845 and little is known about either parent aside from their emigrating to Australia and settling in Lochiel. When they died, leaving at least four adult Hehir siblings living on the one property, J.J.

decided to depart for if not greener, then less inhabited pastures. He married and went up north to Cambooya in the Darling Downs of Queensland. He applied for a publican's licence but didn't get it. In those days you needed to be a fit and proper person. This was Steele Rudd country, where Dad and Dave lived – and it was there that my grandfather was born and grew up. The family moved back to Lochiel in 1920 when J.J.'s brother died of Spanish flu, which was all the rage back then.

When I say little was known about J.J.'s parents, that is true only of their lives. Of the death of J.J.'s father, we know quite a lot because it got a nice write-up in the local paper. Apparently, he set himself on fire with his pipe after falling asleep at the reins during a horse-and-cart trip home late one night from the Snowtown Hotel:

### A GRIM TRAGEDY.

A tragedy, shrouded in mystery, was enacted on the Snowtown-Lochiel-road on Tuesday (says the Stanley "Herald"), when Mr. M. Hehir, an old resident of Snowtown and Lochiel, was burnt to death. It is presumed that the old gentleman had put away in a pocket a lighted pipe, which ignited his clothing. Mr. W O'Niel, who was returning from Lochiel, noticed Mr. Hehir's buggy coming from the opposite direction. Obviously something was wrong, as the horse was restive, and ultimately broke into a frenzied run. Mr. O'Niel was able to stop the frightened horse, and saw that the occupant of the now blazing buggy had succumbed. He unharnessed the horse, but could not approach near enough to extricate the body, and the vehicle burned until it and its terrible burden collapsed. Mr. Hehir, who was 76 years old, had resided for nearly 50 years in the district, and left two sons and four daughters.

It's hard not to believe alcohol was involved, even as an accelerant. It might also explain why J.J. was so upset about my mother playing with those kerosene lamps.

J.J.'s grandparents had come to Australia because, as Catholics in Ireland in the early 1800s, they weren't allowed to own land, rent property, vote, go to school, or live within five miles of town; also the British government's faith in the laissez-faire system as a cure-all for the mass starvation caused by the Potato Famine wasn't really working for them. They accepted Australia's offer of paid passage and some free land they could not only own but grow something on they could actually eat. The Hehirs spread out to areas in and around Kadina. Big farming families with the oldest boy tending to inherit the land made for some of the later Hehirs being better off than others. My mother's family were from the less well-off lot and even four generations later she grew up in a house with no running water or electricity.

Tradition and the pioneering spirit of his ancestors aside, my grandfather felt he was destined for better things than eking out a meagre living on some crummy farm and he did his best to mix with those with whom he felt he had more in common. He married the boss's daughter at the salt company, rose up the ranks, and for most of his life was an inveterate club joiner and club secretary, fetching and carrying for men of station and always pleased to be mentioned in their dispatches. Recognition from those he considered the right sort of people was important to him. When he heard I was going to law school, he made a point of introducing me to Judge Stanley, whom he knew from the Probus Club or the Reid Park Bowls Club, or Rotary, or the Knights of the Southern Cross. He was so proud of me and, I regret to say, I was a little embarrassed by the fuss. It meant so much to him – far more than it did to me – and, not yet twenty years old, I was not mature enough to let him share in the moment. He offered several times to pay for the wig and robes I'd one day need for my court appearances, but I always declined, thinking – rightly, I suspect – that it would have been too expensive for him. He was not a man to splash his cash around and that he even offered to pay for them was a sign of how much he wanted to be a part of what he thought was going to be my career. I see now it wasn't my place to deny him that and I'm sorry I didn't let him buy them for me.

Approval and endorsement. I guess we all need them. Some more than others. My mother never quite got her due from my grandfather, for her good marks and report cards. Oh, he loved her all right but his expectations and ambitions for her were not all they might have been had she been a boy. Back then the idea of going to university wasn't even considered if you were some poor farm girl from Nowheresville. The loftiest ambition my grandfather had for either of his children was that they work in the bank – my mother until she got married and her brother until he sat his public service examination, which he did, eventually ending up as a local magistrate. I was just about to graduate from law school when my uncle died suddenly of a heart attack. Perhaps that's why my grandfather wanted to help me.

I was at my grandparents' house that night of my uncle's death. My mother had asked me to stay over, perhaps hoping I'd distract them. The house, never crackling with conversation at the best of times, was terribly quiet. My grandparents and I sat in the lounge room watching a Danny Kaye special – well, they sat in their chairs on opposite sides of the room, not talking, and I lay on the floor watching Danny. He was conducting the New York Philharmonic: not quite as funny as *The Court Jester* but I'd been looking forward to it all week. I should have been talking to both of them and offering some measure of comfort, but I really didn't know what to say. Neither of them laughed or, indeed, said a word for the whole program. When Danny finished up, we went to bed – my grandparents each to their separate rooms, me to the room where my grandmother painted. It was my uncle's childhood bedroom. Canvases lay about, one featuring an impossibly orange sunset over Kowloon, another a lonely cottage in the woods and, on the easel, an unfinished poodle.

The next day I went with my grandfather to church – my grandmother never went – and we sat in the pew reserved for the collectors; I remember him leaning into another of the team who had nodded a passing hello and whispering: 'Terry died.' Now, that's quite a lot to take in and you're not really expecting to hear something like that when you're handing over the collection baskets, so the man didn't understand what was being said. 'My son,' explained my grandfather. Still the man didn't seem to register and my grandfather had to spell it

24

out, and louder: 'MY SON, TERRY, DIED LAST NIGHT.'
I guess my grandfather needed to talk to somebody and I had
been of little or no use.

As the men counted the money after mass, I heard my
grandfather say to another official, 'You don't expect to bury
your son, do you?' The other old man, probably also in his
late sixties, agreed. As my grandfather and I walked to the car
afterwards, I tried to talk about my Uncle Terry but I didn't
really have the words. We never much talked about serious
things. Like my grandfather, my uncle had been funny and
liked jokes, so I reminded my grandfather of a joke that Uncle
Terry liked telling:

*What's the difference between a riddle and an elephant
sitting on a bun? One's a conundrum and the other's got a
bun under 'im.*

My mother came from English stock as well as Irish. The
English were on her mother's side and perhaps the anglicised
spelling of 'Sean' is some sort of gesture towards détente. She
was a smart kid and found time between doodling my name
to excel at school, gain her Intermediate Certificate and sit
the public service examination, eventually getting a job at
the bank in the back room, as in those days it was thought
customers would lose confidence in the institution if they saw
a woman handling their money. A married woman was, of
course, even more of a concern and according to bank policy

my mother had to leave her job after her wedding. She became a receptionist for Mr Catchpole the optometrist but had to give that up as well when I came along. Twenty years later, when the world had wised up a bit, she would retrain and return to the now deregulated banking industry as a qualified mortgage broker and eventually start her own business training others. She's still doing it at eighty. Without the hiatus she'd have probably ended up in Christine Lagarde's old job.

My mother is also funny and I liked making her laugh. Like my grandfather and my Uncle Terry, she liked jokes, particularly those featuring puns. I never found puns *hugely* funny but would end up laughing along anyway because she enjoyed them so much and laughter, like the Spanish flu, is infectious. We were not a demonstrative family and laughter was how we showed our affection for each other. Maybe that's why I like hearing it so much from audiences today. My mother also liked jokes that were a bit wicked – things that were 'only jokes' and so couldn't be taken as out-and-out rudeness but that nonetheless might make you wonder if you thought about them later. I learned from her that you could misbehave with a joke, not only hiding behind the warmth of the laughter but also revelling in its implicit approval of the transgressive thing you'd done or said.

I saw much of my life through her eyes in the early days. I went everywhere with her: the Four Square shop, the hairdressers, the local deli, the library, the greengrocer, the butcher who said 'Hot enough for you?' all the time, even into the city by bus to the big department stores, oftentimes to visit my grandmother, who worked in the fabric department of John Martin's, or sometimes to ride on the Ferris wheel on top of Cox Foys or, on a few occasions, even to buy something. While window shopping one day, walking alongside my mother down Rundle Street as she wheeled my baby sister in the pram, my head down and watching the white rubber wheel as it turned around and around along the pavement, I suddenly looked up to see that it wasn't my mother next to me at all. I had been watching the wrong pram wheel. The pavement was crowded and I was small and I couldn't see above the forest of legs and coats as I looked about for my mother. She was nowhere to be seen – well, she might have been but, as I was to discover a few years later when I started school and sat an eye test, I was short-sighted as a bat. The next thing I remember, I was atop the shoulders of a policeman, looking about at his urging for some sign of my mother. Of course, I still couldn't see her at all. Fortunately, she saw me and I recall a blurry arm waving its way towards us through a sea of blobby heads and we were reunited. At least, I assume we were reunited. Perhaps the woman the policeman handed me over to was not my mother at all but some crazed lunatic; it would certainly explain a lot of things. In any event, I did not end up at the Goodwood Road orphanage (though once when rifling through a cupboard for some wrapping paper, I found a card to my mother from one of her bridesmaids congratulating her 'on the arrival of your baby boy, Simon'. My so-called mother claims it was a joke).

On the way home from these bus trips to the city, I would often ask her: 'Have I been a good boy?' – and she would answer: 'What do *you* think?' That I needed to ask this question says a lot about my need for validation and approval even at an early age. My mother's response, though, while probably helpful in the long term, was not what I wanted to hear. When you're a child, you can do without that sort of moral relativism. Still, I don't blame her for trying to make her answer more layered and interesting. She'd probably grown tired of constantly having to say, 'Yes, Shaun, you were *very* good.'

## CHAPTER TWO

# A tendency to be silly with his friends*

MY MOTHER'S FRIENDS had all married Australian men, so apart from my father and his family, we didn't know anyone else who was foreign except for our next-door neighbour Mr Zelensky. He spoke with an accent (a Polish one), had a big loud voice and enjoyed a drink. He drove a bus and would let my mother and me travel for free if we happened to get on his bus to go to town. He was a nice, gregarious man and I liked him, but he was nothing like my father, who was much quieter and didn't drink anything harder than Adelaide tap water.

Like the Hehirs, the Micallefs came over to Australia on paid passage, but much later on: in the 1950s. Malta had been a British dominion since 1800 after the Maltese rose up against the French occupation and, with the help of Nelson, forced a

---

* This comes from my Grade 3 report card. By Grade 5 I had apparently developed 'a morbid preoccupation with death', but I thought using that might be a bit of a downer so early in the book.

surrender. The Treaty of Paris made it all official in 1814 and, apart from his overthrow of King Louis XVIII, the War of the Seventh Coalition and the Battle of Waterloo, Napoleon was never heard from again. Malta became a seafaring nation and for a succession of Micallef men stretching back generations (well, two as far as I'm aware) it was the life of a ship steward for them, starting off with my great-grandfather Giovanni in about 1890 and ending with his son, my grandfather, Carmello. Micallef is a very common name in Malta and one, according to every Maltese person I've ever spoken to, I've been mispronouncing my entire life. Apparently it's Mi-kuh-*lef* and I've been saying Mi-*kar*-lef. I feel like such an idiot.

My father was fourteen years old when he left for Australia with his three brothers, two parents and one sister, practising his English on the way over with others on the ship. He was in steerage but the better English speakers were on the upper decks, so that's where he hung out, even though he wasn't supposed to and they kept sending him back. Once here, he went to work straight away as a stock clerk at a motor mechanics and with his first pay-packet bought a smart new sports jacket to wear to parish dances. He was very cross one night when he returned home from work to find one of his brothers had already gone out wearing it. He lay in wait until his brother returned and they came to blows, their mother screaming and their father having to break it up. It was probably the only time in my father's life he ever raised his hand to anyone. Years later, when I would raid his cupboard for anything and everything that would fit me, he was far more understanding – even when I borrowed his wedding suit to go on a pub crawl. He barely managed to raise an eyebrow.

As well as learning how to speak English (kind of), my father also learned to play the trumpet and joined a band. He met my mother at a parish dance and sold his trumpet so he could take her out. He never bought a new one. 'I lost my lip,' he would always say.

Though he started off as a stock clerk, he eventually worked his way up over the years through the motor mechanic hierarchy to become manager of the spare parts division. He was still working at eighty-five. Unlike my mother, he didn't get to sit his Intermediate Certificate, his school years back in Malta having been interrupted by World War II and the various bombs that the Italians and later the Germans dropped on the naval facilities at the end of Stuart Street, where he lived (as did many aunts, uncles and cousins, all of whom had livelihoods connected in some way to the to-ing and fro-ing of British ships). The Italians would circle half-heartedly and drop their bombs in the water; the Germans, it won't surprise you to learn, took their work more seriously.

Running for an air-raid shelter on New Year's Eve of 1942, my father-to-be, then only six years old, tripped and fell but was scooped up by an older brother and carried to safety. Thank you, Uncle John. They spent the night in an underground bunker, returning home the next morning to find their roof missing. Other homes in Stuart Street were gone completely, along with many Micallef uncles, aunts and cousins. The little island colony came in for a lot of grief during the war. Even today, the columns of the Royal Opera Theatre are still pockmarked from strafing by Messerschmitts.

Once the roof was put back on, my father and his brothers would take up their positions on it and watch the dogfights between the Bf 109s and the Spitfires. As an adult my father subscribed to a magazine called *Aviation* and tried to interest me in reading it with him but I couldn't get into it. Had I known then what I know now about his childhood I would have at least pretended to be interested. I don't think he would have ever told me anything about those years were it not for the interview I conducted with him for *Who Do You Think You Are?* Half an hour uncut, it was probably the longest conversation we've ever had together. Getting anything out of him about his childhood was like pulling teeth.

I once found a box of his old, exquisitely detailed, hand-painted model airplanes with little pilots inside the cockpits. These were from when he was a teenager. It seems that when he wasn't blowing his dough on zoot suits and reeds for his horn, he was spending up big on Airfix kits. What a no-good punk. He caught me playing with them and told me they weren't toys. They sure looked like toys to me. After a conversation with my mother, he spent all day suspending them from the ceiling of my room. Of course, they weren't anywhere near as much fun way up there where I couldn't reach them. At least not without standing on a chair.

Food was scarce during the Siege of Malta and there wasn't much more of it after the war ended. My father hated lining up for bread. Apart from the time he snuck in to see Maria Callas perform in that scarred opera theatre, he has few fond memories of those days.

The Maltese were useful to Australia's post-war economy. Most of the men either had worked in the shipyards and were mechanically minded or good at administration, or they'd made their living in the merchant navy as stewards, like Giovanni and Carmello, and so were used to a chain of command where someone with a fairer complexion than theirs was giving the orders. Giovanni had been serving sandwiches to the captain of the *Black Prince* in 1916 when it was sunk during the Battle of Jutland. Plus, being from a British colony, they could all speak English (kind of).

A mother brought up in a house with no power or plumbing and a father who had to dodge falling bombs and didn't have enough to eat – and there I was complaining about an itchy cardigan.

| | | | /—

Pretty soon I was too big to wear the itchy cardigan anyway. In fact, the whole family was growing. I've mentioned me (and will continue to do so throughout this book). I've also mentioned my baby sister, but she was growing too and her place in the pram was eventually taken by another baby sister – and then another. It was like my parents were *trying* to get rid of me as the centre of attention. Eventually they got me out of the house entirely for at least a few hours of the day by sending me to school.

I tried out a few of the local Catholic primary ones until we found one my mother liked and which I could catch the local Harcourt Gardens bus service to and from. It cost five cents in the new decimal currency but you could use the sixpences that were still around. The bus driver was not our friendly neighbour Mr Zelensky but a gnarled old grump named Tofty. He mumbled a lot and I could never understand what he said. He had, in fact, driven my mother to school when the family had moved down from Lochiel, so he must have been ancient. Though he came across gruff he would sometimes let me on the bus for free if I had lost my money and once, when I was the only passenger left on board, he drove me all the way home and dropped me off in our driveway.

When I see TV shows set in the '60s, everything looks fresh off the cover of *Modern Living*. Everyone's lounging around in Eames chairs, wearing hats, pipes hanging out their mouths and drinking martinis. In truth, at least in Australia – or certainly around my neck of the woods – the decor tended to be a hodgepodge of whatever people had been given and whatever they could afford. Furniture, homewares, kitchen appliances, manchester and cutlery covered every decade back to the 1920s, and not in a good, antiquey way.

Although born seventeen years after the end of World War II and on the other side of the world, I may as well have been growing up in post-war Britain. And not just because of the furnishings. All my books were hand-me-downs from an older cousin and as he seemed interested only in soccer and Boys Own Adventures, I grew up with a working knowledge of Bobby Charlton and quite keen on the idea of routing out Nazi spies. My bookshelf also featured some of my mother's old Rupert annuals, which had come to *her* from an older cousin. I liked Rupert but, again, the adventures of an anthropomorphic bear from the '30s who lived in a world that was part Tudor England and part medieval – he even owned a small pet dragon – only led me astray from the time I was actually growing up in.

Because we didn't then have a TV, our radiogram was my window to the world. I enjoyed watching the records turn as I listened to Al Jolson, Herb Alpert and Bert Kaempfert (my father's favourites) but most of the time my preferred position was lying under it, listening to what the local ABC station had to offer. If I wasn't playing with my cars, I was looking up the radiogram's underneath at all those glowing tubes. There may have been a nod to the '60s with *Round the Horne* and *Hancock's Half Hour* but mostly I listened to *Men from the Ministry*, *ITMA*, *Much-Binding-in-the-Marsh* and, my favourite of all, *The Goon Show* – all shows from the '40s and '50s. The absorption of all this audio into my brain resulted in an ability to parrot catchphrases from a previous generation and do voices. I can still do a spot-on impression of Kenneth Horne – probably the most useless skill I have.

*Hello everybody and, of course, today is Festoon a Gnome with Bacon Rind Day ...**

Of course, a life spent gorging yourself on comedy will get you nowhere and my parents were keen to teach me skills that would actually prepare me for the real world. My mother thought I should learn how to read properly. School wasn't really doing it for me and despite all the books I had in my room, most of the stories I'd just been following, or more usually making up, by looking at the pictures.

I mean, I *could* read. I just couldn't do it that well. I really had to concentrate – and things were never fun for me if I had to try. If it didn't come naturally and effortlessly, forget about it. Reading was complicated. Words in a sentence would seem to me to be in a lump which I sometimes recognised and other times didn't. Individual words I could sound out and remember how to pronounce if they were in a list, but when placed in a row they would suddenly seem unfamiliar. Although no one knew it at the time, my eyesight was weak, so this may have had something to do with it. Either that or I was dyslexic. Whatever the reason, no amount of the handwritten tests my mother set for me would make the spelling or the sound of the words stick. Eventually it was just accepted I

---

* Obviously, that impression is going to work better in the audio book.

wasn't the sharpest note in the symphony and any expectation of achievement was shifted to my younger sisters, who did not disappoint.

If not a scholar then perhaps a sportsman. Skilled at any number of ball sports and physically fit, my father still played soccer with his brothers at a local club and so I was taken along to watch in the hope that I would be seized by the muse of whichever one looked after sport (Nike?) and want to join in. Looking at a bunch of guys kicking a ball around never did much for me and I was soon back under the radiogram, now taping what I heard with a small reel-to-reel tape recorder I'd been given for my birthday.

My inability to catch a ball even in the backyard was concerning; no matter how gently my father threw it to me, I couldn't seem to coordinate my hand with my eye. Even when I got my first pair of glasses from Mr Catchpole halfway through my first year of school, things didn't improve. Skinny and clumsy, I was taken to gym classes by my father in an effort to make me less like Jerry Lewis, whose movies I was just starting to enjoy on the new TV we had and, frankly, would have much preferred staying home and watching.

Hundreds of boys in a cavernous gymnasium, leaping and tumbling and yelling and landing with thuds on plastic mats. I could just about stand the nauseating smell of sweat and the interminable waiting in line; what I didn't like was being barked at by the guys in t-shirts and whistles as they taught us our tricks. I did what I was told and tried my best but didn't exactly blossom in the assembly-line atmosphere of the whole enterprise. I hated being assessed, and 'D Squad' doesn't sound impressive no matter how enthusiastically you're congratulated and referred to as 'Muscles'. My father must have seen how miserable I was from the bleachers, where he sat with the other dads, because after a few weeks I suddenly didn't have to go anymore.

Meanwhile, back at school, my writing had become a problem as well, at least according to my Grade 3 teacher, Mrs Woolgar. 'Illegible,' she said. I didn't even know what that meant. Work was often returned with a line through it and the command 'RE-DO!' written across the page in virulent red. Even at seven years old I thought this seemed excessive. Fortunately, my mother came to the rescue: turning up at school – for some reason the mental picture is always of Margaret Hamilton riding her bike in *The Wizard of Oz* – and telling Mrs Woolgar how I had been born with inverted thumbs and had spent my first year in plaster casts to help open out my hands. My thumbs had got better, my mother explained, no doubt with a catch in her voice, but I still had terrible trouble holding a pen.

The next day Mrs Woolgar made a beeline for my desk at the start of her lesson. 'Why didn't you tell me about your poor hands?' she said, her mouth contorted hideously in what I guess was her smile. 'You just do the best you can, okay?' As her voice had a sympathetic tone to it, I looked back at her as pathetically as I could (I'd just seen *Oliver*). The truth was I didn't know anything about ever having had inverted thumbs.

When I got home that night I pressed my mother for more details about my affliction and she went to my cupboard (the one with the itchy cardigan in it) and from an old shoebox took out the two tiny plaster casts I had worn on my arms as an infant. Man, what a prize I was. A prem baby, near-sighted, with inverted thumbs, the motor skills of a lobotomised monkey and the IQ of Lennie from *Of Mice and Men*. Plus, I'd been recently diagnosed with a hiatal hernia, which meant that whenever I went to bed I vomited and so had to sleep inclined on a large wedge-of-cheese-shaped pillow.

I abandoned cursive writing forever and stuck with printing in an effort to improve my penmanship. My atrocious spelling remained, as did my inability to recognise words in a sentence, and so I was put in the remedial reading class. It won't surprise you to learn that I was equally abysmal at maths and still can't do long division. Many a night was spent staring uncomprehendingly at the tear-sodden page of incomplete sums I'd been given for homework, my shame returning years later when my own children would come to me for help with their arithmetic and I still didn't know what the hell was going on.

I was always much better on my feet than I was at my desk. Not on my feet shooting hoops or taking marks, obviously, but standing up in front of the class and talking off the top of my head. All that radio and television in my brain meant I could give off the air of someone who was quite eloquent and smart.

I was good at stringing together sentences if I was speaking them. As it turned out, while I was nowhere near as clever as I appeared, I perhaps wasn't quite as stupid as the tests suggested either. Of course, the good thing about people underestimating you is that it's much easier to impress them when you suddenly do something half decent. Not that there was much chance of that happening in a Catholic primary school.

I did eventually win a school prize but it was for Christian Leadership, which even at the time I knew wasn't for anything, really. Nonetheless, I was allowed to pick any item off a table in the library to go along with the certificate. Given what I'd won the prize for, I thought I'd better pick the rather impressive-looking crucifix that was on offer. Brother Jordan suggested the book of science fiction stories instead. Perhaps he knew about my reading level and thought I could do with the practice.

By dint of the natural flattening of the bell curve in our class and no actual effort on my part, I worked my way up from dimwit to a solid C student. Still more interested in standing up in class than sitting down, I enjoyed being called upon to read out my own creative writing – which, unlike Mrs Woolgar, I had no trouble reading – *and* it was my first experience performing my own material. I had an audience. Whereas in the schoolyard I would clown around only with my chums, the classroom gave me a chance to get laughs from kids I didn't know all that well: the smart ones, the sporty ones, the quiet ones – even the teachers joined in. I could make them laugh and they would get to know me without me having to get to know them; for a shy, gangly boy like me, it was a pretty sweet deal.

The surest way to get a big laugh was by doing an impression of a teacher. I had a few in my repertoire, including our headmaster, Brother David. To be fair, Brother David was pretty easy to do. He had a wooden leg and always carried a tan briefcase containing a leather strap he called Percy. To instil in us the level of fear he felt necessary to maintain order, he would sit down at the start of the lesson, open his briefcase on the desk and arrange Percy so that his head poked up and could watch everybody. Brother David also had a car aerial which he pretended was a pen, extending it to several feet in length before 'writing' your name in his book if you misbehaved. The implication was that one day, when your name had sufficient marks against it, you would be summoned to appear before him and savagely beaten by Percy.

As all of this was done with a twinkle in his eye, I don't think anyone took it seriously, but Brother David certainly left an impression on you – and, like I say, if you had the props and could do a reasonable limp, it was an easy one. But I could do his voice as well and that made my impression a cut above the others. It was the low, sinister whisper of the snake in Disney's *The Jungle Book*. If Brother David called you by name to his office through the classroom intercom, it put the fear of God into you. Sometimes, if a teacher had to leave the class, he'd use the same system to listen in and then maybe turn up at the classroom to hiss out your name in person, jotting down your details with his aerial and whispering your transgression to his briefcase, presumably for Percy's benefit. At the time all this seemed perfectly normal. He was certainly more benign than my Grade 6 teacher, Mr Wilczek, who would hit you across the knuckles with a ruler if you got a word wrong in the spelling bee. As a teaching strategy I question its efficacy. To this day I cannot spell rhythm or rhyme without double-checking that I've put the 'h's in the right place. I had to do it just now.

It took until Year 9 to happen across my English teacher, Mr Hooper, and he was *that* teacher that some of us are lucky enough to get maybe once during our school lives: the one who understands and inspires you. Like Robert Donat in *Goodbye, Mr Chips* or Sydney Poitier in *To Sir, With Love*. Mr Hooper was the one who called on me to read out my compositions and he would laugh along with everybody else, often louder at some of the more obscure jokes. He was nicknamed 'Crom' by some of the older boys because he resembled Oliver Cromwell. I assume in regards to his political beliefs, but it may have been his haircut. He always wore a purple three-piece suit. Always. To the point we started to worry. He was eccentric and funny and as much about amusing himself as amusing the class. Without him I would never have learned to love language and appreciate how it's the key to everything.

Another teacher I remember quite well introduced me to politics. He would hold lunchtime classes for any students keen to learn how parliament worked. He was a much-liked teacher who took a keen interest in his students whatever they were doing. We noticed this while we were showering at the school camp. He would also take students across his knees to smack them with his open hand if they misbehaved in class. He was Dutch and we assumed this was a cultural thing. My friend Peter Ricci and I were too tall for him to discipline in this way, so on the rare occasions we were considered to have misbehaved he'd just hit us with the yardstick. I remember him administering a bout of corporal punishment in his traditional over-the-knee fashion to some poor kid when I looked up and saw Crom watching what was going on through the glass of the connecting door to the neighbouring classroom. The expression on his face, framed as it was by the window, was worthy of Edvard Munch. The Dutch teacher disappeared soon after that. No explanation. No announcement. Not a word. These days *Four Corners* would get at least two episodes out of it.

Then there was old Mr Wignall, our commerce teacher. A fascinating creature who blustered about with all the haughty pomposity of Arthur Lowe in *Dad's Army*. Horace Wignall: a man who, despite having had both his knees shot off in the war, insisted on wearing shorts all year round. He may have been a good teacher once, but those days were long gone by the time he got to us. Many Catholic primary school teachers were dragooned back into service from retirement to make up the numbers at new schools like ours, often regardless of ability or, in the case of the nuns at the Dominican schools I'd been to earlier, even teaching qualifications. I liked Mr Wignall and would draw pictures of him during his lessons to pass around the class. One, with voice balloons extending from where his knees would have been, explained Keynes's Law of demand and supply. It made Phil Kiley laugh so much that Horace demanded the drawing be brought to him and I was sent to the red chairs outside Brother David's office.

The red chairs were where only the naughtiest boys were sent. Those banished there would disappear for a lesson or two and return with heroic tales of being caned or strapped by Percy or, slightly less heroically, with a note for their parents. Most boys saved their parents the bother of reading the notes by destroying them on their way home from school.

'Show Brother David your artwork, I'm sure he'll be impressed,' Horace had said indignantly as he handed back my cartoon.

This was not going to play well. I was usually pretty good at talking my way out of things but having to explain a drawing making fun of my teacher's war injuries to a man with only one leg was a bridge too far. I binned the cartoon as I made my way to the office and decided to confess to the lesser crime of talking in class. I'd probably get a note. Horace wouldn't be privy to it and I wouldn't get into too much trouble at home. The perfect crime. When I got to the red chairs, though, the bursar wasn't there to announce me. I went round the corner, knocked on Brother David's door and, receiving no reply, nudged it open. Empty. I mean, there was stuff in it but no Brother David. Perhaps he had gone down to the TAB. The Marist Brothers were notorious gamblers and, as it was Friday afternoon, perhaps they were off letting the school funds ride on a longshot.

I considered returning to the red chairs and waiting but decided instead to check out the big intercom system behind Brother David's desk. It was of professional interest to me as I was a member of the library's Audiovisual Club. I gently switched the intercom to ON for Room 7 Red and listened in. Hearing nothing from my class, I flipped the switch to what I thought was OFF and got some feedback. I was live. In a fit of daring that I would never again display in my life, I tried out my Brother David impression:

*Would Horace Wignall please come to the office. Horace Wignall.*

Losing my nerve, I ducked back out to the red chairs. Through the window I could see the knee-less Mr Wignall hurrying across the quadrangle at a speed that was probably not safe for him. Slightly out of breath, he nodded politely in my direction as he hobbled in – his eyes were also not great so I could have been anybody – and made his way past the bursar's office to the headmaster's, from whence I heard a brisk knock and then the sound of him entering. A few seconds later he returned, puzzled.

'Hello, Mr Wignall,' I chirped, alerting him to the fact that it was me sitting there.

'Did you see Brother David?' he asked when he realised who I was.

'Oh, yes,' I lied.

He gave a ponderous nod and cast a look towards the office. 'Well, uh … where is he?'

'He's in his office,' I lied again. I really hadn't thought any of this through.

Horace nodded again and then actually went back to check, thinking perhaps that Brother David had been hiding when he went in the first time. At that point I could, through the other window, see the definitely-not-in-his-office Brother David limping across the car park with his tan briefcase and thought I'd make myself scarce.

By the time Mr Wignall returned to the classroom, the bell had rung and we had all escaped to other lessons. He seemed to have forgotten about it all – or perhaps still hadn't quite worked it out – when I saw him for commerce the following week.

Approaching the pointy end of my secondary education, my thoughts turned to life after school. Rather full of myself after my Christian Leadership prize, I thought I would answer the call we were always being told about and decided to enter the seminary once I graduated. I began carrying around the biography of Pope Pius XII and hearing confessions from my fellow students from behind the lid of my desk. As the self-anointed school chaplain, I played peacemaker on the playground between warring gangs. Anthony Cacciotti, the toughest kid in the class, even took to calling me Monsignor. When Brother Jordan called the class in for one-on-one careers advice and asked me what I wanted to be when I left school, I gave him the good news about becoming a priest.

Brother Jordan, or 'Brick' as the older boys called him, was a short slab of a man and it may well be he earned the nickname simply on the basis of his shape. Or perhaps the colour he went when he got angry. Or what it felt like you'd been hit with when he punched down knuckles-first onto your head after some minor infraction. Anyway, Brick sat there looking at me, trying to work out whether I was being serious or not. I had already earned a reputation for irony so perhaps this was another of my attempts at mild subversion. When he saw I was legit, he leaned in to me. 'How old are you?' he asked. When I told him he gave a slow nod. 'Yeah,' he drawled. 'Just wait a couple of years and see how you feel about it.'

## CHAPTER THREE

# Girls! Girls! Girls!

GIRLS HAD NOT been a mystery to me until I started noticing them. My mother had enrolled my three sisters into ballet classes and so a goodly proportion of my after-school childhood was spent waiting in the car reading comic books while they attended their lessons. Sometimes in the summer, when the car became hot enough to turn me into a Teochew dumpling, I would be allowed to come inside and sit on the benches near the mirrors where the class did their barre work. By the time I was fourteen, the tall bun-haired girls *petit jeté*-ing about on the parquetry were at least of equal interest to me as my bumper editions of *Whizzer and Chips*.

Occasionally I would be pressed into service for the end-of-year shows put on for the parents to justify the fees they were paying. I was taught some basic tap dancing – step-ball-changing mostly – and soon enough found myself backstage being made up as an Arab slave boy for the big Scheherazade finale while fifty girls slipped into their culturally inappropriate belly-dancing costumes. It was all a bit of a blur until the curtain call when, after our bow, I mistakenly ran offstage in the opposite direction to the other slaves, doubled back and got a big laugh. Then the whole thing came into sharp focus.

By the time my next job in the theatre came along, though, I had been either promoted or demoted, depending on how you looked at it. Either way I was no longer required onstage. In fact, I was about as far away from the stage as you could be while still remaining in the auditorium. Unpaid spotlight operator at the Royalty Theatre in Angus Street, just down the road from where my father worked.

It was the school holidays. The show was *Pippin* and starred a young John Farnham – 'Johnny' in those days. I don't now remember how I got the job. One of my sisters was a dancer in the chorus, so I guess my mother arranged it because I would have been hanging around anyway and it was probably safer and slightly less boring for me than having to wait in the car until the show had finished.

The spotlight was housed in a small room above the lighting box. It was all metal, including the handle, and I often burnt myself on it. My job was very simple. In between burning my arm, I had to point the spotlight at whoever was singing – usually Johnny, sometimes Colleen Hewett or Nancy Hayes, who were also in the cast. I couldn't turn it off because it was plugged into the room below me, so when the spot wasn't required, I was told I should close the iris. Unfortunately, the spotlight was so old and warped that the iris didn't close properly, so I would have to hide the remaining shard of light somewhere it wouldn't be noticed, like in the lamp on the piano in the orchestra pit or on the back of the conductor's bald head. The next time I saw Johnny was twenty-five years later in the ABC cafeteria and as he didn't bring up my shoddy work on the spotlight in *Pippin*, neither did I.

Most of the things I ended up doing at that age were attempts by my parents to get me out from under the radiogram or away from the TV. It's probably how I ended up onstage in the Arts Theatre auditioning for *Jack and the Beanstalk*. My mother has always insisted that it was *my* idea, but I seriously doubt it.

'What would you like to do for us?' asked a voice from the stalls. I didn't know. 'Can you sing?' asked the voice. I said I couldn't. 'Dance?' No, I couldn't do that either. 'What *can* you do?' asked the voice, understandably flummoxed as to why on earth I was there. I shrugged. In the end I sang a verse of 'Happy Birthday' while swaying a bit and then left the stage as bamboozled by the whole thing as they were. So naïve was I that I wasn't even humiliated by the experience. I met my parents at the back of the theatre, walked out to the car and went home. No one had thought to tell me what an audition was.

In the end, they sent me off to the Bunyip Children's Theatre, where I learned to project my voice and hide my tone-deafness in the back of a chorus line. Not only did these acting classes involve having an audience and the chance to make the other students laugh, but also a lot of those other students were girls. I did many shows for Bunyip – not for the money, which was just as well as the student-actors seldom received any, but for what turned out to be the fun of it. I really did enjoy prancing around onstage and showing off, which is all acting is, really. When I wasn't drawing attention to myself, I was often pressed into service pulling curtains or tearing tickets and over the years I learned everything: how to run a sound desk and a lighting board, how to stage-manage, do front-of-house, paint a set, and even run a fly gallery.

I never ended up doing a show for the owner of that voice in the Arts Theatre stalls, which was just as well too because he ended up in trouble with the law for various offences, the least of which was trying to rob a bank in West Lakes. Newspaper reports said he used gelignite, which sounds a little melodramatic. But then, he was used to doing pantomimes where everything was always way overdone.

Bunyip Children's Theatre was a far more professional and less criminal enterprise. We were drilled in enunciation, breathing, posture and movement – all things that I'd been doing my whole life without thinking and, as was soon pointed out to me, quite wrongly. Once corrected, I learned how to perform dialogue, stand on stage properly and, as I mentioned and most importantly of all, use my diaphragm to project my voice so it could be heard at the back of a theatre. Of all the things I have learned about performance, being able to talk loudly without yelling has been the most invaluable. Yes, *volume* is the single greatest weapon in an actor's arsenal. Olivier, Pacino, Barbara Carrera, Rod Steiger – all really loud. Without that skill, my friends, you have no right to call yourself an actor.

The shows were fun and performing before large audiences developed my timing as a comedy performer. Any sense of comic rhythm I may have today is entirely down to what I learned in my teenage years and I really have learned nothing else of substance since. I'm sometimes asked for advice from aspiring comedians and I always tell them the same thing because it's all I know: get in front of an audience as soon as possible; a crowd is the best editor of material and you can tell pretty quickly what they like and what they can do without.*

Doing these pantomimes during the school holidays, I would often take on the mannerisms of whichever comedian I had been watching on TV that morning. Thus, Mr Plod in *Noddy in Toyland* became Groucho Marx; Tom the Piper's son in *Tales from Mother Goose* was Jerry Lewis; Eeyore from *Winnie the Pooh* resembled Stan Laurel; even Humphrey B. Bear, whom I played for some scenes in *Humphrey Bear and the Wishing Tree* while the real actor was in his dressing-room rehydrating, was more reminiscent of Curly from the Three Stooges than the fun-loving bear the children had just seen exit the stage moments earlier. Also, my costume was older and

---

* Whenever asked, Peter Sellers' comedy advice was to 'always keep your head still'. He's quite right.

more moth-eaten than the one worn by the real Humphrey.

The head of the costume was also quite complicated. In order to see, I had to look through the meshed-over nostrils in Humphrey's nose, which meant I had to keep my own head down while holding Humphrey's head up if I wanted to avoid walking off the stage into the orchestra pit. Plus, the mouth was operated by moving one's chin up and down on an ancient foam pad in such a way that I had to open my mouth in order to close Humphrey's and close my mouth so as to open it – all while looking down and holding the head up so I was able to see through Humphrey's nose. Basically, I had to retrain my entire nervous system. Most of the time I just let the mouth hang open as it was the only way to let fresh air into the sweltering hide. Unfortunately, the spotlight would sometimes catch the lenses of my glasses and reflect it back out into the audience, momentarily blinding anyone in the first few rows. On these occasions, Humphrey was like Godzilla from *Destroy All Monsters* (1968), emitting a radioactive beam from his mouth as he battled his enemies. I also developed pyorrhea from the bacteria-infested chin pad, something else that distinguished me from the real Humphrey.

With all the poise, erudition and confidence born of holidays spent treading the boards, you'd think I would have been regularly beaten at school by the less sophisticated, football-playing rubes who comprised the bulk of my classmates, but no, it made me popular. Making my pals laugh wasn't quite in the same league as making the girls laugh in acting class, though, and while a Marist Brothers–run all-boys primary and middle school education was preparing me well for life in the Victorian era as a barely literate mudlark, it was teaching me nothing about human sexuality and gender, which were the sorts of topics I was really interested in.

Apart from a night when the Year 9s had to attend the science laboratory with their fathers to watch a film projected on the wall about meiosis, there had only been one rather curious religion lesson we'd had from our deputy headmaster, Brother Leo, the day before our school dance, where he wrote the word FUCK on the blackboard (which he pronounced 'FOOK') and asked us to list all the euphemisms there were for having an erection. Many I had not heard before, but Brother Leo helpfully wrote them all up on the board, presumably for us to memorise and use the following night should the occasion call for it.

A mountain of a man in a gleaming white soutane, he warned us all in stentorian tones about something terrible, but in language so vague that it was difficult to know just what it was we were all supposed to be ashamed about. Whatever it was, he made it known that it was quite appalling and that these poor girls we were about to meet deserved better. With a final warning that we were not to ride off on our motorbikes from whatever we'd done without a look over our shoulder – something none of us were capable of doing as we were all too young to have even a learner's permit – Brother Leo turned an alarming shade of puce and stormed out of the room, leaving our regular religious master to quickly erase everything on the board before it caused even more damage.

It was at the school dance in Year 10 that I met the first girl I liked enough to actually ask out. Though I cannot now for the life of me remember what she looked like (I think an overbite was involved), I was smitten enough to risk dancing the Madison with her every time the DJ played *Nutbush City Limits*, always pocketing my glasses first so I would look more handsome. Come to think of it, maybe not having my glasses on whenever I was with her is why I can't remember what she looked like.

It wasn't until the school holidays a month or so later that I plucked up sufficient courage to look her up in the White Pages and call. In those days you had to guess the suburb and work your way through the list of surnames. I asked her if she'd like to go to the pictures and she said no, that her father wouldn't approve. A few months later I nerved myself to ask her to a dance, but again she declined, again citing her father and this time adding that he was in the Lions Club. I still have no idea what she meant. I never went out with her. It really wasn't much of a relationship.

My school turned co-educational for the last two years of my time there, which of course was great for everybody's concentration and commitment to studies. Brother Leo had sensibly been forbidden to talk to us further about whatever he had been trying to talk to us about the previous year and we were all left to work things out for ourselves.

I had many friends who were girls; in fact, I preferred their company to the boys'. We'd sit in a circle at lunchtime and talk about our hopes and dreams and I'd try and get as many laughs out of them as I could. It was like *The Breakfast Club*, except we were all too well behaved to ever be on detention.

After school camp in Year 11, I kissed one of my friends at a party. Actually, I'm pretty sure she kissed me as it had never occurred to me that our friendship could be anything else. Assuming we were now boyfriend and girlfriend, we did the usual things boyfriends and girlfriends did such as going to a 'rock' mass and to the pictures to see *The Hound of the Baskervilles* starring Peter Cook and Dudley Moore, the latter of which I enjoyed enormously, particularly the scene where Denholm Elliott is holding a wildly urinating dog. I don't remember her laughing quite as much as I did. We also went to the Royal Show. My father drove us and waited outside while I went to collect her from her house and meet her parents for the first time. I declined all offers of drinks and biscuits and even a chair, preferring instead to stand nervously in the lounge room while she finished getting ready. Several of her older brothers, draped like James Deans over various items of furniture while they watched *Hey Hey It's Saturday*, cast me the occasional side eye, conveying a mixture of both relief and disappointment that the guy taking their sister out was such a jerky-looking nerd.

At the end of the year, on the very afternoon of New Year's Eve, I went down to the phone box at the end of our street to ring and ask her out. Given I had left it so late, she had not surprisingly already made plans. She also told me that she didn't want to go out with me anymore because she didn't want to be tied down. I said I understood and walked home with something in my eye.

In my final year of high school, I continued to win friends and influence people despite never having read the book. I was even elected college captain after a speech I gave, cribbed largely from Peter Cook's Miner sketch.* My plagiarism fortunately went unnoticed and they voted for me. Once people expected me to be funny, I found I could get laughs simply by reading out a straight announcement using the same cadence the headmaster had used to welcome me to the dais. Yep, I played that Year 12 cohort like a harp from hell.

---

* *Beyond the Fringe* (1960).

## CHAPTER FOUR

# Subpoena Hard Day's Night*

IT'S AN OLD bromide that your school days are the best days of your life. I guess whether that's true depends on how miserable the rest of your life is.

I had by year's end sufficiently navigated my academic blind spots to get into Adelaide's only law school, a besser block of brutalist modernism plonked in the middle of Adelaide University's otherwise delightful nineteenth-century gardens and ivy-covered walls. As if to assert its disdain for the Gothic architecture surrounding it, it even had a Henry Moore sculpture out the front (although in my view, it looked nothing like him). I don't mean to sound snide; I was damn grateful to have got in. My second choice was journalism at Hartley College. God, can you imagine? My third was Wildlife and Park Management.

---

* This one was the name of one of our Footlight's revues, which gives you some idea of how funny we all were.

My mother and father were equal parts proud and relieved that I'd made the cut. They'd done their best to give me the opportunities they never had and to cocoon me from reality in an idyllic world of movies, radio, TV, books, comics, homework and pretend. I still had no idea about what differences in race and money meant. I had grown to adulthood blissfully unaware of class or that anything at all might turn on where you were born or what was in your pay packet. Only at university did it become clear that these things were important to some people. It was the first time I was called a wog – in jest, I was assured – and I was the subject of mild ridicule when someone turned up to my twenty-first birthday and cracked wise about my choice of celebratory spumante. I found it curious that these people I was knocking around with felt the need to make me aware that there were some things about me that put me outside the group. *Their* group, I suppose.

Meanwhile, back when I was not yet even eighteen and finishing up with what was still then called 'matric', I'd abandoned my theatre training classes because I had to get serious about my study or, according to my grandmother, I'd end up a road sweeper. At the beginning of my year as a 'fresher', I joined a Young Christian Students group in the hope of meeting some new like-minded friends. Well, some new like-minded girls. The girls I'd gone to acting classes with were all friends, so that ruled them out as romantic prospects; ditto the girls I knew from school; and the girls at law school were all strangers whom I couldn't get to know because I had not yet joined the Footlights club and impressed them with my onstage hilariousness. The Young Christian Students group was perfect.

I had, of course, done a lot of growing up in the three-or-so months since high school finished. Gone were the short back and sides, replaced with a helmet of hair that now almost covered the tops of my ears. My neat school uniform, jumper, tie and prefect's pin had given way to brown cords, a short-sleeved tangerine body-shirt and a pair of beige Ciaks. Plus, I had the beginnings of a moustache. Yes, I was quite a catch.

A few evenings into discussing how the Holy Bible could be used as a roadmap to navigate the secular world, I chanced my arm and asked a girl I liked to the law school ball. My parents knew her parents and our families went to the same church. If I craned my neck around my father during the sermon, I could just see her from our pew. Having learned my lesson that previous New Year's Eve about leaving things to the last minute, I wanted to give her a good seven days' notice.

After our weekly meeting, as we were waiting in the car park of Christ the Worker for our fathers to pick us up, I was making small talk about the law ball with her. 'So, do you want to go?' I asked casually.

'Yeah, I better,' she said. Her father had just pulled up with a crunch of gravel and she started walking off.

'No, no – I meant to the ball,' I explained, panicking a little.

'What?'

'With me. Do you want to go to the law ball with me? I mean ... if you're not doing anything else ...'

Her father beeped his horn.

'Oh ... um, when is it?'

'Next Friday.'

She paused a moment and, perhaps unable to think of an excuse quickly enough, shrugged. 'Yeah, sure ...' And with that she got in the car with her father, a doctor, and swept away.

A law ball probably sounds more impressive than it is, particularly if you've never been to one. From the way my date was dressed when I picked her up, I think she thought it was some sort of turn-of-the-century cotillion instead of the drunken *Animal House* toga party she ended up having to endure.

'Would you like to go outside?' I yelled over the music. I'd unwisely chosen a banquette under a loudspeaker and felt we could talk more easily without Dire Straits blasting all over us.

'No thanks,' she yelled back, no doubt suspecting I wanted to get her alone for some non–Young Christian reason.

'Okay,' I replied, mortified – and then tried to ignore my friends, who were off in the distance making lewd gestures which to this day I hope to God she didn't notice.

The poor girl. It must have been a dull night for her, the monotony relieved only by the trip home. As I still didn't have a driver's licence, one of my lewd friends was driving us. He decided he would avoid the breathalyser ahead by suddenly squealing down a side street. The cops, rightly surmising that something was up, turned on their siren and gave chase, eventually cutting us off and forcing the car up onto the kerb. Names and addresses were taken, and after I saw my shell-shocked date to her door, my friend tried to cheer me up as we drove away by saying it would make a good story that she and I could tell our grandchildren one day. Unfortunately, as I never heard from or even saw her again, I never got a chance to find out if he was right. By year's end, I'd left the Young Christian Students and taken up with a whole new crowd.

I'd been told by the brochures that university life would introduce me to a world of fresh opportunity and give me a chance to meet interesting people from backgrounds vastly different from mine. Catholic, *Goon Show*–loving and late of Sacred Heart College, Gary McCaffrie, though, was about as close to being like me as *I* was, except for his smoking habit and standing a good four inches shorter (these things perhaps being connected). McCaffrie was also two years older than me (and still is) and so was already halfway through his law degree when he sidled up to me at the urinal of the downstairs Ligertwood Building toilets and invited me to see the Footlights extravaganza for that year, *They Route Horses Don't They?* (Why it was spelled that way I have never been able to work out. Perhaps they were being coy.)

I saw the show. A little too much singing and dancing for my liking but there were some funny people in it, including

SUBPOENA HARD DAY'S NIGHT

McCaffrie. I went backstage after the show and he introduced me to everyone, most of whom were in their final year and would soon be leaving the club. Vacancies were opening up, and McCaffrie encouraged me to put my name down.

I was reluctant. McCaffrie made no secret of the fact that the only reason he had decided to attend law school was so he could join Footlights and inveigle his way into their revues. He knew exactly what he wanted to do for a living and that was to make comedy. I, on the other hand, was going to law school so I could become a lawyer because as much as I loved comedy, I never thought of it as something that could pay for things like food and shelter. McCaffrie insisted I at least drop by the first Sunday writers' meeting in the new year to see what I thought. I figured this would probably mean missing out on the movie matinee double feature but okay – Oxbridge Footlights was where Peter Cook and Dudley Moore and *Monty Python* and most of the *Not the Nine O'Clock News* people came from, so maybe it'd be fun.

A few weeks later, I put on my tangerine shirt, cords and Ciaks and caught a couple of buses to the rich side of town where the meeting was to be held. I was early but the guy whose house it was invited me in and we were making small talk in the lounge room when his girlfriend sashayed in and took her top off so he could massage her. It was so beyond the realm of my experience that I continued the conversation as if nothing was happening. I even read out one of my scripts. She had a few notes and I did my best to look her in the eye and nod. Mercifully the others arrived, and she put her jumper back on.

Auditions were held the following week. McCaffrie assured me it would be a mere formality as far as I was concerned.

There I met someone who was about as *unlike* me as anyone could get without belonging to a different phylum. Firstly, he actually had some talent; several, in fact: his audition piece was a spirited rendition of Herod's song from *Jesus Christ Superstar* while accompanying himself on the piano. Plus, he could play the clarinet and the banjolele. For me, comedy was a default setting; I couldn't do anything else.

This guy was sophisticated, able to speak not only French but also Russian while I was still trying to get my head around English. Posh too, having gone to an expensive school in the eastern suburbs instead of the stick-in-the-dirt joint McCaffrie and I had mooched around in. His name was Francis Greenslade. During our many post-show dinners, he'd eschew the beer we'd got for the table, order himself a Chablis and, smouldering Gitane between his fingers, regale us all with stories of his youth on the island of Guadalcanal, where his parents were entomologists and he'd had a rare beetle named after him. It was like he'd been written by Evelyn Waugh.

When he was inevitably elected president of the Footlights Club (the best I could manage was club secretary), Francis always made sure our wrap parties were classy, well-catered affairs with enough prawns and Veuve Clicquot to choke a horse. Our time together in Footlights proved ridiculously enjoyable, and somehow McCaffrie and I have managed to trick Francis into squandering his gifts on our work in the forty years since.

Francis and I might not have been the funniest people auditioning that day, but we wanted it more. The best of the lot of us was a guy named Al Ward. When his name was called, he entered the room, threw himself on a bank of stacked chairs and then did an impression of two pieces of plasticine arguing with each other in Italian. *That* was his audition. He was and remains the funniest person I have ever seen. Mercifully, he didn't pursue a professional comedy career and Francis and I never had to compete with him.

Footlights also introduced me to alcohol. This made meeting new people much less complicated. Onstage I could pretend not to notice I was being observed by playing a character; offstage, I avoided the problem by rendering myself insensible with wine and beer.

The revues afforded me the chance to play to larger and larger groups in actual theatres. It was perfect. Not only did I not have to meet those showing their appreciation for me, I didn't even have to *see* them, thanks to the auditorium lights being off and leaving my glasses side-stage before I walked on. For someone who found it hard to strike up a conversation with four or five people after a tutorial, I had no trouble acting the goat in front of a thousand strangers, wearing my father's tracksuit and my mother's old wig. Even today, I'm more comfortable being 'on' than not when I'm with others. People assume I'm an extrovert because of the way I carry on on TV, but really I'm an introvert *pretending* to be an extrovert. Actually, no – I'm an extrovert *so worried* about looking like a show-off that I present as a faux-introvert masquerading as what I really am so I can pass it all off as an act if anyone calls me on it. That's not to say there was nothing for me to be painfully shy about when I was younger; it's just that I was self-aware enough to know that people found my natural clumsiness or the way I looked funny and so I would lean into those things for a laugh.

It's exactly this sort of meta-paradox that makes me such a fascinating subject for a book.

My friends at uni were by and large those I rehearsed, wrote and performed with: like-minded fans of comedy. Some were good actors who could deliver a joke; others, like me, cared about acting only as much as was necessary to get the laugh and as many more as could be grabbed on the way. The script we'd laboured on for all of two weeks was merely the starting point. As soon as that blurry blob in the auditorium started responding, I considered myself free to ignore what was written, change it, subvert it, ad-lib and improvise in order to wring out every possible reaction. Looking back, I can see how this lack of discipline might have irritated those keen on serving the text. But unless it was a different show every night and I was enjoying myself, what was the point?

My old high-school friends slowly fell away and this new lot replaced them. We got together after our exams, swapped jokes, workshopped material, wrote things out, practised the sketches, glued up posters, handed out flyers, put on the shows, went to afterparties, ate pizzas, got drunk, waited for the reviews, commiserated with each other, got drunk some more, and woke up the next morning under a table.

We didn't socialise much between shows. Putting on a show – whether it's a university revue or a TV show – tends to hot-house your friendships, but they seldom last once the season is over. The familiarity, the closeness, the camaraderie are all in the service of the thing you are creating together and, once it's done, the friendships go on hold until next time. If there is no next time, you just never see them again. It shouldn't come as any surprise to learn that you don't really get to know anybody that well when you're pretending to be someone else all the time. The exception was probably McCaffrie, who was both law student and Footlighter, although we would tend to catch up only in the photocopying room of the Sir John Salmond Library as he xeroxed my notes at exam time. Perhaps we would have seen more of each other if he'd actually attended some of his lectures.

Since the debacle of my first law ball, my idea of a fun weekend was going to a Marx Brothers or Woody Allen film festival by myself. So uncertain was I about initiating anything even vaguely romantic with anyone that it was easier to just not consider it, waiting instead until someone expressed some interest in me first. Of course, because there was no real emotional underpinning to my contribution, these relationships would sputter out soon after in a mess of awkwardness, with me not quite knowing how to act and the other party thinking my heart wasn't quite in it, which of course it wasn't. For most of my time at university, the closest I ever allowed myself to get to a woman was the night I danced with Princess Diana.

[needle scratch]

Oh, yes. It was 1983 in the Helen Mayo Refectory. The Student Union threw a disco and invited the Prince and Princess of Wales, who happened to be in town at the same time. For some reason, they accepted. I assume the equerry responsible was later executed. Anyway, the night was rolling along and the royal couple had arrived fashionably late – though, unfortunately for them, not so late as to have missed the evening entirely. They were mingling with various quasi-dignitaries when suddenly the DJ put on Haircut One Hundred's 'Love Plus One'. Charles and Di took to the floor to much cheering. Within seconds everyone was up dancing and I, invited as a duly elected member of the Student Union, found myself bopping along in the proximity of the royal couple. The Princess, of course, was dancing with her husband, but at one point she spun around at the exact moment I did and if you had taken a picture of it and cropped everybody else out, including Charles directly behind her, it would have appeared as if Di and I were grooving together. Our eyes met for the briefest of moments and who knows what might have transpired had things been different. But it could never be.

She was a princess married to the next in line to the throne and I was an idiot in a yellow velour jumper. She smiled that shy smile of hers more or less in my direction and I grinned gormlessly back, showing her I was still wearing braces. We turned back to our respective dance partners in time with the music: Charles was still there and whoever I was dancing with had sensibly gone off to get a drink.

| | | / ⁄_

I had joined a few clubs and societies when I started at university but seldom attended meetings. I even inadvertently signed up with ASIO one year. Presumably, I am part of a sleeper cell and I will get an email activating me at some point. Some memberships, though, I did take seriously: the Australian Union of Students executive which got me invited to Charles and Di's hootenanny, for example; also, the Law Students' Society council which, every winter, allowed us the opportunity to try and capture Chancellor J.J. Bray as he roamed the campus in search of food. I also wrote the occasional piece for a university newspaper, one of which, in my final year, taught me more about the laws of defamation than the actual course on the topic I'd had to sit through as part of my degree.

Adelaide, as I'm sure you're aware, is *the* place to be if you want to be murdered. It has plenty of other things going for it too, of course: WOMADelaide, the Schützenfest, frog cakes,

Cowley's pie cart, Tom Roberts's *A Break Away!*, that Stobie pole Clifton Pugh painted that time – but mainly it's murder on a dark and grisly scale not seen since the days of Jack the Ripper.

One of the most fascinating cases ever to baffle the police involved a woman by the name of Emily Perry. Her brother had died of arsenic poisoning, her late first husband had suffered from arsenic poisoning, and her second husband too had, it seemed, gone to his reward having been poisoned. When her third husband turned up at hospital suffering from poisoning by arsenic, the authorities swung into action. She was arrested, charged with attempted murder, arraigned, convicted, imprisoned and eventually let out again by the High Court. Something to do with not being able to rely on similar fact evidence (I forget exactly). Her third husband, happily recovered, stood by her through it all.

Of course, I thought it was all very funny – and indeed by Adelaide's usual standards of homicide, it was – and so I wrote what I believed was a satirical transcript of her examination-in-chief in the style of *Punch*'s A.P. Herbert for the university's weekly broadsheet. I'll spare you the details. Suffice to say my version of Emily Perry was quite happy to admit her crimes and several others which hadn't been attributed to her but were on the books at the time. She professed an unquenchable desire to murder everybody and anyone at any time using not only arsenic and other substances but also knives and axes. Despite her confession under oath, she was acquitted. The law is an ass. The end.

Or so I thought.

The real Emily Perry and her still very much alive third husband happened through the university cloisters one sunny afternoon as part of their daily constitutional and came across a big pile of unread uni rags. Perhaps in need of some lining for an aviary back home, they picked up several copies and— well, you can guess the rest. Lawyers became involved and the Adelaide University Union, as publisher, was sued; as were a couple of good friends of mine who happened to be the editors. It was an indication of just how good a couple of friends they were that they did not give me up and so I managed to graduate from law school without having my name blackened in court, which could have made getting a job in a law firm more difficult than it might have been already because of my less than stellar academic results.

Unfortunately, my first job ended up being at the same firm that was defending the university union and its editors. I was called in to the managing partner's office and told in no uncertain terms that I was to have nothing to do with this matter and that I must not, under any circumstances, go anywhere near the court while the hearing was taking place. Of course, I went down straight away with another articled clerk and watched most of it from the gallery in the manner of Atticus Finch's children in *To Kill a Mockingbird*. I even photocopied the transcript from the file when I got back to the office. The real one was much funnier than the one I'd written. The case was eventually settled for a modest sum without my identity ever being revealed. Even today, some forty years later, no one knows that it was I – Shaun Micallef – what done it.*

| | | /⁄⎽

I met Leandra on my final day at law school and it was only then that life – and not just my personal life, but Life in general – started to make some sort of sense. Though I met her after my last ever exam and was, as was my wont, as drunk as Oliver Reed, she was not so appalled that she didn't want to talk to me the next time we met; in fact, we talked all night. She was beautiful, funny and smart. We shared many of the same friends and it turned out we not only came from the same side of town but had even both been to Sacred Heart College, albeit three years apart. We loved the beach, films, ideas and a life without airs and graces. She wasn't at all needy or obsessed with attention either, so me larking about onstage was given its proper inconsequential weight.

Over the next forty years, Leandra would be the keystone in my various attempts to become a more complete and better person. She taught me to value myself from within, rather than rely on my worth to others – which is why I don't read reviews today (or at least pretend not to). My emotional growth would be slower than hers but we grew in the same direction. Though I'd like to think I was as much a helpful stake in the ground alongside her as she was for me, I suspect that's wishful

---

* I checked. They're both dead. Natural causes, I assume. Unless …

thinking. As inextricably intertwined and entangled as our two lives have become, I can't help feeling I'm the wisteria in this relationship. On any reckoning, I'd not have had the life and career I've had or become the husband and the father I am without her. I owe her everything. Plus, when we met, she had a driver's licence and an XT Falcon with mag wheels.

We were married just six years later in the chapel of our old school and the elderly organist played Leandra down the aisle to the 'Trumpet Voluntary' (with a few extra notes of his own thrown in). We honeymooned in Hong Kong and stayed at the same hotel as Inspector Clouseau in *Revenge of the Pink Panther*. Students were protesting over something or other but we were young and in love and had sights to see. A media blackout as we left for a tour to the mainland meant we had little to tell the protesting students we met in Guangzhou when they asked what was going on. Change was in the air and the mood was optimistic. We could feel it. We took their pictures, they gave us some of their protest flags and we went off and bought things at markets. Busloads of young people waved their flags as they passed and we waved ours back. As we boarded the return ferry our flags were confiscated by border guards. The tour guide had to give his name. Back in Hong Kong the students were now on strike. Then a hunger strike. By the time we were in Singapore having our picture taken at a zoo with an orangutan, Beijing had declared martial law, and a week after we got home the massacre at Tiananmen Square took place. Our photos had just been developed when Bob Hawke wept in parliament and offered asylum to the 42,000 Chinese nationals in our country. When democracy has always been with you, it's easy to forget that someone somewhere sometime had to fight for it. It's hard – if not impossible – to imagine an Australian government today being so free with its permanent visas.

## CHAPTER FIVE

# Tentative strides

*FAST FORWARD* WAS a very successful and popular sketch comedy show on Channel 7 during the late '80s and early '90s. It launched the careers of Steve Vizard, Magda Szubanski, Gina Riley, Jane Turner, Michael Veitch, Marg Downey (my favourite) and Peter Moon. I was not in it.

What I was in was the much less successful and not quite as popular sketch comedy show *Full Frontal,* which replaced *Fast Forward* when it finished. It was much the same show and had the same directors and producers and crew. The first season, in 1993, had guest appearances from the big-name *Fast Forward* team, but I wasn't in that version either.

I came along in the second year of *Full Frontal* after the big names had moved on. I wasn't even in the cast when I started. I was a writer. My contract was for $120 a week and I earned additional money doing occasional work as a background extra. My first appearance on the show was holding an umbrella in a golf sketch featuring Eric Bana.

This wasn't my first time on television, though. When I was about six years old, I appeared on a show on Channel 9 in Adelaide called *The Magic Circle Club*. The woman who claims to be my mother had taken me along to watch the show being made, and during the segment where a superimposed halo would appear over the head of a child in the audience, I was selected. There was applause and much urging from my mother to go with the floor manager and join the hosts, who included a clown called Bobo who was so famous he had his own brand of cordial. I went up and sat next to Bobo, who was much bigger and more terrifying than the soft-toy version which sat on my pillow at home. It didn't take me too long to realise that Bobo was just a man dressed up as a clown rather than an *actual* clown. I could see him sweating a little under the lights and he reminded me of the clowns I'd seen at the circus, who I'd also noticed were just men wearing make-up and costumes and weren't really all that funny.

The grey-haired host with the craggy face asked me a few questions and Bobo laughed and clapped his hands at my perfectly straight answers. It was a short interview; I was asked what my name was (Shaun) and where I lived (I didn't know). I was then invited to have a go on the Test-Your-Strength machine and maybe win the prize: the toy speedboat that was circling the inflatable wading pool next to us. This seemed a pretty good deal and so I agreed, to the delight of Bobo.

*Pung!* I'd brought down the mallet they'd given me onto the steel plate but the bell didn't ring and the audience let out a disappointed 'ooooh'. I had seen this happen on the show before, so I wasn't too worried. As expected, I was encouraged to have another go – but again, no bell. I started to get a little concerned now because I'd really put a bit of effort into that last swing. I was urged to have a third try and, as I sensed this was my final chance to win that boat, I brought the mallet down with all my might and sent the puck higher … but not high enough.

This time, though, the sound of a bell could be heard through the PA system and the audience cheered. I pointed out to Bobo that the puck hadn't hit the bell and he laughed and clapped. The lady host said it was okay and that I'd won the speedboat, but I was quite sure the bell had not been struck and pointed vaguely up into the studio roof, trying to explain the bell noise had nothing to do with me. The craggy-faced man got up, grabbed the mallet from me and smashed it down onto the steel plate with such force that it startled Bobo and he stopped laughing and clapping. The bell rang out clear as a bell. I was given the dripping speedboat and hurried off so they could cut to a commercial.

My mother was so delighted you'd have thought *she*'d won the prize, but it occurred to me as I sat back down that this whole TV thing might not quite be what it appeared – a feeling that persists to this day. Worse still, I never really enjoyed playing with the speedboat because I felt I didn't deserve it. It mostly sat in my cupboard and for years after I had feelings of guilt when I happened across it. Fortunately, my golliwog cardigan was also in there to soothe me.

The next time I was on television was as part of the ABC's attempt to turn *Theatre Sports* into a TV show. I was by then in my early twenties, the innocence of my youth switched for the glib cynicism of an articled clerk in a medium-sized Adelaide law firm. By day, I went down to the post office to get the franking machine filled at the request of my secretary; by night, I performed comedy with the cavalier derring-do of someone who didn't actually have to do it for a living. Our impro team, however, composed entirely of lawyers but for Francis, did not do well and we were bounced from the competition pretty early. No speedboat for us.

'Back to obscurity,' sighed the captain of one of the other unsuccessful teams as we shared the lift down to the ABC car park. The implication that what we'd just been doing had even fleetingly elevated our profiles was optimistic at best. Perhaps even deluded. Either way, I thought I was done.

Then, a few months later, in one of those moments that only ever seem to happen in Judy Garland–Mickey Rooney movies, I arrived back to my office after lunch to find a note on my desk telling me that Andrew Denton had called. This was the equivalent of Flo Ziegfeld sending his card to your dressing-room. Andrew had been in one of the other *Theatre Sports* teams and we'd got to know him a little. He had since gone on to host *World Series Debating* for the ABC. I rang him back immediately, trying not to sound too excited. We exchanged pleasantries and quickly got down to business. They were shooting a debate in Adelaide in two weeks; someone had just dropped out; they needed a last-minute replacement and Andrew was wondering whether I had Francis Greenslade's phone number.

Concealing my disappointment with way too much enthusiasm for how wonderful Francis would be, I flipped through my Filofax for his number and passed it on. Despite my boiling jealousy, I managed to watch the show when it eventually went to air and not leave the room or start talking to Leandra when Francis came on. Seeing the video cassette of the episode for sale at Christmas was a bit too much for me, though, so I just avoided buying presents that year.

At the time I'd really thought that I would remain in the law for the rest of my life, rising up the ranks to partnership, perhaps going to chambers as a barrister, eventually becoming a judge, getting appointed to the International Court of The Hague as chief justice, even ending up as UN secretary-general – and yet here I was, only ten years later, writing for the poor, backward cousin of one of the most popular and successful shows on Australian television. I really had no business being there.

For a start, I had no experience writing for television apart from a few scripts I'd sent in to *The Big Gig* for Glynn Nicholas. I knew Glynn from Adelaide and thought he was a genius. Still do. Glynn had seen my performance during the Adelaide

Fringe Festival one year as a children's show presenter who read stories that would turn unsettling after a few lines and get increasingly bloodthirsty as they went on, ending in some stomach-churning denouement. He'd obviously liked the idea because he promptly used it in his own show the following year. Given I'd pretty much stolen the idea from Peter Sellers anyway ('Auntie Rotter', 1958, Parlophone), I gave Glynn the script I'd used ('The Fish that Was Naughty', based on *Jaws*), together with the prop book I'd pasted it in so I didn't have to learn it, and wished him well.

Writing for *Full Frontal*, though, was a different proposition to writing for *The Big Gig*. *The Big Gig* was a live-to-air variety show with some filmed inserts and it more resembled the cabaret shows I was used to writing; *Full Frontal*, on the other hand, was a proper television show which had the look and feel of the movies, commercials, news bulletins and TV series it was parodying. I wasn't going to be able to just submit the sort of revue material I'd written at university and expect them to shoot it.

Mind you, I was to find that out later; at the time, I thought that was *exactly* what I could do. It hadn't even occurred to me that I might not be good enough to do it and that my inexperience would trip me up. It wasn't so much arrogance on my part as sheer cluelessness. I simply didn't know what I didn't know.

When I'd popped over from Adelaide a few years before to watch an episode of *The Big Gig* get made, I was introduced to the head writer, Patrick Cook. He was a pretty big wheel back then: a well-known satirical cartoonist for *The Bulletin* and a writer and performer on another ABC show, *The Dingo Principle.* I told him that I wanted to write TV comedy for a living and asked his advice. He didn't mince words. He told me my material was derivative (he must have had a copy of 'Auntie Rotter') and that if he were me, he wouldn't be giving up his day job and moving to Melbourne just yet.

Patrick's discouragement didn't bother me. Looking back, it probably should have. In fact, I'm amazed I was so impervious to it. It certainly wasn't because I had unshakeable faith in myself as a writer; I wasn't at all confident I could make a go of it. I knew I had some ability as a performer because I could get laughs from an audience, but at thirty years of age, I thought that speedboat had well and truly sailed. An Adelaide theatre critic, who drew the short straw one night and had to review one of our Footlights shows, once said of me:

*Shaun Micallef appears just in time to save rotting sketches.*

What he didn't know was that I'd written the sketches.

By 1994, *The Big Gig* was over. Glynn, Wendy Harmer, the Empty Pockets, the Doug Anthony All Stars, Jean Kittson (my favourite) and Anthony Ackroyd had all moved on. So too *The Late Show* starring Rob Sitch, Jane Kennedy, Mick Molloy, Judith Lucy, Santo Cilauro, Tony Martin (my favourite) and Tom Gleisner. It was the last episode of *The Late Show,* in 1993, that made me realise that if I wanted a career in comedy, I'd better get off my arse and do something about it. The cast had come from university revue like I had and, although a couple of years younger than me, already had two TV shows* under their belt, both of which were funny – as much as it pained me to admit it. With *The Big Gig*, I just took it on trust it was funny; with *The Late Show* I could actually tell.

I hadn't watched a lot of *Fast Forward* because, as with *The Late Show*, as much as I enjoyed the performances, I felt threatened by it; the cast were close to my age and doing what I wanted to do. Steve Vizard had even gone on to host his own nightly chat show, just like Don Lane (or, as it turned out, David Letterman). There was a big picture of Steve advertising *Tonight Live* in the lobby of the Piccadilly Cinema on O'Connell Street that served only to make me more green eyed.

My old Footlights friend McCaffrie had been true to himself: he'd never practised law and had instead gone off to write for both *Fast Forward* and *Tonight Live*. It was on his recommendation that I got the job on *Full Frontal*. He suggested that I at least watch some of it before I came over and started writing, so I made sure I sat myself down to watch the last few minutes of what turned out to be the last episode for the 1993 season. I'm afraid it wasn't really my cup of tea.

While I'd never really understood what all the fuss was about with *The Big Gig*, I could at least tell the performers

---

* The other being *The D-Generation* (1986–89).

were skilled and committed to what they were doing; with *The Late Show*, there was an endearing unpolished, low-rent quality which helped connect the performers with the material they had obviously created themselves. With *Full Frontal*, though, it just looked like the performers were doing what they'd been told. There was no ownership of the material. The final sketch of that final show: a song sung straight that the credits rolled over, ended with the singer exploding, followed by a Spike Milligan–esque close-up of his smouldering boots. *The Late Show*, by contrast, had the actual Don Lane on to sing 'Saturday Night (Is the Loneliest Night of the Week)', taking over the camera like he used to do on his own show and giving away a gold necklace. Whatever you might have thought about closing numbers, it was clear that the cast were in on the joke on one show and largely irrelevant to it on the other.

As I hadn't been asked to write on *The Late Show* and it had finished anyway, I packed my red Ford Capri and, with my Amstrad word processor on the back seat and an ironing board sticking out the window, drove the 730 kilometres from Adelaide to Melbourne (actually, 940 kilometres because I made a wrong turn at Tailem Bend and accidentally took the Great Ocean Road).

||| /⁓

Having spent my whole life in Adelaide, moving to a new city to start a new career was a big deal for me. I was leaving everything behind: my family, my friends, my house, the only job I ever knew, and – amazingly, now that I think back on it – Leandra. But this whole thing had been her idea in the first place.

The way forward had been paved by a conversation we'd had the night we got engaged. We'd been a couple for about five years, give or take a break-up or two when we tried not to be. The break-ups hadn't worked out, so we found ourselves outside a health food shop in Hindmarsh Square wondering what to do next. I was twenty-five and she was twenty-two. Should we get married? I confessed to her I was thinking of quitting my job. She couldn't see how me quitting my job was relevant. What if I didn't have any money? *It didn't matter.* What if I didn't make it in whatever it was I tried next? *That didn't matter either.*

We were en route to see Ibsen's *Rosmersholm* – a fun night out in anyone's language, particularly if it's Norwegian. During one of its more tedious scenes, we proposed to each other and were married twelve months later. Six months after that, not quite being brave enough to quit my job, I took a year's sabbatical during which I wrote a couple of never-to-be-performed plays, made exactly the same dinner every night, appeared as Venticello 2 in an amateur production of *Amadeus* and popped over to Melbourne to have my dreams crushed by Patrick Cook. I ended up following Patrick's advice: I returned to my old job and worked there for a few more years while doing comedy on the side until Leandra, seeing clearly what

I wanted but dared not admit to myself, suggested I have a proper crack at it. Quit for good this time, try out the comedy thing for twelve months, and if it didn't work out then at least I wouldn't die wondering.

I can honestly say that if it hadn't been for Leandra, I'd be secretary-general of the UN today.

I might also be single, as one of the other problems we worked out together was my drinking. Because I didn't have a driver's licence when we started going out, I was able to drink as much as I wanted, knowing Leandra would be driving me home. I wasn't a particularly good drinker and it wouldn't take much to have me on my ear, yet I would continue to drink even after I was drunk as I was under the impression that it made me even more charming. Frankly, there didn't seem much point to drinking unless it was to excess. I certainly didn't enjoy the taste of it. Mainly, I think I was doing it out of habit. Only ever socially. I wouldn't drink at home. There was no audience there.

Things came to a pretty pass the Friday night I was supposed to meet Leandra and pick up a couch we'd bought from Le Cornu's. It was the first item of furniture we'd picked out together during our engagement. It was pink and had flowers on it. That wasn't the reason I didn't turn up. No, the reason I didn't turn up was that I was passed out upstairs near the lift at work. Drinks sessions with colleagues were not unusual for a Friday night. The conference room had a bar and the alcohol was free so we'd often load up and go out bar-hopping afterwards. Why I had drunk so much on that particular evening is a question I don't have an answer for.

I was roused after midnight by Leandra and her mother and her mother's poodle (brought in to help with the search). I remember little apart from hearing the word 'disgusting' from my soon-to-be mother-in-law, but that was probably enough. I stopped getting drunk after that. Eventually, because there didn't seem too much point having a drink unless it was to have too many, I stopped drinking altogether. It was only later that Leandra told me she wouldn't have hung around if I'd continued.

I'm afraid I have no wild hell-raising stories for you, unless you count the time after a revue when my Footlights friends and I danced around the empty streets of Adelaide at three in the morning doing *West Side Story*. I sang 'Something's Coming' to the statue of Colonel Light on Montefiore Hill. He points to the south, roughly the direction I would one day set off in to make my future. We crammed an empty KFC bucket on his finger so it looked like he was holding it and, pleased that we had made some vaguely satirical point about Colonel Light promoting a product normally associated with Colonel Sanders, danced into the dawn.

## CHAPTER SIX

# Welcome to television ...

I HAD BEEN concerned about how my parents would react to my leaving the law. From their perspective, they'd worked and saved my whole life so I could go to university and enjoy the fruits of their labour as a professional man in the city; from mine, it just sort of happened and the taxpayer footed the bill. Either way, I worried that news of me abandoning it all would disappoint them. My mother especially, because I think she would have loved to have gone to university and me going was the next best thing. As it happened, she was perfectly okay with it, perhaps blitzed by the other news that I would also be leaving the state; though she took that news pretty well too – and if she went through any inward turmoil about any of it, she didn't let on.

I make jokes about my mother (giving up on THAT would definitely be a disappointment to her), but she has never been anything less than supportive of whatever I have wanted to do in my life. I wanted to be in a pantomime, she arranged it; I wanted a red jumper like the one Jerry Lewis wore in *The Big Mouth*, she knitted it; I liked drawing, she signed me up to the Paul Rigby cartooning course. The James Bond *You Only Live Twice* Corgi diecast Toyota 2000 GT convertible in the toy shop window that I'd gazed at longingly on the way to church? She helped me save for it.

My mother taught me there was nothing I couldn't achieve if I wanted it enough. If a TV comedy writer was something I felt I could be, then there was no doubt in her mind that I would become one. It remains the greatest gift she could have given me. Although that James Bond *You Only Live Twice* convertible, which I'm sure she chipped in for when I wasn't looking, comes a close second.

My impressions of Melbourne had come mainly from seeing it on TV. I knew that Graham Kennedy and Bert Newton and one of my heroes, Barry Humphries, came from Melbourne and that *The Don Lane Show* (which I enjoyed) was made there, as was *Hey Hey It's Saturday* (not so much). I had the feeling that Melbourne was the place where funny people made funny TV shows. And radio too – though Fred Dagg was an émigré.

I'd picked up that there was some rivalry between Melbourne and Sydney. When I was about twelve, I'd watched the 1966 movie *They're a Weird Mob* on TV and seen Graham Kennedy pull up in a car, wind down the window and ask for directions to TCN 9 in Willoughby. A local, barely looking up from his paper, tells him he should drive 2000 miles to Cape York.

Graham mutters, 'They don't appreciate art in Sydney,' and then drives off. I'd asked my mother what they were talking about, and she explained that people from Sydney looked down on people from Melbourne. This thought nagged at me a little as I packed my bags; if Sydney didn't think much of Melbourne, where all these funny people and TV shows came from, where did Adelaide stand, given it didn't seem to make anything funny apart from Hills hoists and FruChocs?

After I passed through Bordertown, another thought took over. I noticed signs every now and then warning me about 'hook turns' in Melbourne. The signs featured an alarming diagram indicating that if I wanted to turn right in the city centre, I had to pull over to the left and somehow get in ahead of the cars already travelling across in front of me, also from my left. What the hell kind of city was I going to live in that not only had such a ridiculous road rule but felt the need to start warning you about it nine hours before you get there? By Ballarat, I'd resolved to deal with it simply by sticking to the suburbs.

Unfortunately, when I finally arrived in Melbourne, I went down the wrong off-ramp from the West Gate Bridge and somehow ended up on the Flemington roundabout, a multi-laned centrifuge fed by five major arterial roads and a set of tram tracks. It was a nightmare for born-and-bred Melbournians, never mind someone who'd been in town for thirty-five seconds. I tried to change lanes a few times but wasn't quite brave enough and so settled into a holding pattern on the inside lane with my hazard lights on. Eventually I committed to a left-hand move, flipped on the indicator, looked in the wrong side-mirror and wrenched the steering wheel. There followed a regatta of horn blasts and the scent and sound of skidding rubber. An apoplectic motorcyclist sped up and thumped my bonnet with his fist. 'Fucking South Australian,' he yelled and then gobbed on my ironing board.

Still, a lot friendlier than they'd probably have been to me in Sydney.

| | | | / ⁄—

*Full Frontal* starred Jennifer Ward-Lealand, Rima Te Wiata, Kim Gyngell, Glenn Butcher and Ross Williams for a while; then John Walker, Denise Scott and Sue Yardley; then Daina Reid, Julia Morris, Kitty Flanagan and Darren Gilshenan; then Gabby Millgate and Jackie Loeb. Even Francis Greenslade was on board for a year. And, of course, it launched the career of Eric Bana (everybody's favourite). It was a factory. Apart from a few greenhorns like me, most of the twenty-odd writers, like McCaffrie, had worked on *Fast Forward* and *Tonight Live* and were very used to churning out material day after week after month to toss under the mill wheel. *Full Frontal* was a commercial hour – forty-three minutes plus five ad breaks – every week for twenty-six weeks a year. Now, forty-three minutes doesn't sound like a lot when you have twenty-odd writers, and indeed it isn't. It's very easy to fill that amount of time; what's challenging is making sure it's funny. In charge of this were Andrew Knight and Doug MacLeod.

Andrew, who had written with the D-Gen and John Clarke and had a ponytail*, was an executive producer and co-owner of the production company with Steve Vizard, though we didn't see Steve very much. Doug was what the Americans call the showrunner and he was the one we presented our scripts to. As an experienced TV writer and the author of a few books, he was a stickler for correct spelling and good grammar; it would, for example, have rankled with him that my previous sentence ended with a preposition. In fact, it wasn't even just the English language he was keen we know how to use; the first time I said the word 'ingénue' out loud was in front of Doug and I had pronounced it 'in-*yoo*-jenny'. He was one of the first in the industry to realise that beneath the head that bore the bookish glasses and hair flecked with experienced grey beat the brain of a moron. Fortunately for me, he never let on to anyone else.

We worked next to Channel 7's South Melbourne studios, just on the corner of the lot, in a jerry-built fibro hut everyone referred to ironically as 'the Castle'; someone had even put a sign up on the building to that effect, thus ruining the joke. It was cold and cramped, painted police-station blue and filled with mismatched tables and chairs and not enough Apple Macs for everyone. As my Amstrad floppy disks were

---

\* He later went on to lose the ponytail and write the Academy Award–winning *Hacksaw Ridge*.

incompatible with Apple Macintosh (and indeed every other word processor in the world) and I therefore couldn't work from home, I had to get in early to secure a spot. Up the back was what looked to be a cupboard, and inside a man named Alf, who had nothing whatsoever to do with the show, would sit at an editing desk transferring 16mm footage of old VFL games onto video tape. He was a reminder to us all of the outside world.

Those writers who worked from home only ever came in to submit their material, which we all did by dropping it in a cardboard box outside Doug's office. Doug would empty the box a couple of times a day and work through the material. If it passed muster, he might make cuts or add things, give it a tick and send it upstairs to Andrew, where it might have further changes made to it and be given a second tick. Thereafter it would go into 'the system' and end up with Ted Emery, the director, who would shoot it – or, if he didn't like it, wouldn't get around to shooting. Sometimes, Doug would give your script a tick and Andrew would give it a cross and there might be a few comments to help you with a rewrite. Other times, you'd just get a cross with 'sorry' written under it. Scripts with crosses would be put on a clipboard up on a wall under your name. It was the first thing you would see when you walked into the Castle. McCaffrie called it 'hanging out your dead'.

In my first week I reworked what I considered to be all the best material from my university revue and cabaret days. This was the stuff I knew was funny because we had performed it in front of an audience and they had laughed. I had about twenty-five of these babies lined up and my plan was to mix them in with my new scripts over the first year so that even if I had a lean week there would always be at least one or two sure-fire laugh-getters in there. But then I got overexcited and submitted all twenty-five of them on the first day.

The next morning, I walked in to see my clipboard groaning with dead scripts. All twenty-five of them. The comments on them from Doug were gentle but there was no getting around it: my stuff stank.

Doug stuck his head out of his office and invited me in. He went through a few scripts and explained why he'd rejected them. Fortunately, I was too stupid to realise what a terrible first impression I'd made; I assumed everybody's first day was like this. Upstairs I went to Andrew, who wrote a sketch with me. Again, I was too stupid to be embarrassed that I was being given a remedial class in How To Write a Script for TV.

Unbeknown to me, McCaffrie was assigned to teach me the ropes. This was fine with me; he and I had written together in the old days and it just felt like an extension of that. It was only later I learned that I was being babysat. Had McCaffrie not vouched for me, I'm sure I would have been let go.

Eventually I was submitting things that were approved by both Doug and Andrew and went into the system. Now my only obstacle was Ted, but that wouldn't be for a few weeks.

*Full Frontal* was still in pre-production – by which I mean we were just writing and scheduling but not actually shooting – when Steve Vizard ambled in to raid the growing stockpile of scripts. He was looking for material for another show they were making named after its Irish comedian star, Jimeoin. Steve picked a few of my sketches (one, about a vegan restaurant that sold only meat dishes, was a bit ordinary, but the acceptance speech of a young Lifetime Achievement award winner depressed that he'd peaked so early wasn't too bad). The scripts were given to Jim's co-star, Bob Franklin, to perform. I was now officially writing for *two* shows. I got to know Bob and Jim and also Glenn Robbins, who was on this other show too and was already quite famous from his time in *The Comedy Company* (yet another show I could never bring myself to watch). Everyone appearing in *Jimeoin* was a funny writer as well as a performer and I felt more at home working on this show than I had so far on *Full Frontal*, where you were either one or the other.

Jim, Bob and Glenn would test out their material at a hotel down the road from the studio and I would tag along to watch, eventually getting up onstage myself to try my hand at stand-up. It was fine every now and then, but I could never imagine myself doing it for a living. There was something dark and depressing about it, and many of the stand-ups I met seemed to hate what they were doing. They only really enjoyed themselves after the show, when they could schmooze, tell war stories and bag each other. Before the show, they would pace around in whatever grim holding cell management had provided, beer in one hand, notes in the other, haunted looks on their faces as they listened to the audience responding (or not) to whoever was on stage. This was not necessarily a show of support or schadenfreude; rather, they were getting an idea of what they were in for when they went out there themselves.

For me, all this was a foreign country. Thanks to my sketch revue background, I was used to everyone going on at the same time and performing together; almost no one ever went on by themselves in an ensemble cast unless it was for a song or monologue so the scenery could be changed behind the curtain. While I could admire the timing and inventiveness of the stand-ups, I thought it a very lonely way to experience the pleasure of making someone laugh.

Jimeoin loved it, though; in fact, I think he preferred it to making the TV show, which seemed to be the glittering prize craved by most of the stand-ups. But TV is a complicated machine where a hundred or so people all play a part in telling the joke; onstage, it's just the comedian. They are completely different disciplines and not everyone can adapt.

As part of Jim's entourage, we would go along to the Athenaeum and watch him perform sold-out shows. The crowds loved him. Material that, on paper, looked like nothing at all to me would bring the house down. It taught me very early on that whatever rules I thought there were to comedy didn't mean anything at the end of the day; a funny enough person could go off-road whenever they wanted and make an audience laugh by sheer force of will. If the audience liked you and you were committed to the joke, the audience would go with you.

Jim was a rockstar, by which I mean he was so self-assured and so brimming with confidence that to me he seemed to be from another planet. Eric Bana had the same quality; Mick Molloy too. Even before they made it big, they carried themselves with certainty. I found this so difficult to relate to that I never really got to know them that well when I worked with them. I found I had more in common with Bob and Glenn; maybe it was their admission of self-doubt now and then. The audience would tell us what was funny – until then we were all really only guessing.

Glenn was a good guide – everyone looked up to him and valued his opinion. It was hard to make him laugh, not because he was a tough audience but because he had seen so much comedy that he couldn't help but approach it like a scientist. He'd listen thoughtfully to the joke, mull it over a moment and say, 'Yes, that's funny' (the best response), or he'd dissect it for you and explain why it wasn't (just as valuable). The other thing that was great about Glenn was that he'd be that way with *everybody*, regardless of where you were on the ladder. I don't think he even thought there was a ladder. He'd as happily entertain an idea from someone with no runs on the board, like me, as he would from Steve Vizard.

It was Glenn who introduced me to Steve as the one who'd written the scripts he'd raided from the *Full Frontal* box. I was manning the bar in the green room after one of the live night records. Glenn suggested I had a good voice for voice-overs. 'Your gin and tonic, sir,' I said in a deeper voice than usual, handing over his drink. Steve agreed, and the next day I was suddenly the voice-over guy on *Jimeoin*. Writers were often happily lured into sketches in bit parts or as extras, and pretty soon I also found myself acting like a seagull in a sketch with Glenn and fellow writer Dave O'Neil.

My big break on *Jimeoin* came when I had to pretend to be a political satirist while Bob and Jim upstaged me in the background. This was the first time on TV I'd been front and centre and introduced by my real name. My job was to do dry political 'jokes' while the real comedy was happening behind me: i.e. Jim and Bob appearing from under a counter wearing a variety of amusing hats. It got good laughs from the studio audience but at one point I had mistakenly referred to the former ambassador to Ireland during the Whitlam era as Vince *Gore* instead of Vince *Gair* and asked if we could do a second take. They all looked at me as if I was insane.

Perhaps I was. Alone in a new city, there was literally nothing to do but hang around the studio, living and breathing whatever was going on there. I had gone from doing comedy in my spare time to having nothing but spare time and I couldn't stop myself from gorging on it all. I hadn't realised just how hungry I was.

By the time *Full Frontal* started taping, I knew quite a few of the writers and became the go-to voice-over guy on that production as well. One of the senior writers had written a sketch that was entirely voice-over: a station announcement that Mr Bean was up next but instead of a brief outline of the episode, there was a complete and detailed description of every scene, including the physical gags. It got nice laughs on the live night and I sought out the writer afterwards. 'Hey, I thought that Mr Bean thing went well,' I said nonchalantly, as I passed him in the corridor. 'Yeah, thanks,' he said, on his way somewhere else; then, perhaps sensing my need for validation, he added over his shoulder: 'Nice read.'

Nice *read?* I had done more than *read* it. I had given it life! It would have been *nothing* without my performance! I wandered off in search of more effusive compliments.

There is no shortage of places to go and hang out at a TV station. There was the control room, where Ted would sometimes let me do the iso switch – by which I mean he would do the on-line switch between cameras during the sketches and my job was to make sure we recorded other angles that might be helpful if he changed his mind in the edit. Should he be after an out-of-focus shot of a door or a series of exactly the same shots he had already, then mine was the cut he could rely on.

By day, I could also be found loitering around the scenery bay and the workshop, where I could watch a set get built for a sketch I'd written. So much money and effort for such a dumb idea, I remember thinking, as they constructed the entire edifice of an office block I'd have someone jumping off later in the week. The studio floor was where I could go and watch the actors; the edit suite was where I'd watch Andrew or Doug or Ted cut an ordinary sketch into a better one, or a rubbish sketch into at least something shorter.

It was in the edit suite where I really learned to write for TV. The rhythm, the beats, filling a moment during a laugh, the importance of cutaways, reaction shots, quick set-ups, getting out early, not telling a joke in five lines if you could do it in two. I understood why all my scripts had been rejected that first day: they'd been way, *way* too slow. I'd been writing pieces for the stage, where the audience could luxuriate in a performance and be won over slowly. TV was fast. All the things that I might naturally do as a performer to material as I delivered it (dropping a line, condensing others, pacing things up) I would have to anticipate as best I could as a writer and put into the script beforehand.

The post-production sound mix was also educational, and Ted would often invite me to join him in making fart noises, whether the sketch called for it or not.

The most fun to be had at the studio, though, was in the cafeteria. This was where the writers could sit around and try and make each other laugh. I was reasonably good at throwing in the odd quip, but the stand-ups were better at telling stories. We all carried tiny notebooks and when funny thoughts occurred to us, we would write them down with our equally tiny pens. I think we'd all seen Glenn Robbins do this and so we thought we'd better copy him. It was disconcerting, though, if, in the middle of a conversation, one of the group would suddenly write something down in their tiny book because it felt like some moment of inspiration had been missed by the rest of us. Worst of all was when you were talking to another writer about nothing and they would suddenly stop you and say: 'Can I use that?' I always felt obliged to say yes, but others would happily say no and write it down themselves. Eventually I dispensed with the tiny book, figuring that if I had a half-decent idea, I would probably remember it anyway.

Gradually, as I had done on *Jimeoin*, I crept my way on camera in *Full Frontal*. After I had done my time standing in the background holding umbrellas, I was cast in a live night sketch. While I can't remember the sketch (I hadn't written it), I do remember that I got some laughs and felt very disappointed when my bit was cut out when the sketch went to air. I asked why and Andrew told me the audience wasn't always right. This is complicated but true. Also, I had been getting laughs independently of – or perhaps in spite of – the material; and there is nothing that annoys a writer more than an actor who mugs all over your script. Of course, I mug like crazy in *Mad as Hell* – but only in the gaps *between* the jokes, never *during* them (unless I'm desperate).

## CHAPTER SEVEN

# Character building

AS SCRIPT EDITOR for *Full Frontal*, Doug MacLeod would have an overview of how things were shaping up week by week and would occasionally commission certain types of sketches he felt were needed for a particular show. It might be a parody of an annoying ad or newly released movie (he once got Dave O'Neil and me to write one about *Cliffhanger*; given neither of us had seen the film, it did end up relying a bit too much on Eric Bana's Stallone impression*). Sometimes, he'd just need a short piece to break up the longer ones, and one week he whipped up a series of easy-to-shoot quickie sketches in the form of a serial called *The Bank,* which centred on two dull admin workers in neighbouring cubicles who, after a dramatic opening title sequence, talk about nothing for a

---

* None of us had time to go and watch the films. We once did a parody of *Die Hard with a Vengeance* (1995). In between set-ups for something else, Ted watched eight seconds of the trailer on a VHS tape before turning to me and saying, 'It's brown.' He was spot on. My impression of Jeremy Irons, though, wasn't.

couple of seconds, followed by dramatic outro music and a voice-over promising more next time. He cast me as one of the workers. Poor Denise Scott, from the actual cast, had been saddled with this interloper from the writers' room to do seven of these damn things, which Doug planned on using across the series. Andrew, though, liked them so much he used them all in one episode.

I was praised by Ted for my 'eye-acting' – which was a polite way of referring to my mugging – and he started casting me in more and more things. He liked the broader, physical stuff I could do, and I was happy to oblige. He didn't like stuff that was, as he described it, 'up your bum'. I'd once written a five-minute monologue called 'Ex Tempore Misjudgement' which amazingly had managed to get past Doug and Andrew and into the system. Ted returned it with the words 'Aren't we clever?' scrawled over it.

Ted and I shared a love of silent film comedy and sight gags and I have him to thank for whatever I know about telling a joke using the visual part of the TV medium. Frankly, I don't think sketches like 'Ex Tempore Misjudgement' would have taken me very far. He also showed me how cast and crew could work together as a crack unit with the same objective in mind, like the sketch you were shooting was a military operation. Ted didn't talk much about his past but it was rumoured he'd flown choppers in Vietnam. I assume for the Viet Cong.

With so many minutes to fill every week, *Full Frontal* had a proper big-budget movie-sized production team. There was not only a main unit, with trucks and buses and lights and catering tents, but also a sleeker and more agile second unit. This usually comprised one camera, no lights, and you'd have to change in the car. Today the second unit has become the industry standard, and back in 1994 it was the unit I graduated to on *Full Frontal*.

Doug, Andrew and Ted began encouraging me as a performer and they let me do some particularly empty things in the quickie-filler style of *The Bank* – but as a TV reporter called David McGahan, named after a boy I went to school with whom everyone teased because his name was so unremarkable. Whoever was fronting the news desk on *Full Frontal* (usually Rima Te Wiata or Kitty Flanagan) would say something like, '... and now David McGahan reports to us live from a bakery,' and we would cut to McGahan in front of a bakery, but there was no report. He would merely confirm he was indeed in front of a bakery and then throw back to the studio.

The spots grew longer, with McGahan going into greater and greater detail as he confirmed where he was and why he wasn't perhaps somewhere else. He would use convoluted metaphors and unnecessarily complicate things, often talking himself into a corner before petering out and throwing back. Eventually he had his own segment called *David McGahan's World Around Him*, a nod to Channel 7's long-running *World Around Us* series, which was usually named after whichever newsreader was at a loose end at the time. McGahan would present an extremely short documentary film, usually running no more than ten seconds, with much the same build-'em-up-give-'em-nothing format of *The Bank,* but longer and emptier: titles and grand music in the style of Carl Orff, followed by a by-now almost incomprehensible McGahan trying to explain what we were about to see, which would be virtually nothing, then a redundant and meaningless back announce by McGahan and the *Carmina Burana*–like play-off.

After thirteen episodes, McCaffrie and I were put in charge of producing *Full Frontal* (with no change of pay). We took to it like hopped-up Visigoths: trimming the cast, changing the opening titles, pissing off most of the writers by not using their material and generally transforming the show into something far less popular by abandoning the sort of comedy audiences had been enjoying for the past three seasons in favour of more arcane fare. My six-minute sketch about the police investigating a kidnapped tooth and McCaffrie's *Sale of the Century* parody using entirely rhetorical questions were typical of our reign. The next season saw us demoted back to writers (with no change in pay) but I was invited to join the main cast as a sort of consolation prize. This delighted my mother back home in Adelaide even more than that speedboat, and she took to ringing me immediately after each show to tell me which of the sketches I'd appeared in that she'd liked. She tended to prefer the ones McCaffrie had written.

It turned out I was perfect for television. Just as my whiteness, maleness, tallness and deepish voice had enabled me to pass for a lawyer, they also helped me look and sound like what people mostly expected when they watched television during the '90s. With the right lighting, I could even pass for telegenic. My hair was dark and flecked with George Clooney silver, rather than the Leslie Nielsen white of today. I could play newsreaders, reporters, TV presenters, dads, husbands, boyfriends, police officers, politicians, priests, doctors, anybody with authority that could be undermined. I could also do clownish, undignified buffoons without looking like I was stooping to do so. Doug played out a pretty long leash for me to run around on, long enough for me to hang myself with occasionally. I was finding out what I could and couldn't do. Regrettably, some of what I couldn't do went to air. Knowing that stuff that hadn't worked might make it into the show made me more careful with what I submitted. A sketch where I played a priest who loses a baby down the drain during a christening remains the worst thing I have ever done on television – and this is coming from a man who once sang a duet with Tottie Goldsmith on the Channel 7 Good Friday Appeal.

As a writer, I had been told along with everybody else that we needed to come up with regular characters for the cast, as this was the best way for the audience to connect with the show. I hadn't done a lot of this, although I had written a few sketches for Eric Bana's foreign man character, Eddie, and had suggested that his bogan character, Poida, wear a wedding suit as this would be the only one he owned (though I'm pretty sure Paul Hogan had done the same thing). As a performer, I set about trying a few of my own characters to see if they worked.

I already had David McGahan, the idiot journalist, and McCaffrie wrote another one for me named Brian Quist, who was an art critic forced by the network to conduct post-match interviews with football players. He was the polar opposite of McGahan: intelligent, pedantic and patronising, he picked up the players on their poor grammar, mangled metaphors and reliance on cliché. He didn't last very long as the studio audience tended to side with the football players. McGahan, meanwhile, moved from presenting his own documentaries – which had taken on an Ernie Kovacs feel with tilted and sometimes rotating sets – to acting in his own TV series, *Roger Explosion: Secret Agent*, which people seemed to like.

My first real comedy character in the *Full Frontal* style was based on the Italian-American romance novel cover model Fabio. It wasn't a parody as such because I didn't know much about him and so hadn't attempted an accurate impression, but he had an interesting look and had just released a spoken-word album outlining his philosophy of love, which is why we called the segment *Fabio's Love Tips*. Every sketch was basically the same: he would introduce himself as Fabio, the Most Beautiful Man in the World – although this would later be extended to the cosmos (including the black holes) – and, as with McGahan, it was a set-'em-up-knock-'em-down structure in that he would announce a high-falutin' objective (e.g. melting a woman's heart by sharing with her your deepest desires), followed by a crass and offensive execution (i.e. him bursting through the door, yelling 'Root me!'). I wore a long blond wig and a large plastic fake chest made for Nick Giannopoulos from *Acropolis Now*. Over time, Fabio acquired a stuffed monkey called Claude and an accent like a Maltese Dracula. In essence, though, he was little more than a toned-down version of Steve Martin's Festrunk brother from *Saturday Night Live* and was wisely retired after a season or so.

Another character I liked doing but which didn't really have legs was based on the US Air Force fighter pilot Scott O'Grady, who had crashed behind enemy lines in Bosnia and survived by drinking ditch water and eating ants. O'Grady had sticky-out ears, an underbite and was a bit of a hillbilly; at least, that's how I portrayed him. After the character's first appearance talking about his heroism in an interview with Kerry O'Brien (Kim Gyngell), we replaced his uniform with a maroon cardigan, morphed him into an Australian, and changed his name to Nobby Doldrums. He was our all-purpose idiot expert during interviews and could hold forth on any subject, at least until Kerry had had enough of it.

Another all-purpose idiot that our audience couldn't seem to get enough of was Milo Kerrigan, created by McCaffrie and me one week to get ourselves out of a hole. As punishment for having almost destroyed *Full Frontal* the previous season, we were given the responsibility of script-editing the regular news segment, which cropped up about halfway through each episode. We had to collate the better news jokes and interviews submitted by the writers and link them together with more jokes and interviews and maybe a weather segment. Given neither of us were that interested in the news, the additional jokes we supplied were usually of *The Two Ronnies* type rather than anything too topical and we were running on empty about a quarter-way through the season.

To kill a few minutes of airtime, McCaffrie wrote yet another interview with an inarticulate sportsman, only this time he made him an incomprehensible boxer. Making him incomprehensible saved us the trouble of having to write any lines apart from the questions and McCaffrie, quite taken with the voice I was doing as we wrote it, suggested I play him. His voice and general enthusiasm were based on a Melbourne taxi-driver who'd driven me back from the airport that week. Like the sexism inherent in our version of Fabio, the implicit brain damage of Milo didn't seem to bother audiences of the time as much as it might today. Not that we were thinking about any of that back in 1995. In fact, we didn't give much thought to anything when we were writing news jokes. That came later. Milo was just a natural comic extension of the sort of fighters you'd see in films like *Raging Bull*, *Rocky*, *Requiem for a Heavyweight* or even Brando's Terry Malloy in *On The Waterfront*. The punch-drunk boxer had pretty much been a stock comedy character forever. These days, of course, we *would* think about it – and we wouldn't do it. Part of your job as a comedian is to read the room.

For me, Milo was a clown. In a crew-cut wig, with putty nose, broken teeth and crossed eyes, I could indulge in the sort of rough-house physical comedy I loved watching as a child. The smashing and the clattering and the quadruple-takes owed less to the grace of Keaton and Chaplin and more to the Three Stooges. In appearance and manner Milo resembled a cranked-up version of Jerry Lewis's impression of 'Slapsie' Maxie Rosenbloom in films like *Sailor Beware* and *The Family Jewels* combined with the look of Peter Sellers' Irishman from *The Naked Truth*. Surprisingly, for such a noisy fellow, he also owed quite a bit to Harpo Marx and Marcel Marceau.

Over a couple of seasons, Milo moved on from talking about boxing to singing about boxing and then to presenting the weather. Soon came his own segment, separate from the news, where he demonstrated his skills at fitness training, snooker, table tennis, bowling, gambling, poker, acting, cooking, ballet, music, art and micro-surgery. The sketches were heavy on slapstick and often involved Milo destroying the set by walking, cycling or driving a car through walls, or attacking furniture with a baseball bat or roast chickens with breakaway bottles. Mannequin heads would frequently fly off (having been punched or yelled at) and trays were upended for maximum clatter. Eventually things grew too violent, unwieldy and expensive to do on live nights, so we retired him but for cameo appearances. In his last full-blooded appearance, he demonstrated the art of sculpture by letting off a few rounds from a semi-automatic weapon. This was deemed too violent for the children who increasingly comprised our audience and was duly cut.

Doug's faith in me by this time was almost worrying. He'd ring and ask if I had a McGahan or a Fabio or a Milo for that week, scheduling it without even needing to see a script. The more I wrote, the less I was available to perform other people's material or work with my cast-mates as part of the ensemble. I was almost exclusively performing material written by either myself or McCaffrie and was starting to dominate the show in terms of not only screen-time but, as my sketches grew bigger and more ambitious, the resources that went into making it. Though we weren't aware of it, I had developed into a solo act and McCaffrie and I were ready to produce our own show.

| | | | /⁄–

We got our chance to do just that at the end of 1996. It had been a good year; not only had Leandra packed her bags to join me in Melbourne but our twenty-six-week season of *Full Frontal* that year had been extended and the last two episodes would be specials: one hosted by Eric Bana and one by me. This was a great opportunity. Word was that the network was looking to have one of the specials spin off into a new series, so of course McCaffrie and I set to work constructing a show that would please only ourselves and appeal to the narrowest possible demographic.

We agreed that we would combine the David McGahan and Brian Quist characters into one arrogant idiot with my name and he would host it, whatever it was. One of us wanted to make the show a faux telethon called the *Shaun Micallef Mortgage Benefit Concert* where we would present sketch comedy, stand-up, musical numbers and mock interviews. In the end we settled on a faux variety show based on the revival of *In Melbourne Tonight* that was running on rival network Channel 9. We called it *Shaun Micallef's World Around Him* as a nod to the McGahan segment that started it all.

We decided to take some of the better unused studio-based pieces we'd written for *Full Frontal* and mix them together in a single show. As we thought it might be unrelenting to do only this and difficult to transition between the pieces anyway, we ran another show parallel to it which consisted entirely of our unrelated non-studio-based sketches. It was only later I realised the structure was very similar to *Jimeoin*.

In many ways, the special was simply a consolidation of what I'd been doing on *Full Frontal*. We used most of the same cast (plus Bob Franklin) and all my regular characters. Eric's show, on the other hand, was far more adventurous, used a completely different cast (including Roz Hammond and Robyn Butler) and featured characters played by Eric that we'd never seen before. It also showcased Eric's sense of humour in a way that *Full Frontal* had not. It should have come as no surprise therefore that it was Eric who was invited to front his own show. McCaffrie and I were disappointed but philosophical about it all.

Soon after, though, we *were* surprised to receive a call asking us to meet with the station manager.

'I've got a great idea you are both going to love,' the station manager told us as we were ushered into his huge corner office. We sat down at his urging and he offered us a beer, which in our excitement we agreed to despite it only being 3 pm. He knocked the caps off a couple of Heinekens and threw them at us. 'How would you guys like to produce a football show?' he asked, loosening his tie and opening a packet of Cheezels.

My heart sank – my lack of interest in sport, particularly football, had by now turned to a mild loathing. McCaffrie, ever the yin to my yang, *loved* football and for years had been wanting to do such a show with some proper comedy in it, instead of the dreadful blokey cross-dressing rubbish they usually served up. He leaned forward on the couch we were sharing, displaying what for him was an unusual level of interest in what someone in authority was telling him. He may have even considered eating a Cheezel.

The station manager paced about, pitching his idea not so much to us as to the many pictures of footballers and team scarves adorning the walls. 'It'll be hosted by Milo Kerrigan,' he explained – at which point McCaffrie slumped back into the couch; he was out. 'A panel of footy players talk about the upcoming games …' the station manager went on, absent-mindedly picking up one of his signed Sherrins and spinning it about in his hands; '… and Milo can give away prizes to the punters in the audience who win the handball competition or something.' I was worried for a moment that he might try and handball the Sherrin and expect me to catch it, but he just looked at us both with a slightly crazed expression.

I asked how Milo could present a show when no one could understand what he said. The station manager shrugged and said we could iron out these sorts of details once we went into pre-production. 'Have you seen the tape?' What tape? He yelled for his PA. After a long delay wherein he tried to operate the remote, surprisingly long for someone who ran a TV station, a big screen over the bar fizzed into life and on came an un-subtitled Italian TV game show which we watched in silence for thirty minutes. It featured a sleazy host with a hand mic and some very excited female contestants. After it was over, McCaffrie and I told the station manager we'd definitely talk about it further, shook his hand and never saw him again.

The next year rolled around and *Full Frontal* started up again but my heart wasn't in it. Eric had moved on to bigger things (and even better things after that), Kitty Flanagan announced she'd be leaving halfway through the year (to join the cast of *The Sketch Show* in the UK), Daina Reid had done a directing course (and would later go on to earn Emmy nominations for her work in the US) and I started to get restless.

My frustration was compounded by another project that had stalled. Over the break, McCaffrie and I had written a telemovie about a whistle-blower cop who's sent down to archives as punishment and ends up solving a thirty-year-old cold case. It was a drama and unlike anything we'd attempted before, but Andrew Knight liked the idea and encouraged us. Although it would eventually get made seven years later as *BlackJack,* starring Colin Friels, for the moment it was just sitting on someone's desk going nowhere.

It was the same place I was going. I was stuck in a rut repeating my old characters, yet I couldn't bring myself to embrace the chance to do something new when given the opportunity to perform someone else's material.

It all came to a fine how-de-do when I was cast in the big TV parody for that week's show. Usually, I managed to escape such things because while I was okay at doing impressions of my old headmaster and the occasional movie star from the 1940s, any pop-culture figure since then was beyond me. With Eric gone, though, I was expected to step up.

Thus far, it hadn't gone well. In past seasons, Eric had done a great impression of Glenn Ridge in innumerable *Sale of the Century* sketches and Ted had asked me to take over the part. I couldn't get the voice and, worried that it wouldn't be as good as Eric's version even if I did, ended up just doing it as myself with a sign around my neck saying 'Glenn Ridge'. That level of postmodernism was out of kilter on *Full Frontal* and the sketch didn't make the cut.

This time, though, it was the main sketch of the night and I'd have to do it properly: a spoof of *The Nanny* with

Kitty in the Fran Drescher role and me as Mr Sheffield. I was concerned about the sketch from the get-go because the source material was itself a comedy and I'd always felt that parodying something that was funny was pointless; the joke always ended up being about how unfunny the original show was, which seemed a bit rich coming from us. I complained to anyone who would listen and a few, like McCaffrie, who were too busy to. 'You can't parody a comedy!' I told them. That I had done exactly the same thing only a season before, impersonating Billy Connolly in his *World Tour of Australia,* made no difference to my convenient self-righteousness.

I had never seen *The Nanny,* and even though we were always sent reference tapes, I couldn't bring myself to watch it this time. I kept blowing my lines too. Despite how ordinary I was, the sketch still went to air. Even worse was the following week's parody of *Independence Day* where I was playing either Bill Pullman or Jeff Goldblum. I couldn't tell which one and neither could the audience.

It was time to go.

## CHAPTER EIGHT

# Travels with my Auntie

I HAVE A recurring dream that usually comes on whenever I change jobs. I'm back in Union Hall at Adelaide University. We're putting on a show and I don't know what it is. Not only do I not know my lines, but I'm late and I can't get to the stage. Sometimes I can't even get into the theatre; other times I'm lost in corridors or other rooms or on the wrong floor; often I'm trapped in the walls and have to climb up to the top of the building to the room where we used to rehearse. The theatre has grown over the years to include the insides of many of the other theatres I've performed in – never TV studios – and will even occasionally include the office I worked in as a solicitor. I'm sitting at my desk, filling in time slips. I forgot to do them before I left and am trying to remember what work I did and for how long and for what file.

Andrew Denton and I were once being interviewed for a newspaper feature on our competing chat shows and were posing for a joint photo. In between talking the photographer out of poses where we pretended to box each other, I told Andrew about my dream and in Andrew's lovely way of making people he's talking to feel special and important, he helpfully interpreted it for me. Either that or he was trying to psych me out.

He said that my dream represented a subconscious fear that I didn't belong in the world in which I'd found myself; that my attempt to climb to the top from within the walls of the theatre, instead of entering by the stage door and taking the stairs like other performers, revealed a deep-rooted anxiety about whatever success I felt I was enjoying; that I believed it ill-deserved and that I was a fraud who had no right to be where he was.

Andrew, of course, was quite right – as was my subconscious – and my chat show was axed after only thirteen weeks due to dwindling ratings, whereas his went on for several more years to much acclaim and a positively galling number of awards.

After I left *Full Frontal* for an uncertain future, my dream came on again, as it had when I first left Adelaide. Any normal person in my position would have had a ruthless manager to plot their career path with Machiavellian guile (or entered into a Faustian pact with the devil as Karl Stefanovic was rumoured to have done), but here was I just making it up as I went along, approaching my work in the same cack-handed fashion I'd tried to get onto radio back in the '80s (i.e. by dropping off audiocassettes to the station, Rupert Pupkin–style).

I posted off a VHS copy of my *Full Frontal* special to the ABC in the hope they would want to make a series of it. Astonishingly, they said yes. The head of comedy at the time was one of the judges who had gonged us off *Theatre Sports* some thirteen years before, so perhaps he was trying to make it up to me.

Now all we needed was a production company to do all the things that McCaffrie and I weren't interested in, like drafting budgets and negotiating licence fees and monetising costs and pocketing a 14 per cent margin. The ABC arranged a meeting with Gary Reilly, who had produced *The Naked Vicar Show*, which I enjoyed very much, and a radio series called *R.S. Playhouse* with Graham Kennedy, which I thought was excellent. Unfortunately, he had also produced eight seasons of *Hey Dad..!*

Gary Reilly was a nice enough fellow but when he started talking about putting together a writing team for me, I knew it was never going to be. McCaffrie and I wanted to be in complete creative control, as Doug and Andrew had been on *Full Frontal*. Our solution was to lure Ted away from Channel 7, and he brought with him all the heads of department and production teams we'd worked with previously.

McCaffrie and I then set to work rejigging the structure of the special into a half-hour series and toyed with the idea of making the whole thing into a terrible variety show like *The Norman Gunston Show*. I wasn't sure that my McGahan/Quist persona would be able to sustain a full half-hour in the way that Garry McDonald was able to do with Gunston, given that we didn't have the helpful tension of interviewing real guests as he did; our guests would be fake or worded up to play along. There had been an American chat show parody in the '70s starring Martin Mull and Fred Willard called *Fernwood 2 Night* which I'd liked but it had relied on a lot of improvisation whereas ours would all be scripted. Someone else then showed us *Knowing Me, Knowing You* hosted by Steve Coogan's Alan Partridge character. This proved that a fake chat show could be entirely scripted and done brilliantly, but it raised the problem of doing such a show at all given that Coogan had already done it and so well.

In the end we decided to revert to the format of the special and keep the sketches, but have the show within the show sometimes admit it was a comedy show by throwing to the sketches now and then; the rest of the time it would be a news program, a quiz show, a telethon, etc. as we had originally envisaged with the special.

All this freed us up from just having to be a parody – or indeed doing any parody at all since that had been *Full Frontal*'s shtick-in-trade – and ultimately *The Micallef P(r)ogram(me)* became a showcase for the many types of comedy that McCaffrie and I grew up on; for example, my interview with Australian classical pianist Roger Woodward, which ends up with him playing 'Lara's Theme' on a melodica while I blow into it, was a nod to Morecambe and Wise's famous Grieg piano concerto sketch with André Previn. Structurally we did our best to step around those that had come before us, though not always successfully. Some thirty years later, I can now see that the show it owed the most to in terms of its shape and pace was the show that our special had most resembled, *Jimeoin*. So thanks again, Jim.

For two guys who wanted to move on from *Full Frontal*, we seemed to go out of our way to bring as much of that show with us as possible. I guess we liked doing what we knew we could do and wanted to see how far it could take us. Plus we liked working with people we trusted and who understood our sense of humour. As well as having the same director and many of the same production teams, a large number of scripts for the first series were adapted from ones we'd written for *Full Frontal* but not got around to using. We also featured old characters like Milo, McGahan and Sergeant Spoog quite prominently; even my impression of newsreader Jim Waley made an appearance, as did some of the cast from the special (a couple of whom had been regulars in *Full Frontal*). For the ensemble cast at least, we looked a little further afield: Francis Greenslade (well, not too much further afield), Roz Hammond (who had been in Eric's special) and Wayne Hope (who was in a show I'd co-written with Glynn Nicholas the year before*).

---

\* A word or two about *The Glynn Nicholas Show*. It starred Glynn, Alison Whyte, Bob Hornery, Tracy Harvey, Merridy Eastman, and Wayne Hope as Jeff. I was to have co-written the whole series with Glynn but ended up writing only first drafts for half the episodes. Francis Greenslade and I appeared in one episode as Amway-selling Mormons who enter Glynn's flat by osmosis. Not exactly crowd-pleasing stuff. Nonetheless, the ABC wanted to do a second season but Glynn, for some reason, decided not to. This suddenly created a hole in their schedule for 1998. The next day a VHS of my special landed on the commissioning editor's desk. In the script for the telemovie based on my life, this scene would be cut for being too corny.

The ABC had a very hands-off approach, which was fine with us because what we really wanted was to call the shots like we had back in our university Footlights days. All they asked was that the show be a half-hour topical news satire. Apart from that we were free to do what we liked. McCaffrie and I still weren't that keen on news satire, so we ignored that part of the proviso and just went with the half-hour and 'free to do what we liked' bits. Come to think of it, I don't think I even mentioned the news satire element to McCaffrie.

As it turned out, it was impossible to make the show topical because scheduling meant we had to pre-record the entire series before they put it to air. When we pointed this out, the ABC were very understanding, giving us their blessing to do as we saw fit. But they did want to see the scripts before we started shooting.

This perfectly reasonable request rankled for some reason. Was it the prospect of being assessed and found wanting by men in t-shirts again? McCaffrie and I had already spent a number of years having Doug and Andrew pass judgement on our scripts, but at least we knew them – and it was *their* show, so fair enough. This time around it was supposed to be *our* show. Of course, it wasn't our show at all; it was the ABC's show, much in the same way that *Full Frontal* and *Fast Forward* had been Channel 7's shows. McCaffrie and I just weren't used to dealing with the networks; that was something Doug and Andrew did on our behalf. Now we were grown up, we had to do it ourselves.

Instead of growing up, we got Doug, as executive producer for the production company, to submit the scripts and run interference for us. We were the creative producers – the showrunners – and would concentrate on that. To this day, I don't know who received the enormous pile of scripts we had begrudgingly submitted, but whoever it was dutifully read them all and returned them with copious notes and suggestions that I refused to even look at.

'They really like the Pope Pageant sketch,' Doug rang to tell me, so we would have some idea of what the ABC thought if we bumped into anybody from the so-called comedy department.

Pope John Paul II had just passed away and I had written a Miss Universe–type contest to choose his successor with a fashion parade and an oral section. I had quite liked the sketch, but now that it had met with approval by the higher-ups I was instantly suspicious of it. In an act of childish contrarianism, I deliberately left it out of the show. We eventually used it in the first season of *Mad as Hell* some thirteen years later.

'They also really liked the Tilted Room sketch,' Doug went on. 'Although they reckon it should end when Roz asks if you've been drinking.'

This was another of my Ernie Kovacs–style pieces. A man comes home from work into a house built on a 45-degree angle which he pretends to his wife is normal. It's mainly sight gags – making tea, answering the phone, 'straightening' a picture, sliding across the set and out the window – most of which occur *after* Roz asks her question. What was, in fact, the premise of the sketch was read by the reader as its punchline. It confirmed to me that whoever was doing the reading had no idea about comedy or, at least, the comedy that we wanted to do. Anyway, as there was no process in place to follow up these notes and suggestions, they were never bothered with again. I don't think I mentioned these to McCaffrie either.

I also didn't mention other things that I knew would annoy McCaffrie, like the elaborate sketches I'd written for David McGahan, a character he had grown weary of even when it was on *Full Frontal*. On one of his rare visits to the studio, he was greeted with the sight of an enormous courthouse set being built across the soundstage. It featured several offices, a courtroom and an elaborate circular proto–West Wing corridor that would enable endless walk-and-talks. He wandered about, taking in the opulence of it all, looking up at the detailed olde-worlde woodwork which must have cost a fortune.

'What sketch is this for?' he asked, genuinely perplexed.

'It's a surprise,' I replied, feebly.

He went back to the office and wrote an eight-second sketch that would require a helicopter and another that required an aircraft fuselage submerged in the ocean.

The budgets for all three seasons of *The Micallef P(r)ogram(me)* were, by today's standards, astronomical. Not only were we building sets from scratch in the studio for two shooting days a week, we were off on location for another two days a week with the equivalent of a drama film crew. Nothing was denied us. Everything we wanted was supplied. If a script required a hundred horsemen riding out of a valley so I could pretend to flub my lines at the end of it, we got it; if I wanted to be nailed up on a crucifix at the crack of dawn, flanked by two others, in a chilling recreation of Golgotha so a small corgi could trot up, drop a tennis ball and have Jesus say 'Not now, Pogo', we got it. No idea was too stupid, slight or unpromising to have way too much money, time and effort lavished on it. It was the last decently budgeted sketch comedy show ever made in this country, at least until Foxtel's *Open Slather* came along in 2015 and ruined it for everybody for at least another thirty years.

I'd never been happier in my life. Plus, at thirty-six, I had just become a father.

| | | /—

I had been worried that if I had a child, I would suddenly lose my sense of humour. I'd seen enough comedy routines about the travails of being a parent to know how woefully unfunny it could make a person. So too those newspaper columns by stay-at-home comedian dads and mums carrying on like they were the first ones ever to become parents. I vowed to never *ever* do material about having a baby.

[SMASH CUT]

Interior. Hospital. Day. Leandra has been in labour for about twelve hours, but the nurses are very attentive, popping into the birthing suite every now and then to see if I'd like a coffee or something to eat. Leandra, though, has had enough.

'I'm going,' she announces as she tries to get out of bed.

She is attached by wires to various machines and pulls them along with her around the birthing suite as she collects her things.

'Huh?' says I, looking up from my toast.

'I'm going home.' She ejects the Inese Galante CD from the portable player, returns it to its case and starts packing her bag.

Leandra is the sensible one of the two of us. Yet there she is in a hospital smock, towing a CTG monitor behind her as she makes for the door.

'What about the baby?' I ask.

'No.'

'Shall I get anyone?'

She's already in the corridor.

It dawned on me that I needed to take charge. I had up until that point been treating the whole giving-birth-to-a-baby process like it had nothing to do with me. I'd been led to believe that my only real job was to look after the volume on the relaxation music and rub my partner's wrists during the more intense contractions. Clearly we were in a situation that called for more than that. Try as I might, though, I couldn't recall what I'd been told to do if the mother attempts to escape from the hospital, so I ushered Leandra back into the room and pressed the call button for the nurse.

'More toast, Mr Micallef?'

'No, thank you, but I think Leandra needs to be induced.' I was very serious and nodding like Dr Miracle.

'Her waters have already broken, Mr Micallef,' explained the nurse, patting my forearm. 'And her contractions are already close.'

'But, I—'

'It won't be long now.'

'But look at her,' I pointed. 'She's trying to put her jeans on.'

The nurse talked Leandra into staying and checked her progress.

'She's fully dilated,' the nurse reassured me, but then noticed my blank look. 'She's nearly ten centimetres.'

Nonsense. She was much taller than that.

A pull on some forceps later by someone who actually knew what they were doing and Leandra and I had a son.

We called him Joseph Gabriel, as we couldn't decide which of our two favourite names we preferred.

As it turned out, my sense of humour did not disappear. What did vanish, though, was any notion I had that I might occupy the centre of my own universe. As I held Joe in my arms it dawned on me that the whole point to my life was him and that from then on, I couldn't help but see the world through his eyes, so I'd better do my best to make it worth looking at. Most important of all, I knew there were vastly more important things than writing jokes and pulling faces but that I'd have to keep doing both as there would now be more bills to pay. It was as good an excuse as any to continue on as if nothing had changed.

| | | /⁄—

Towards the end of *The Micallef P(r)ogram(me)*'s run, I was asked to play a straight role in someone else's TV show. I welcomed the chance to do something different. Like all Australian actors, I'd had a guest role on *Blue Heelers*, but this time round I would be playing a romantic lead: the new love interest for Sigrid Thornton's character Laura in the wildly popular ABC drama series *SeaChange*.

It was Andrew Knight, my mentor from *Full Frontal*, who approached me at a Christmas party on the roof of the ABC. 'How would you like to be the most boring man in the world?' he asked.

I didn't know it was a part he was offering; I thought it was a life choice. I accepted anyway.

The role of Warwick Munro required me to be an actor rather than a comedian and, while I'd never harboured any desire to play Hamlet, the idea of pretending to be someone more real than the sketch characters I'd been doing since my late teens had begun to appeal to me. Perhaps I *was* growing up.

Warwick was supposed to come across as the perfect man for Laura Gibson: dependable, caring, kind, decent and good … but ultimately a bit dull. Andrew had mounted a cynical case against romantic love and I was his patsy. Obviously at the end of the season, Laura would end up with the ruggedly good-looking Max Connors. She'd already missed out on Diver Dan. To go from David Wenham to William McInnes was one thing, but to end up with me was too steep a fall for Australia's Sweetheart.

Sigrid had casting approval, so I dropped by the ABC casting office during a break in our *Micallef P(r)ogram(me)* taping to read a few scenes with her. This wasn't an audition, they'd assured me. Sigrid just wanted to meet me.

I'd auditioned a few times for plays at the Melbourne Theatre Company, usually for bravura director Simon Phillips. I knew him in passing from his work in Adelaide many years before and we'd always have a very enjoyable chat at the start of the audition, followed by me performing the piece I'd been told to prepare. Simon would give me some direction and then I'd do the piece again with no discernible difference. I'd have another go and then another, give exactly the same performance each time, and then Simon would thank me and I would leave. This process repeated itself over a number of years, with each audition growing shorter and shorter until eventually I'd walk in, have our chat and then leave without even having to perform anything. Ultimately I suggested to my agent that there probably wasn't much point putting my name forward anymore.

I'd also done the odd audition for various film and television roles, but never managed to sufficiently impress anyone to land a part. I could never really commit to learning the lines or doing what was asked with the necessary brio. It was the old problem of being assessed again; and while the casting directors weren't wearing white t-shirts or blowing whistles at me, the process still left me feeling small and interchangeable.

When the director or writer was running the audition, it was even worse. I'd try and talk to them as equals. Reading for the role of Julian Burnside QC for the miniseries *Bastard Boys* I was urged to try the big courtroom scene one more time but to make it more theatrical.

'Really?' I asked as I returned to my spot.

The director blinked a couple of times. 'Yes, please.'

I did another version virtually indistinguishable from the last. I'd been a barrister; I knew how they behaved in court.

'Yeah. Try it again but really enjoy it this time. You're showing off to the jury.'

'Well, there wouldn't be a jury,' I pointed out. 'This is an industrial dispute.'

'Okay, you're showing off to the judge, then,' directed the director with a certain directness.

'You're grandstanding,' added the man next to him, thinking he was being helpful.

I held up the script. 'The language is already pretty overblown,' I explained to the man who, judging from the instant hardening of his features, must have been the writer.

'Burnside would probably know the judge. I think he'd be a little more understated in a closing submission.'

Both men half-turned to each other but didn't say anything.

'I *could* try it more wryly,' I suggested, now directing myself.

They said that wouldn't be necessary, cast Rhys Muldoon in the role instead, and the whole thing did perfectly well without me.

Anyway, Sigrid didn't know any of this. We met, she gave her approval and I got to do the third season of *SeaChange*. That it was also the final season was a complete coincidence.

Towards the end of the shoot, Leandra and I had a second son. As we'd already used our two favourite names and could only think of one new one we really liked, we repurposed our first boy's middle name as a Christian name and called his brother Gabriel Elias.

## CHAPTER NINE

# Channel 9

I WAS GETTING better known.* *The Micallef P(r)ogram(me)* was liked by comedy nerds and won a couple of Logies. The Working Dog people I had so admired in *The Late Show* asked me to appear on their new show, *The Panel*, when Kate Langbroek wasn't on. But it was *SeaChange*, as the highest-rating show in the country, that propelled me to the being-stopped-in-the-supermarket-and-asked-what-my-name-was level of recognition. I was also asked to host the Logies.

This was back in the days when the Logies meant

---

* For what fame is like, may I recommend the lyrics to *Rock 'n' Roll Is Where I Hide* by Dave Graney:
> Ah it's not such a bad thing
> To be seen as a guy who thinks he can't be seen
> Even though I know I can ...
> Like they think I can't see 'em
> It's like I'm blind
> Like I'm invisible ...
> Everybody's looking
> Because they think I think nobody's looking
> So I can't not be seen so I'm not looking at them I know exactly where they are

something. Long before Tom Gleeson kicked the crutch out from under it. I mean, don't get me wrong, the Logies were always meaningless garbage, but towards the end of the last century audiences still enjoyed watching the ceremony and the people receiving the awards were still prepared to turn up. In other words, everybody involved was happy to play along. Then Andrew Denton stuck his oar in.

Television's night of nights had for many years been hosted by Daryl Somers. Andrew dared to point at the emperor and say that he should at least put a towel around himself. I think even Daryl knew the event was nothing more than a tawdry Z-grade burlesque of the Emmys, but saying it aloud was a bit like waking your children up on Christmas Eve to tell them Santa Claus was invented by the marketing department at Coca-Cola. Channel 9, who hosted the ceremony, sensed a publicity opportunity and offered Andrew the chance to produce the show for them. Andrew, with an excellent publicity radar of his own, agreed. He assembled a team of writers, including me, and hosted a meta version of the Logies in 1999 that took a large hammer to the event.

Andrew was supposed to host the Logies for three years running but decided to declare after two. You can only really smash a statue to pieces so many times, I guess. With a half-decent Logies acceptance speech on my résumé and the reflected glory of *SeaChange* still glistering about me, I was put forward as host for Andrew's final year, and Channel 9 accepted.

Like Andrew, I assembled a writing team and worked closely with the network. We had to take the debris Andrew had left behind and glue it into something new. Just as the sketch show I had made for the ABC was a mash-up parody of several types of TV, our Logies would be a straight-faced send-up that still managed to be functional. Andrew had told the audience the show was crap and its premise worthless; we would present it as if it was the greatest thing in the world, albeit hosted by an idiot.

The Nine Network are not known for their sense of humour, as anyone who has watched any comedy show they have ever produced can tell you, but to their credit they let us do pretty much whatever we wanted. Andrew had softened them up for us, and the Logies unit became a self-contained rag-tag team of renegades working out of the same rundown shack at the back of Channel 9's Bendigo Street studios that had been Graham Kennedy's dressing-room back in the '60s. We were literally breathing the same asbestos.

Meanwhile, there was trouble at the ABC over the soon-to-be-broadcast third season of *The Micallef P(r)ogram(me)*. During some pre-publicity, I'd been asked by the *Border Mail* of Albury-Wodonga whether there was anything outrageous in the new series and I had obligingly said: 'Yeah, we've got a documentary about how Weary Dunlop was a transsexual.'

Of course, there was no such thing. What there was was a sketch in which I threw to an *apparent* documentary about Weary Dunlop being a transsexual. We only get as far as showing the opening title when we cut to the ABC switchboard lighting up with calls from outraged viewers and then we cut back to me in the studio abandoning the whole idea. That was the joke, such as it was. It was about people overreacting.

Rather than run the interview in the entertainment section where it might have had some context of light-heartedness, the *Border Mail* ran it on their front page and the story fast became one about how irresponsible the ABC was for allowing such a documentary to be made. The fact that no documentary actually existed was irrelevant. The RSL got involved; the ministers for defence and communications got involved; management rolled over and we were told the sketch would have to be cut. No amount of explaining or pointing out the irony of what was happening would shift the ABC to a position behind us.

I removed the offending item but made sure the audience knew something was up by leaving a few seconds of test pattern with the words 'sketch removed' on it. I put the sketch back in for the DVD release and no one wrote in to complain. These days, the most offensive thing about it is the assumption that being trans is an acceptable comic contrast, but back then people seemed more concerned about making sport of our war heroes.

There were some half-hearted calls for me to be replaced as host of the Logies, but Channel 9 weathered the squall. They also remained very trusting of the material we had planned. This freedom was the legacy of Andrew Denton and because I was there in his stead, it was all mine. Only two jokes were vetoed by the head of light entertainment. One was for me to have a random member of the public read out the winner of the most popular reality show category, and then on my way down from the Palladium Room to the lobby of Crown Casino, I would pass anti-gambling advocate Tim Costello and we would nod to each other (Tim was up for it). The other idea was me walking around a table of network executives with a baseball bat, reciting Al Capone's monologue from *The Untouchables* and then laying into a dinner-suited mannequin with a watermelon for a head. Frankly, these were both lousy ideas and I'm grateful I was prevented from doing them.

The Logies is a three-hour broadcast – though it seems much longer – and live-to-air. There are a lot of moving parts. I wasn't that nervous until about a minute before I went on. I stood in the wings, by myself for the first time in days, the sound of the audience receding as I focused on the nail half-sticking out of the piece of wood next to me. The crew had had only two days to install the set and someone hadn't hammered it all the way in.

This could be the end of me. Why on earth was I doing this? Certainly not because I believed in any of it. I couldn't care less about these sorts of shows. I was doing it simply because they'd asked. Because they'd shown some interest in me and I felt obliged to show them the same interest back. Because Andrew Denton, whom I admired, had recommended me. I'd gone from Andrew ringing me to get Francis Greenslade's phone number to him ringing to get me to write for him, and now to him asking me to take over for him. But Andrew had it easy – he only had to follow Daryl Somers. I had to follow Andrew Denton – and everybody had loved Andrew. Someone could easily snag themselves on that nail.

The emergency exit was just behind me. And I'm not being metaphorical here; there was *literally* a door only a couple of metres away that would let me straight out into the street. I could just leave, cross the road to the No 106 tram stop, take the ten-minute journey home and not answer the phone for a few days. I seriously entertained the idea for a moment or two.

But then I realised that once they saw I was missing, they'd just go into the auditorium and ask Rove to host the show instead. The newspaper headlines the next day wouldn't be about my mysterious Stephen Fry–like disappearance but how wonderfully Rove had done – and with only a minute's notice. Fuck that. I went on.

For someone who had never done it before and would never do it again, I think I did a pretty good job. There was talk of me hosting again the following year, but they asked Wendy Harmer instead.

*C'est la vie.*

| | | / ⁄ ⁔

What the Logies did lead to, however, was an offer to host that year's Midwinter Ball in Canberra. And Alexander wept, for there were no more worlds to conquer ...[*]

---

[*] I am, of course, referring to Alexander Downer.

For those of you who don't know, the Midwinter Ball is a big black-tie shindig for Australian federal politicians, their staff and the journalists from the press gallery. They get a chance to set aside their differences, dress up, let down whatever hair they have left and celebrate their unspoken complicity in the erosion of our democracy. It's generally agreed between those attending that what happens in the Great Hall stays in the Great Hall.

I've dutifully remained silent for twenty years but feel I must now lift the veil on what went on that evening in 2002. Sure, there's a good chance I'll be arrested and tried in secret by some sort of Star Chamber, possibly even put to death. But it's a chance I'm prepared to take because if pretending to be a journalist and playing the occasional politician over the years has taught me anything, it's the importance of appearing to tell the TRUTH. Plus, it's just between you and me, and I feel that at this stage of the book I can trust you to be discreet. If the ADF come calling in the dead of night and bundle me into a van, though, I'll know it was you who ratted me out.

So, there I am in the wings of the Great Hall of Parliament with no bent nail to distract me. They're playing a montage of news footage from the last twelve months and as 'Wind Beneath My Wings' wells up, the audience is treated to a five-minute package of the Twin Towers being hit by planes from multiple angles and then collapsing in slow-motion several times. As I hear myself introduced, I know I'm dead.

My job was pretty simple. Tell a few jokes roasting the pollies and journos, introduce the then leader of the Opposition Simon Crean and the then prime minister John Howard, thank them for their speeches no matter how dreadful, and then throw to Mental As Anything. Instead I'd unwisely prepared a twenty-minute absurdist monologue about why I was unqualified to be hosting the lame Washington Correspondents' Dinner rip-off they were holding. I back-announced the 9/11 tribute with, 'Sure, it looked like a fun year, but it had its serious moments too ...' and went steadily downhill from there:

*Hey, if Alan Reid were still writing today, I'm sure he'd be treated as something of a medical curiosity: a zombie journalist. Can you imagine? It would have been a hideous existence for him and I think it's a mercy he went when he did. And not in Haiti either, where he could have been revived. The press freedom over there is terrible – and in such small portions ...*

I then went on to insult each of the evening's sponsors:

- *Qantas – yes, if you're thinking of flying, do so by aeroplane. Qantas: the only real choice. They've certainly made sure of that.*
- *Gavin Anderson and Company – a great song-and-dance act, folks. They did* A Chorus Line *at Jupiter's Casino last*

*year. Gavin played Kristine – he was superb. Great legs – and that voice. He makes Ethel Merman look like Don Lane – yes, he's a very gifted plastic surgeon as well.*

- *The Seven Network – makers of ... er ... [can't think of anything]*
- *The Nine Network – where old footballers go to earn millions in exchange for their dignity. That's Entertainment? I hardly think so.*

I also accused the Hyatt, which was catering the event, of using condemned meat. During a break, I was told that the Hyatt management were miffed at my sallies and that I should make it clear I was only joking, but I was already waist-deep in blood (the meat was *so* undercooked ...):

*But no, it's great to be here and to meet not only so many journalists but also politicians. I'm not political myself. In fact, I try and avoid politics if I can. I'll give you a case in point. A few months back I was contacted by the Governor-General Peter Hollingworth and he was keen to know whether he had the power to sack the Prime Minister. Now I have had some experience many years ago in politics: I was the one who took that shot at Arthur Calwell in '66; and, you know, Bob Santamaria used to ring me from time to time before his broadcasts to try out his latest filthy limerick (I'd usually counsel against using it). But I got scared off politics and I'll tell you why ...*

The lights were all up in the Great Hall and I could see everyone's faces quite clearly. Eric Abetz appeared to be enjoying himself, but I assume it was at my expense. Undeterred, I ploughed on:

*I'd been employed by Fred Daly to follow Whitlam around and write down any of his stray bon mots. Normally this was easy, but this was December of 1967 and Gough was preoccupied with finding a way to deal with the inexplicable popularity of Harold Holt.*

There were a few laughs for this. All of them uncertain.

*Anyway, during a particularly uninspired visit to the men's urinal in Sydney's fabulous Wentworth Hotel, I filled the lull by jokingly suggesting to Gough that someone get rid of Holt by secretly tying weights to his legs next time he went swimming.*

A sharp intake of breath was audible from Max Moore-Wilton's table, which at least proved some of those sitting there were alive.

*Gough pulled the chain imperiously and left. Two weeks later Holt disappeared.*

*Now I'm not saying Whitlam murdered Holt – he would have got Mick Young to do it – but the coincidence was enough for me to get out of politics. Except for one instance in*

*1975 when Sir John Kerr asked me for advice on what font*
*he should use in his letter dismissing Whitlam. We settled on*
*Courier as he was, after all, using a typewriter. He wanted to*
*use Zapf Dingbats. The man was an idiot.*

I have it on good authority that at this point Janette Howard
leaned over to her husband and scoffed, 'He's not even old
enough to have known Sir John.'

*So I told all this to the Governor-General but made it clear*
*I didn't want to get involved. As I say, I'm not a political*
*animal — more a political mineral.*

A good laugh, if memory serves, from Malcolm Farr.

*Anyway, the Governor-General never took up my suggestion.*
*Although the situation's hotting up for him again so ... maybe.*
*I guess I should warn you, Mr Prime Minister ...*

And Mr Howard smiled alarmingly at my reference to him.

*... that if the Governor-General rings up and asks you to go*
*swimming at Cheviot Beach, I would seriously think about*
*being busy that day.*

The end of my tale was greeted with lawn-bowls applause
which I seamlessly bridged by launching into my introduction

of the prime minister (John Howard), who was still looking very unsure about the whole thing. I think I saw Janette taking advantage of the confusion to fill her purse with bread rolls.

*It's no secret that our next speaker has a serious drinking problem – oh, sorry. It is a secret. I misread my notes ... please welcome the Prime Minister of Australia, Mr John Howard.*

The PM mounted the stage with that youthful run he would sometimes employ during election campaigns, gave a polite nod my way and took to the lectern. Sensing I was still lingering behind him, he turned back as the applause continued, walked over and shook my hand firmly. 'Good on you,' he said. I took this as a warning to behave myself during his speech, which I duly did.

Apart from Simon Crean's speech, everyone seemed to enjoy the rest of the evening. As Mental As Anything launched into 'If You Leave Me, Can I Come Too?', Kim Beazley came up to me and said how much he enjoyed my joke about Albert Camus. Well, he would, wouldn't he.

||||/–

I'm not sure if I've ever seriously subscribed to the view that a comedian – or indeed anyone who takes to the stage – feels the need to perform because of some yearning for approval. That might account for their drive and ambition to play to bigger and bigger audiences or their appetite for adulation or their ruthlessness in getting to what they regard as the top, but I don't believe it's what makes somebody funny. I think that's just a talent, much in the same way that being able to sing or dance or act or draw or paint is a talent. The desire to display that talent too isn't necessarily, in and of itself, about seeking validation; it seems to me to be the natural thing to do with it. There's no point telling jokes, singing, dancing or acting in a room by yourself. Ditto never showing your paintings and drawings to anyone. They *might* be good; you *might* have a talent for it – but you can never really know unless your work connects with somebody. Art needs an audience.

This is especially true of comedy. Not only is there no point to it without an audience, it literally ceases to exist without their laughter. Of course, the background of the comedian, their tribulations and upbringing and schooling and relationships, all inform their comic material, but their sense of humour is something innate. The scope of that sense might be attuned to their family dynamics as they're growing up and the breadth of it will depend on the various disciplines they master along the way, but there's no giving it more depth. You're born with a sense of the comic or you're not, and how much of a comic sensibility you have depends on your genes: enough and you'll end up as a comedian, not enough and you'll be hosting a game show. How funny you end up being, though, is largely up to your audience. It's a complicated relationship.

Gershon Legman, the famous cultural critic and degenerate, has a theory that comedians do what they do to reassure themselves 'on the subject of [their] most desperate fears'; that, as they tell their jokes, they are 'whistling under [their] rictus-mask in the darkened parts of [their] own soul that nauseate and frighten [them] the most'.* I'm not so sure about that. I think when the tramp asks Harpo to help him out so he can get a cup of coffee and Harpo produces one from his pocket and gives it to him, Harpo is just being funny. He's not dealing with the shame he felt as an impoverished child growing up in Flatbush.

Legman, though, might be onto something when he says:

*The whole tragedy of the comedian or teller-of-jokes is ... he can never really be shriven at all, since his true guilt is inevitably concealed from the audience by the very mechanism which excites the audience's laughter. The cycle of telling and listening, listening and telling, must therefore be endlessly and compulsively repeated for a lifetime, the teller visibly taking the least pleasure of all in the humor at which he struggles so hard, and which, at the end, he stands like the hungry child he is, darkly famished at the feasting while the audience laughs.*

While I'm not with him as regards the guilt, there is, I think, in comedians something of a compulsion to perform. What

---

\* *No Laughing Matter: An Analysis of Sexual Humor*, Vol. 1 (Indiana University Press, 1982), p. 19.

would become quickly annoying at the office or worksite becomes perfectly acceptable, in fact demanded, on the stage. The misbehaviour that is the comedian's act too becomes permissible and desired in the performance space, yet it is true the comedian must be seen to take the least amount of pleasure from what he or she is creating, lest the joke be spoiled. A comedian who laughs along with the audience is taking a very big risk: too much and the act becomes indulgent; too early and you're signalling the punchline. Breaking character is sometimes fun for the audience, but it can be a dangerous game, sometimes fatal to the tension you must maintain, particularly if your routine is about you being a kick or two behind the play. If you're suddenly in the moment with the audience, you're peeking out from behind the performance. Worse, if you signal you're *ahead* of the audience then you risk coming off as glib or your act rote. It's a very gifted comedian who can calibrate their act to include all these sometimes contradictory moments without one cancelling out the other or cruelling the pitch of the act entirely. Billy Connolly is the only comic I can think of who could get away with it without losing his edge.

As to what compels someone to perform, I cannot say. I sure as hell don't know why *I* do it. I don't even know where the *idea* of me performing came from. My grandmother would take my mother and me to the theatre to see people like Barry Humphries, Peter Ustinov, Victor Borge and Marcel Marceau. I even saw a rather senior Douglas Fairbanks Jnr shuffle around the stage in *The Pleasure of His Company* but I'm pretty sure *that* wasn't a moment of any blinding realisation (suffice to say that Doug was a lot more energetic in *Gunga Din* forty years earlier). Maybe it was Barry or Peter or Victor or Marcel. Maybe it was my trumpet-playing father. Maybe it was sitting in the audience of my sisters' interminable end-of-year ballet concerts and thinking: it *must* be more enjoyable onstage than it is down here. I honestly have no idea.

I only know that every time the audience laughs it seems to me I'm standing in exactly the right spot at exactly the right time, a bit like the pleasure you feel when you look up at the precise instant the sunset glitters on the water or you're sitting in traffic waiting to turn the corner behind a row of cars and everyone's indicator flashes in unison for that one click. I do it for that moment of perfect synchronicity.

## CHAPTER TEN

# Print the legend

JERRY LEWIS WAS the first comedian in history since Charlie Chaplin to write, produce and direct his own films. In the 1950s, his comedy partnership with Dean Martin was as big as the Beatles a decade later. His solo films were box office hits as well, and while his star had waned by the time I started watching his work on TV in the late '60s, he quickly became the comedy hero of my formative years. Even now there are ineradicable traces of him in my matrix which come out when I perform. My Logies entrance – waiting nervously offstage as I was introduced and then knocking over the Logies table on my way out – was very Jerry; more Jerry, in fact, than Jerry himself had been when he took to the stage a year earlier at the same venue. It had been kind of special for me to wait in those same wings, walk onto that same stage and pace about anxiously in the same dressing-room.

I'd seen his Palladium show and it was the same Las Vegas act he'd been doing since he broke up with Dean Martin back in 1956. There were even a few bits in there he'd done *before* they teamed up. I'd seen him do a version of the show on TV the first time he came to Australia to open the Wrest Point casino in the early '70s. I have to say I was more impressed with the show as a ten-year-old than I was at thirty-six.

Jerry, now in *his* early seventies, had understandably slowed down. He showed clips of his earlier, more rambunctious self between his shtick in order to catch his breath. Still, it had been good to see him live. He'd fallen ill on that last visit and had to cut his tour short. Now he was coming back to Australia to finish it, and I thought it might be fun to actually meet him in person this time.

I used my new-found clout as a minor celebrity to wangle an interview and flew to Sydney on a break from shooting *SeaChange* to attend a press conference and then have a one-on-one sit-down with him. The results would be published by *The Age*\*, who had also arranged a photographer – which was great, because I would have been too embarrassed to ask if we could have a picture taken together.

They say it's never a good idea to meet your heroes, but I knew Jerry could be difficult and was half expecting things might go south. Even at that stage of my career, I'd met enough famous people to know that once they were down off the screen they looked and acted just like regular people. Most

---

\* See Appendix A.

are nice enough, but some behave like they're more important than they are – just as we all do from time to time – and, as in everyday life, come across as dickheads. After putting together the Logies, though, whose roster of stars is composed almost entirely of dickheads, I was prepared for anything.

Back at university, I'd met Gough Whitlam. He wasn't exactly a hero, but I did admire him – and I owed him in a way I would never owe John Howard, because I could never have gone to law school without the Whitlam government's short-lived Free Tertiary Education For Those Who Can't Afford It policy.

Gough was at the University of Adelaide to give a series of lectures about the Dismissal. I didn't bother going, feeling I already knew everything about it from having been forced to read Gareth Evans's interminable *Labor and the Constitution* as part of my course. Gough, though, was nice enough to come and see the show I was in, a law revue to honour the centenary year of the law school called, it pains me to report, *Star Laws* (the previous year's had been *Barrister Galactica*).

The show, which I think was about ET becoming a QC, ran a Logies-like three hours on opening night and Gough had thankfully fallen asleep by the time I took to the stage in a bad wig and an even worse impersonation of him; he had recently done a TV ad for pasta sauce that we thought deserving of our snotty undergraduate scorn. According to reports, he woke up for the finale as we pelted the audience with dog food but was still kind enough to send a note backstage after the curtain congratulating us all on a job well done and offering to take the executive of the Law Students' Society, which included me, to lunch the next day. At the lunch, he was also kind enough not to mention the show and I pretended I hadn't been in it. Instead, we asked him what he thought about the then prime minister Bob Hawke (he was gracious) and I took the opportunity to thank him personally for the tertiary education I was in the process of squandering. Emboldened by house wine, someone even asked about the Italian he spoke in the TV ad: did he speak the language or had he learned it especially? He looked over to me and said, with a half-smile, that he had read it off a card.

The lunch wound up and he called for the bill, explaining that as a guest of the university, he had received 'a modest stipend which will almost cover the cost'. We all laughed heartily – even though none of us knew what a stipend was.

I didn't know if my meeting with Jerry Lewis would turn out as well as the one with Gough Whitlam had, but I was determined that if it was going to be a disaster, it would be entirely Jerry's fault and not mine. I'd read he didn't like reporters consulting their notes during interviews, so I didn't bring any; he was a bit hard of hearing, so I'd speak up; he didn't like talking about his failures, so I wouldn't mention them; nothing about his recent health scare, fine; he could only spare half an hour, I'd be done in twenty. He also hated to be kept waiting, so I made sure I was early.

He arrived early too, dressed in a blue and red tracksuit sporting his own caricature and logo. He and his entourage streamed out of the lift and I saw him deliberately walk into the wrong conference room and start talking to the group of architects in there, pretending he was their next speaker and ad-libbing his way through whatever was on the whiteboard – to much laughter. He left to a round of applause and disappeared through another door.

Inside the correct conference room I could hear a radio mic being attached to his tracksuit. He was talking to Chrissie, his publicist, in an Irish accent. He sounded in a good mood. Great. Someone introduced him and he strode in to some polite applause (the architects had been more effusive). First up he apologised for an unpaid hospital bill from his last visit; a misunderstanding, he explained, which had now been taken care of. No doubt he wanted to clear the air and make way for questions about the tour. Nonetheless, the first few questions were about the unpaid bill and he fielded them with good humour. So far so good. Then the questions got onto the reason for his hospital stay – a bout of viral meningitis. His wife, sitting directly in front of me, shifted in her seat a little. He said he was fine; much recovered, thank you. When was he going to retire, someone asked. He said, pointedly, that he had no plans and that, in fact, he was doing a tour. Was a tour wise when he was so susceptible to illness, implied someone else.

At that point I thought I'd try and help, asking a question about a bug that flew into his ear in a drive-in movie theatre appearance back in 1963. He did a take. 'How can you remember—' he began, but then saw that I was too young to have remembered. 'How do you *know* that?' he asked under the laughter from the room. Crisis averted. The press conference mutated into a plug for Nutty Professor Teeth, which he was encouraged to put in as the cameras flashed. 'Oh God,' he lamented to his wife. 'That'll be the one they'll use.' But really – what did he expect?

After the press conference, Chrissie the publicist tracked me down and took me out to the balcony for the planned photo. Then Jerry came out. He was chewing gum and businesslike. The photographer took a few shots and Jerry pulled a face or two. Then his mood shifted. Our backdrop was Sydney Harbour and Jerry noticed the photographer was using a wide lens. 'He's taking shots of the background,' Jerry muttered, more to himself than me. 'You know your lenses,' I replied anyway. 'You've got to in this business, baby,' he said and then abruptly called an end to the shoot and wandered off.

This didn't bode well for the interview. I'd hoped that if it was going to be a train wreck it would at least come off the rails after I'd asked him a few questions. I commiserated with the photographer, who had hoped for more than two minutes to take his pictures, and then went with Chrissie the publicist to another, smaller conference room.

Jerry walked in with a couple of bodyguards. They were burly, Teamsterish-looking men dressed in tracksuits and they sprawled themselves on some chairs across the other side of the room as Jerry sat down next to me. 'It's me again, I'm afraid,' I apologised.

'You again,' he said flatly. I wasn't sure if he was making an observation or just repeating what I'd said. It was going well so far.

'May I tape you?' I asked, setting up a small hand-held Grundig dictaphone on the conference table between us.

'Hah?' he said, squinting and turning his head.

As I fumbled to turn on the Grundig, I tried to break the ice by mentioning – in a louder voice than was probably necessary – that the long table we were sitting at reminded me of 'that scene from *The Errand Boy*'.

'The Chairman of the Board,' said Jerry, softly.

We spoke of many things in the hour and a half we ended up spending together. He retold old stories, spoke of his fans and the pleasure of meeting his idol, Charlie Chaplin; he gave me some comedy advice he got from Stan Laurel which I didn't quite agree with*, reminisced about his successes, dismissed his critics and talked about the mechanics of comedy. We looked at the *Life* magazine pictures of the *Ladies Man* set I'd brought along and he talked me through the recessed lighting. Over the interview he'd come into focus as the man I thought he'd be: a man who loved comedy and needed an audience – and he didn't get cross with me once. At one point, when he

---

* 'Show them what you're going to do. Do it. And then show them you've done it.' Obviously, he and Stan were not fans of the Lubitsch Touch. Needless to say, I did not mention this to Jerry. I probably shouldn't have even raised it here. FURTHER READING: *The Cinema of Ernst Lubitsch* by Leland A. Poague (A.S. Barnes, 1978).

was telling me about how Chaplin showed him how he broke down shots in his script for *The Great Dictator* – 'a master, a deuce, an over-the-shoulder' – I noticed he'd leaned in quite close and was tapping me on the knee. 'Just how I did it,' he said, smiling again.

I met him only once after that. He was in Australia as chairman of the Muscular Dystrophy Foundation. I was asked to help present a big cardboard cheque for $600,000. He was eighty-five by then and greatly diminished physically. 'How are you?' I'd said as we shook hands. 'How are *you*?' he'd said back. As we were lining up for the photo I told him I'd met him before and how generous he'd been with his time and how he'd told me about Chaplin and Stan Laurel and comedy and his performance at the Olympia in 1972. 'Who's he talkin' about?' Jerry asked his Chrissie equivalent. 'He's talking about *you*, Jerry,' she said, as if to a child. 'He went on so long, I forgot,' replied Jerry, making a joke he often made when people gushed during introductions. I laughed but no one around him seemed to think it was a joke; they were handling him carefully, as if he were senile.

Then the man in charge of the cheque started explaining about the charity. After a minute, Jerry shot me a glance: a combination of a wink and an eye roll. I'd gone on a bit but at least I'd been talking about him. Jerry cut the man off with an announcement that it was time for the photo and, as we posed, started grumbling about how he didn't need to hear every damn detail about where the money came from. Then,

**Top** An extremely European family portrait. My father is third from the right, next to my grandmother Rose. Also (from left) my Uncle Tony and Auntie Carmen and (to the right of my father) my Uncle Joe and Uncle John. My grandfather Carmelo was away at sea.

**Bottom** My mother somehow enjoying herself in the bleak dystopian hellscape that is South Australia's mid-north.

*My mother and I win the Heinz Happiest Mother and Baby competition. The prize was a lifetime's supply of baby food. Well, six months' worth.*

**Above** *This picture was taken for an advertisement in a Maltese newspaper to encourage immigration. My parents were told to make it look like a candid shot of them seeing off some friends. Note my mother gently pushing my head to face the imaginary visitors. Instead, I insist on barrelling the camera.*

**Left** *My first day at school wearing a hand-knitted jumper instead of a store-bought one. I don't remember being set upon and beaten by the other students, but wouldn't have blamed them if they did.*

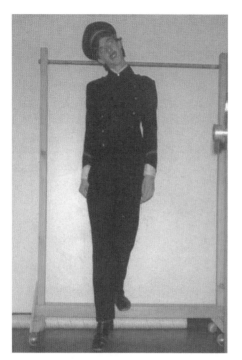

**Top left** *Mid-'70s. I attended acting classes on the weekends for a theatre group that put on pantomimes during the school holidays. I was supposed to be just stage-managing for their production of* Mary Poppins *but the actor didn't turn up so I went on in his place, thus launching a career that was really never meant to be.*

**Top right** *Eighteen years old and ready to take on the world.*

**Left** *My grandfather being warm and affectionate and me being an ironic smartarse.*

*Top right* Leandra (right).

*Middle right* My first union card.
I felt like Che Guevara (without
the moustache).

*Bottom right* I graduated from law
school in 1983 but forgot to get my
official portrait taken. I came back the
next year, borrowed a friend's academic
gown and snuck into their photo session.
Note that I'm holding a program rather
than my degree.

*Bottom* Within a year I had grown
a moustache and long hair and was
appearing in university revues (wearing
my father's tracksuit).

*After I graduated and started work as a solicitor, I continued to appear on stage. Here, Francis Greenslade plays Death and I play the Max von Sydow role in our version of* The Seventh Seal. *I'm wearing Leandra's jumper.*

***Top left*** *An articled clerk earning $120 a week.*

***Top right*** *Daryl Braithwaite refuses to look like himself at his own record launch while I pull the same ironic smartarse act I did with my grandfather a few pages back. My interview with Daryl was broadcast, but mercifully no copy of it now exists.*

***Left*** *Conquering radio in the '80s at Adelaide's SAFM for $20 a sketch. With Mark Thomas (at panel) and Alex Ward. We'd come straight from work.*

*A publicity shot for* Amadeus *(1990) with the redoubtable Edwin Hodgeman (and the doubtful Alex Ward). Only five years earlier Edwin had played Dr Dealgood in* Mad Max Beyond Thunderdome *with Mel Gibson and Tina Turner. I suspect the parfait he is feeding Al had a strong sedative in it.*

*1995. My head is shaved during a sketch on* Full Frontal. *It's not as funny as I hoped it would be.*

*My last year on* Full Frontal *in 1996. You can see the light had gone out of our eyes.*

**Top** Shaun Micallef's World Around Him *(1996), the* Full Frontal *special for Channel 7 that failed to turn into a series but was the unofficial pilot for the ABC's* The Micallef P(r)ogram(me) *two years later.*

**Bottom** *1998. Filling in for Glenn Robbins this time on Working Dog's* The Panel. The Late Show *had spurred me to try my hand at comedy some four years earlier. You can't tell but I am petrified. Rob Sitch looks calm and in control, as is his wont.*

*The only photo I have featuring the full cast of* The Micallef P(r)ogram(me), *(from left) Francis Greenslade, Roz Hammond, Wayne Hope and me.*

*Playing straight to Jerry Lewis.*
*(Simon Alekna)*

*Me ruining* Seachange *in 2000. With me is Australia's sweetheart Sigrid Thornton. We are in character here, she as Laura and me as her suitor, Warwick Munro. The photo appeared in a frame in Laura's living room. I stole it when we wrapped.*

*Top* 2001. I host television's night of nights and get away with it.

<u>*Left*</u> My passport to the big time. Soon to be revoked.

FINAL SHOT 4    f 32 @ 125

**Above** *2003.* Welcher & Welcher *with (from left) Nina Liu, Francis Greenslade, me, Santo Cilauro, Robyn Butler and Anita Smith. I had no idea what I was doing.* (James Penlidis)

**Left** *The first polaroid taken for the photoshoot promoting* Micallef Tonight *(2003). It was downhill from there on.*

*Top* With one of my heroes, and
Barry Humphries.

*Bottom* Shane Warne signing a hockey
stick to confuse collectors on Micallef
Tonight (2003).

**Top** *My first time behind a fake news desk.* Newstopiä *2007–2008.*
(James Penlidis)

**Bottom** *With my sons, who positively revel in the limelight.* (Kane Hibberd / Stringer via Getty Images)

*Above* Excelsior! I win my first and only
Most Popular Logie. One they give to
presenters. Scott Cam has also won one.
(Ryan Pierse / Staff via Getty Images)

*Left* I sing The Who's 'My Generation' on
Rove *in 2010.*

*Top* Francis Greensalde and I have appeared in many things together. What Ever Happened to Baby Jane? *is not one of them.*
(Simon Schluter)

*Bottom* Mad as Hell. *My dream job.*
(Courtesy of ITV Australia)

after only a couple of snaps, he said, 'We're done,' and walked out, leaving his people looking embarrassed. 'He's tired,' said someone, in a way that suggested he'd been tired a few times before.

My last memory of Jerry Lewis is hearing his raised voice outside the door after his publicist had joined him. 'Don't fucking tell me to calm down,' he said without a trace of Irish accent.

When Lewis had been my then age, he had not only just produced, written, directed and starred in *The Nutty Professor*, he had been signed up to host a live nationwide weekly TV chat show. With my acting chops on display in *SeaChange* and proof of my live-to-air hosting skills still fresh in the memory of the 2.049 million people who endured the Logies*, I was ready for big-time commercial television and movie stardom. First, though, I had to do as John Cleese, another comedy hero of mine**, had done: leave sketch comedy behind and conquer the world of the sitcom.

---

\* A lot of people back in those days.
\*\* See Appendix B.

## CHAPTER ELEVEN

# Top of the world, Ma!

'WRITE WHAT YOU know,' they say.

I'm not sure who 'they' are exactly, but I can tell you they clearly have no idea how to write a sitcom. I certainly didn't. Like everybody else who fancied themselves a writer at the time, I'd bought a copy of Robert McKee's *Story*. Unfortunately, I'd loaned it to William McInnes before I got a chance to read it and he never gave it back.*

Despite being McKee-less, I decided to write about my time practising the law, except that because that would have been a bit dull, I wrote instead about a barrister who is in chambers with his wife, also a barrister. It was called *Welcher & Welcher* and co-starred Robyn Butler, Santo Cilauro, Nina Liu, Anita Smith and, of course, Francis.

---

* Obviously, too much time has passed for me to ask him to give it back now. Hopefully, he'll pick up this book in a bookstore, leaf through it looking to see if I've mentioned him, read this footnote, and be embarrassed into returning it. Best he just leave it on my doorstep as it would be awkward if either of us made a big deal of it.

Because I didn't know what I was doing, I just wrote what I thought was funny regardless of whether it was possible to shoot or not. The series was going to be full of elaborate sight gags, word play, marital farce, idiots, arcane film references, dual roles, self-reflective meta-jokes and plain old-fashioned mugging; in other words, pretty much exactly what I'd been doing previously in my sketch comedy work. Although I had called time on *The Micallef P(r)ogram(me)* to do something different I did not seem naturally inclined to follow through.

While I worked with the ABC comedy department's script editor on 'making the characters relatable' and 'giving them arcs' and a whole lot of structural stuff that Robert McKee's book would have taught me had I read it, I received offers to act in two movies.

My increased profile had resulted in requests to audition for various film roles, but I had no more luck at these than I had with the MTC or *Bastard Boys*. As a result, audiences around the world were denied my big-screen appearances in *Son of the Mask* and *Me Myself I* with Rachel Griffiths. These most recent offers, though, were audition-free; I had the parts regardless of whether or not I'd be any good in them.

*The Honourable Wally Norman* was to be shot in Adelaide, so the plan was that on my off-days I would spend some time with my parents, whom I'd really only seen fleetingly at Christmas since moving to Melbourne some nine years earlier. In practice, though, apart from a few dinners, I spent most of my free time holed up in my hotel room rewriting

*Welcher & Welcher*, so that it didn't look so much like a Ritz Brothers movie.

As you may have gathered by now, I love movies. When I was a kid, the family would pile into my father's work-provided Leyland P76 and we'd go to the drive-in: to see Disney movies, usually. The cinema was reserved for birthdays, when my friends and I would be taken to the Saturday matinee double feature, usually battered prints of comedies released a couple of years earlier. When we finally got a TV, I watched everything.

My father loved films too, though he wasn't as keen on the comedies as I was. He liked musicals and ones about the war. If I was watching an Abbott and Costello or a Bob Hope he'd hover around the door to the lounge room only long enough to say 'Is this on again?' and then get back to whatever chore I should have probably been helping him with. He didn't mind rewatching the films *he* liked, though. Sometimes he'd wake me up after I'd gone to bed so I could come and watch the big musical number in, say, *American in Paris*. 'There's some real dancing for you,' he'd say. Often it was Gene, other times it was Fred. Musicals weren't really my thing but I liked that he wanted to share them with me. They always looked great, though, with their luscious Technicolor, and I couldn't help but admire the precision and inventiveness of the routines – the up-the-wall-across-the-ceiling number in *Royal Wedding* I eventually pinched for the rotating room sketches I did on *Full Frontal* and *The Micallef P(r)ogram(me)*.

We once watched *I Was Monty's Double* together and when I commented on how much Monty did indeed look like his double, my father pointed out that both roles were played by the same actor. I was amazed at the cinematic trickery, which of course today could be done by a five-year-old on an iPhone. My father also pointed out that the actor playing M.E. Clifton James – the army lieutenant doing the doubling of the famous general – was the *actual* M.E. Clifton James. 'That's how come they look so much alike,' he explained. I had to think about that one for the next few hours.

Dad was always saying great things like that. Once, we were both watching the sun set over the water at Glenelg Beach. 'There's something you don't see every day,' he said. I resisted the urge to be a smart-arse and point out that a sunset was *exactly* the sort of thing you saw every day. As the sky plunged into a Tiepolo orgy of pink and blue with shafts of golden light stretching out from behind the clouds, I knew what he meant. And it was nice to see things through his eyes sometimes.

We'd often go to the beautiful old Art Deco Capri cinema up the street from the orphanage on Goodwood Road – a revival house with a huge Wurlitzer organ that would rise, Dr Phibes–like, out of the floor as curtains parted either side to reveal glass-panelled booths full of synchronised automata. The Capri showed silent films and the occasional foreign one. Charlie Chaplin and Jacques Tati were my favourites. My fondest memory of my dad is watching the scene in *Monsieur*

*Hulot's Holiday* where an old married couple are walking along the beach at night, the wife in front oohing and aahing over the shells she's picking up, the husband plodding along behind, taking the shells she's handing back to him, giving them the most perfunctory of once-overs and then tossing them away, as the two of us quietly laughed along together.

Ted Emery, who had directed *Full Frontal* and *The Micallef P(r)ogram(me)* and was slated to direct *Welcher*, was also directing *Wally Norman*; he'd directed Jimeoin's first feature, *The Craic*, which had done nicely at the box office, so I felt I was in safe and experienced hands. The film starred Kevin Harrington, Alan Cassell, Greig Pickhaver, Bryan Dawe and Roz Hammond (as a character named Dolly Norman). It was about an average schlub who, due to a spelling mistake, ends up accidentally running for office.

I wondered whether the premise was a little thin. 'Wouldn't they just apply to have the name altered?' I'd asked Ted, after reading the script. 'Nah, they can't,' he'd said. 'They have to go with whoever they put on the ballot.' It didn't seem likely, but I assumed smarter people than me were across it, and hey, it was a film and I got to play the villain (a dodgy politician), so I said yes. The only change I insisted on was that the name of the character I was playing be changed from Ken Oath, which was already the joke name of a popular Adelaide DJ (and no less unfunny when he used it), to the more anodyne Ken Oates. They graciously agreed. I had them in the palm of my hand.

The part had been written with me in mind, so I had no trouble playing it. What I *did* have trouble with was repeating my scenes again and again so that different angles and shot sizes could be covered. I was used to TV, where it was usually one take from multiple angles and that was it. I found it difficult to recreate exactly what I'd done on the first take so that it would match the other takes *and* still have it seem spontaneous and hopefully funny. It was diminishing returns with me; when you've peaked halfway through the rehearsal and you're working with a proper actor who's at their best by take 5, it's never going to cut together as a good scene. In short, I didn't know anything about film acting and it was rapidly flattening out whatever I had to offer comedy-wise.

For example, there was a scene where some lobbyists turn up to my electoral office to put the squeeze on me. I'm not looking forward to it. I'm out on the footpath waiting for them with my chauffeur. Ted thought it'd be funny if I was drinking a cup of tea. I thought it'd be funny if I also had a saucer. Ted said no. So the scene is: I'm sipping the tea, the car pulls up, the lobbyists pile out and walk into the office. On the first take, the chauffeur and I are waiting, I take a sip, make a face and ad-lib to him: 'Did you put sugar in this?' I say it like I'd asked him to but suspect he hasn't. 'Yes, sir,' he ad-libs back. Disgusted, I toss out the contents of the cup as the car pulls up.

Now, for some reason, this struck everybody as funny. There's no pleasing Ken, even when you do what he asks.

It was also a nice story moment; he was about to get a shellacking from his backers and he had to confect a moment of victory over his underling to make himself feel better. Great. Take 2. I couldn't replicate it. I got the line out but my intonation suggested that the chauffeur had put the sugar in when I'd asked him *not* to, so my reaction to his 'yes' is perfectly reasonable. Take 3. I emphasise the 'you' in 'Did you put sugar in this?' which doesn't make any sense. Take 4. I say 'Is there any sugar in here?' which doesn't sound right. Take 5. I come up with 'Is there *any* sugar in here?' which makes it sounds like we've been discussing it for a while and that he hasn't put enough in to be able to taste it. Take 6. Leaning on 'sugar' makes it sound like he should have put something else in. Ted says we have it in there somewhere* and the grips reposition the camera for my single (five takes), the wide shot (three takes), a travelling shot from the car (four takes) and, just for fun and some overtime, a crane shot (two takes).

The other film I was offered was *Bad Eggs*, written and to be directed by Tony Martin. Tony and I had become friends when McCaffrie and I sought his advice on the script for a puppet show we had been commissioned to write for Channel 7 a few years earlier. Yes, a puppet show. He was very polite about it considering how terrible it was. We hadn't at that stage worked together – unless you count the time his cardboard cut-out appeared on *The Micallef P(r)ogram(me)* – and as much as I

* I just checked. He used the unfunny take 2.

162

always enjoyed working with Ted, the prospect of working with Tony appealed to me enormously.

I had read the script before Tony offered me the role and knew it was pretty good. I certainly didn't have to fake my enthusiasm for it as he must have done for the puppet show. Tony and I have quite different comic styles – he hops down into the audience, I invite them up onstage – but we have a shared sensibility when it comes to film; we love comedy and grew up watching and listening to much of the same stuff despite being separated by a few years and the Tasman.

The film starred Mick Molloy, Judith Lucy, Bob Franklin, Bill Hunter, Robyn Nevin, Alan Brough and Nicholas Bell. Again, I was playing the villain (another dodgy politician, although with different coloured hair this time). The plot is complicated but essentially it's about two cops uncovering some police corruption that goes all the way to the top. Judith and I get kidnapped and the bad-guys-meet-good-guys denouement takes place on a dry, desolate expanse of land similar to that featured in *Seven* except [SPOILER] no one's head ends up in a box. Again, I don't think I was great in the role – but I was better than I'd been in *Wally Norman*. I had learned a lot from making the previous film and picked up even more from watching how good Mick and Bob were in our scenes together.

With my place in the Hollywood firmament assured, I left Ted and Tony to cobble together my soon-to-be award-winning performances and returned to the ABC for the final draft and polish of my own sitcom masterwork.

*Welcher* had by this time turned into an office comedy. Unbeknown to us, it was slated to come out at around the same time as *The Office*\*, which, as you might remember, was also an office comedy. Blissfully ignorant, the ABC signed off on the scripts – toned down and a bit more real and with things at stake and the characters relatable and the structure McKee-ed – and we went into pre-production.

At that moment, two more opportunities came my way, but I could only choose one. Both Channel 7 and Channel 9 had contacted my agent with a view to having me host a late-night variety show. Late night in Australia is 9.30 pm. I was living the dream: a couple of blockbuster films waiting to be released, the funniest Australian sitcom ever in the offing, and now my choice of networks and a chance to become the next Rove McManus.

The current Rove McManus was still enjoying success with his weekly chat show and I guess the other networks wanted a slice of that sweet, sweet advertising pie. Such was the poverty of imagination in this country that mine was the only name both Seven and Nine could think of. Happy to be the only fish floundering in the dry creek bed of Australian television, I took meetings with the heads of both networks and revelled in their flattery for a few weeks as I lunched with one and then the other with neither knowing, like Dudley Moore in *Micki & Maude*. Eventually I went with Nine. I felt beholden to them for the chance they'd given me with the Logies, I'd be working

---

\*  See Appendix C.

with many of the same people and trusted them, and it was the network that already had a long late-night variety-show tradition with Graham Kennedy and Don Lane, so it made sense to subvert it where it lived rather than at Seven, which had only ever had Steve Vizard's show, which was already a bit postmodern. Plus, Nine was offering more money. I inked the deal and returned my attention to the sitcom.

As it turned out, our little office comedy had more problems to contend with than just the release of the Ricky Gervais one. I had written it to be performed in front of a studio audience, but Ted thought the mise en scène was so complicated (not that Ted would ever use that expression) and the set-ups so numerous that we'd best shoot it without an audience and then play it to one when we were done. Unfortunately, this decision was made *after* the main set had been built and so it had a very theatrical proscenium arch feel to it, rather than looking like a real office.

We'd also committed to a multi-cam approach and an on-line switch – using multiple cameras and cutting between those cameras as we went, rather than shooting it with a single camera like a film and then editing it later – and while we could and would recut the on-line switch, it meant the studio component of the show had to be lit so that all the shots worked; so it ended up looking like *Frasier*, but without the benefit of an actual studio audience.

Without that audience to guide us, we all ended up delivering our lines more quickly and this did not help the material, because I had written it in such a way that the jokes could land and have some reaction room before we picked up and moved on. Without the laughter the pace became a bit unrelenting, plus the scripts ended up running two or three minutes under, which meant I had to write extra material on the fly to pad them out to the length agreed on in the contract. Worst of all, when the time came to roll the show in front of an audience in order to record their laughter, we hadn't left sufficient gaps, so if they laughed at a joke, the laugh spilled over into the next line and they didn't hear the next set-up or plot point. Riding the levels in the sound mix just made it all sound fake and so we decided it would be best to go without a laugh track entirely.

What we ended up with was a show that looked like a traditional multi-cam sitcom, with big jokes that invited a response that never came. The jokes in the studio felt like they were failing. The material shot with a single camera outside in the real world felt better, because there were fewer joke-jokes and more physical comedy, but there was no blending the two worlds. On watching a rough cut of the first episode, I had my head in my hands most of the time. It was, I thought, a disaster.

Ted missed the screening – he'd been shooting a Volkswagen Beetle spinning on its roof for a scene – and asked how it went. I lied and said it was fantastic. Eager to see just how fantastic it was, he made the editor run it again and snickered all the way through, requesting some tightens here and there but otherwise perfectly happy with the result. I didn't mind it as much the second time around and even the editor, who'd already seen it a million times, had been laughing. Ted's enjoyment of anything, as always, was highly transmissible.

I realised that up until that point, I'd only ever been in an edit suite for *Full Frontal* and *The Micallef P(r)ogram(me)*, shows that had live audience reactions already on the soundtrack. I hadn't realised just how reassuring that element had been and how much I'd relied on it when cutting those shows together. Editing *Welcher & Welcher* was going to have to be a leap of faith. If the material was funny when I wrote it (and I thought it was) and funny when we shot it (and it seemed to be), it would be funny when we put it to air. I stiffened my resolve and for the rest of the shoot and into post-production convinced myself, as I do on most things I'm in the process of working on, that it was the best thing I'd ever done. You have to fall in love with what you're doing at the time, otherwise it's got no chance.

| | | | /⁄—

With two films under starter's orders and the sitcom assembled and scheduled for midyear on the public broadcaster, I moved back to the ramshackle fibro buildings at the converted soup factory in Bendigo Street to begin work on *Micallef Tonight*. Channel 9 had wanted to call the show *Micallef Tonight!* but I felt the exclamation mark was too gaudy and wanted something more subtle; we back and forthed over this for minutes but they finally caved, the worms. This was an even more make-or-break opportunity than the Logies had been. Jerry Lewis's late-night show had been a bomb and only lasted thirteen episodes. I certainly didn't want that happening to me.

That they made us do four pilots should have tipped me off that something was wrong. Clearly, they hadn't been won over by what we were doing, but there'd never be any notes (and I certainly wasn't going to ask for any). They would just request another pilot. We would oblige by shooting virtually the same show over again – and again – and again. It was like auditioning for the MTC.

Eventually they realised that it wasn't going to get either any better or any different, bit the bullet and scheduled the show. I was up on billboards, featured in magazines and even did a network promo dressed in a kilt and playing the bagpipes (I guess they thought 'Micallef' was Scottish). Expectations were high. As part of a publicity blitz on a scale unseen since Goebbels launched Hitler, it was arranged that I would have a special tête-à-tête luncheon with the Hedda Hopper of Australian television, Robert Fidgeon. Robert used to work for Channel 9 when he was young and was now still doing much the same thing through his regular TV column in the *Herald Sun*. If Robert Fidgeon liked you, then you could be assured of glowing reviews week after week during your run. I was forever getting him mixed up with another writer who worked for rival newspaper *The Age* (let's call him Louella Parsons), so before our confab I made a mental note that whatever I did, I must not mistake one for the other.

The day for our lunch arrived, so did I and then eventually our food. Robert was friendly, holding forth on the rich glory days of Channel 9 while shovelling forkfuls of expense-account scampi into his craw. He asked me what I thought of Graham Kennedy. I liked him. Don Lane? Watched his show all the time. Bert Newton? Brilliant. He liked that I'd sent a personal note to Bert asking him to present the Gold Logie when I hosted. I was doing well. What did I think about Mick Molloy's new show? This was a test. He'd dropped it in, hoping to catch me off guard.

Daryl had just left the network after a century of doing *Hey Hey It's Saturday* and Mick had filled the gap with a show that was as different from Daryl's as David Lynch's *Elephant Man* had been from Zoltan Korda's *Elephant Boy*. The thing was, I'd just done a film with Mick and he couldn't have been nicer so I wasn't going to bag the guy just to curry favour with some pompous windbag. 'I liked it,' I said. Really? 'Yes, I did.' He made a face and returned to his scampi. If I'd left it there, I might have been able to remain in his good books on the strength of my admiration for Kennedy, Lane and Newton – but no, I had to mention Louella Parsons and how she had attacked Mick's show week after week in a way which suggested an almost unhealthy obsession. It was only when I clocked Robert's face that I realised I'd got him and Louella mixed up again.

*Welcher & Welcher* exploded onto TV screens during our pre-production period at Channel 9. Neither Hedda nor Louella liked it very much, although I remember more vividly the two-word review from one viewer in an internet chat room which read simply: 'Oh dear ...'

Louella changed her mind about halfway through the season, even favourably comparing one sequence with *Fawlty Towers*, but Hedda took the time and column space to bag the show each and every week, even writing a few longer pieces here and there on how dreadful I was and how it didn't augur well for this new show I had at Nine. I hadn't received negative publicity like that before and the cumulative effect of the eight-week barrage took its toll. It was around that time that I decided to pretend to never read reviews ever again. It works quite well. Some people will always mention a bad review you've had but you can just annoy them by professing not to know what they're talking about. '*Which newspaper is this?*', '*Who wrote it?*', '*Oh really? What does "sophomoric"mean?*' Being obtuse is really infuriating. And fun.

I'm not suggesting for a moment that Hedda and Louella were wrong about *Welcher & Welcher*. The show clearly didn't work. Ted went off and directed the enormously successful *Kath & Kim* so I can't blame him. The cast was top-shelf and so was the crew. It was really down to me.

I'm not an overly sentimental person when it comes to my TV career. Generally speaking, I grow less enamoured with my work as time goes by; unless it's Milo or a rare moment in something where I'm being unselfconscious, I find it hard to watch my younger self without cringing at least slightly. *Welcher & Welcher*, though, contains some of my favourite things:

**FAVOURITE GAG:** Santo plays an IT guy who is always installing the latest tech around the office. He spends a lot of time in the walls* attaching cables to each other and at one point becomes entangled. As he fights his way out, Quentin Welcher is typing away on his keyboard and with each pull of the cable, Quentin's computer moves closer and closer to the edge of the desk. At the same time, the receptionist is away from her station and a client rings the bell on the waiting room counter. As the bell sounds, Quentin pushes back the computer so that in that moment it resembles the carriage on a typewriter. He types some more, the computer edges across the desk, the client rings the bell, Quentin returns the carriage again. Eventually the IT guy falls out of the wall, dragging so much of the cable with him that Quentin's computer scoots off the desk, along the floor and up the wall, ripping a neat line of plaster as it goes, ending up stuck fast in the corner of the office ceiling.

**FAVOURITE SEQUENCE:** In the last episode we use the old trope of Quentin having to be in two places at once. Double booked, but with the courtrooms hearing his cases down the corridor from each other, he must run from one to the

---

* A subconscious exploration of my dream-state career-change anxiety or an homage to Curly Howard in the Three Stooges' *A Plumbing We Will Go* (1940)? Discuss.

other as his junior counsel buzzes him on his phone, to make various submissions or cross-examine someone. At one point he knocks over a water cooler and drenches himself as he attempts to put the bottle back in its stand. The next time he races down the corridor, he aquaplanes several metres across the tiled floor and ends up under a bench. We shot it in a real courthouse and much of the action is spontaneous and ad-libbed and resulted in actual bruises, but Ted did a great job with the direction and I am very proud of it.

**FAVOURITE EPISODE:** The power goes out and everybody has to take the stairs, but the automatic locks kick in and while people can get into the stairwell, no one can get out. They only discover this when they get to the ground level. There is no mobile reception in the stairwell, so they can't ring for help. There are no lights either, so they use the light from their mobile phones to get to the roof. It turns into a version of *Journey to the Centre of the Earth*. There's even a goose called Gertrude. Once on the roof, everyone has access to mobile reception but now their batteries are all flat. The power comes back on but now the door on the roof is locked and they can't get back down because no one has their swipe pass BUT the power-operated high-rise window-cleaning gondola is working, so Quentin uses it to go down the side of the building and get help. Meanwhile the grill in the Welcher office kitchen is back on, and has heated up, burnt the bagel inside and started a fire which spreads to the entire floor. The last shot is of Quentin on the outside of the building looking in as his wife, Kate, steps out of the lift with a potential investor only to be greeted by flames engulfing the reception area as the sprinklers turn on. Kate and Quentin clock each other through the window and he waves.

I'd be perfectly happy to have any of the above feature in an obituary clip package after I'm gone. No doubt, though, they'll just play Milo Kerrigan walking around with a bucket stuck on his foot.

Okay, so the sitcom was a bust. I still had the Channel 9 show and those movies coming out. All was not lost.

CHAPTER TWELVE

# Kaboom!

SO THERE I was in the Channel 9 boardroom, outlining my bold new plans for what they kept calling a 'tonight show'. Listening and nodding were the new general manager David Gyngell, the chief programmer, the head of light entertainment, the head of publicity, head of promotions, head of sales – all the heavy hitters. I explained that what I had in mind would be a little like the Logies I'd hosted, in that it would have some fun subverting the conventions of the genre. Fearing I was losing them, I talked about the big-name guests we hoped to have on the show, like Shane Warne and Barry Humphries. 'Kath and Kim,' suggested somebody. 'Yes, absolutely,' I promised. It didn't feel like the right time to tell them that they were fictional characters.

'Will there be a band?' asked someone with a steady voice and a Montblanc poised over the leaves of a Moleskine.

'There will be a band,' I confirmed. 'We're going to call them ... The Channel 9 Nine.'

There was a dribble of laughter around the room and my joke was duly noted. I thought it best to tell them later that the band was going to be cardboard cut-outs. Perhaps I wouldn't tell them at all and have it be a surprise on the night. Yes, a much better idea. Networks love surprises.

A month earlier there had been a meeting to which I had not been invited. It was about creating a new tonight show with opportunities for synergy; it was also about cross-promotion and big names and sales opportunities and native advertising and product placement and money. Kerry Packer was even there. Having decided on what the show had to do, now all they needed to work out was who would host it.

'Who's the next Graham Kennedy?' Kerry had asked as he stared out the conference room window across the rooftops of Willoughby.

The new head of light entertainment gently cleared her throat to speak. Packer turned like a turret on a tank, lined her up in his sights and rumbled, 'You got someone?'

'I think so, Mr Packer,' she said. People around her were turning white – well, whiter than normal. Blanched almonds in suits, they were. Very few people ever actually spoke at these meetings. Questions from the network owner were usually treated as rhetorical. Occasionally, there would be noises of agreement and maybe even smatterings of applause, but seldom actual words. 'I worked with him on the Logies,' she went on. Packer's pale eyes burned into her soul but the recently appointed executive held firm. 'His name ...' she said, '... is Shaun Micallef.'

The billionaire media baron rolled the name over in his head before he said it aloud. When he did, it sounded ludicrous. A Shaun Micallef was a discontinued brand of automobile from the 1920s or maybe a skin condition. It didn't trip off the tongue like Graham Kennedy.

But Packer had watched the Logies as he'd watched everything broadcast on his network. He was a man who knew what he liked and, while he may or may not have liked the way this Micallef person had hosted, he did like the ratings: the highest the Logies had ever received. 'And he's the new Kennedy, is he?' he growled.

'I believe so, Mr Packer,' replied the young woman, not six months into her job.

The Panzer muzzle smiled and pointed itself back out over the suburbs of Sydney's lower North Shore. And waited ...

The bright young head of light entertainment was my friend Hilary Innes, and while I can't vouch for each and every detail in my fanciful retelling of her meeting with Kerry Packer, I assure you that Hilary put her career at Nine on the line by recommending me for the job. It was an act of faith I have never been able to adequately repay. *Micallef Tonight* just got me deeper into the red.

As airtime approached on the first night, I paced about Daryl's old dressing-room. I was more nervous than I had been for the Logies, which was ridiculous because I'd had to *learn* my monologue for that as there was no autocue. This time we had autocue; how hard could it be to stand there and read it? And it was only five minutes long instead of the fifteen I'd done in the Palladium Room. Plus, I'd already had four pilots' worth of rehearsal and I knew the material backwards; in fact I was considering delivering it that way, I'd become so bored with it. Maybe I was worried about next week's show as we wouldn't start writing that one until tomorrow—

*Knock! Knock!*

What the fuck was it NOW?!!!

All week it had been something or other. First, it was David Gyngell wishing me good luck and telling me to be myself, 'just like Eddie McGuire'. I told him I couldn't do both. He gave me a tight, closed-mouth smile and left. Then Graham Kennedy's old writer turned up to tell me how great Graham was. He seemed to think Kennedy's greatness was in some way because of his writing; I didn't have the heart to tell him it was regardless of it. Someone from publicity turned up to have me sign off on my preferred head shots in a booklet of a thousand proof sheets; I really didn't care. Don Lane's old director popped by to insinuate that people like me were ruining the industry (he was, of course, right). Even the network colourist had spent an hour with me to discuss what tie I might wear for tonight's episode before deciding on exactly the same shade of blue I'd worn for all three seasons of *The Micallef P(r)ogram(me)*. There were others, so many others – some who actually had something to do with the show we were putting on.

I opened the door. Bert and Patti Newton had thoughtfully sent me a hamper. Perhaps I could escape in it like El Chapo. Instead, I tore through the cellophane, grabbed some chocolate and made a beeline for the studio, where I could stand around being nervous and comfort-eat behind the curtain.

*Micallef Tonight*, named partly in homage to *In Melbourne Tonight* but mainly because it sounded a bit awkward, featured Pete Smith, Livinia Nixon and the perennial Francis as our pretend bandleader. Getting Pete to do our voice-overs and absurd prize reads was a coup, as he had done the real ones on *Sale of the Century* for twenty years and had been a mainstay on Nine during its golden age. My God, the man had started working there in 1962, the year I was born! I think he was happy to do it because he knew Tony and Mick and the Working Dog team and thought we were somehow connected with them and therefore to be trusted. Pete would come in and do his stuff live rather than pre-record it, and this helped the timing and allowed for some improvisation and spontaneity. He also arranged for me to get into the network archives so I could watch a swag of previous 'tonight shows' from over the years, including one from Daryl Somers called *Daryl* where interviews were conducted in a conversation pit without any furniture. We got most of our ideas from this show. Livinia was a surprise; she was a network suggestion but turned out to be pretty funny and up for anything. That she had been on

*Hey Hey It's Saturday* helped give the show the look and feel of something familiar that we could then derail.

Our writers included McCaffrie, the playwright Matt Cameron, with whom I'd worked on *Full Frontal*, Michael Ward from *The Micallef P(r)ogram(me)* and Robyn Butler, whose career I had almost destroyed on *Welcher & Welcher*.

The show was an in-house production, by which I mean it was made by Channel 9 on its own and not as a co-production with someone who knew what they were doing. I was employed by the network, which meant that technically I had to do as I was told. But, to their credit, no one ever did. What became apparent very early on was that, at least insofar as light entertainment was concerned, they weren't used to dealing with scripts; or, it seemed, with any written material. They were used to shows where by and large the presenters just said any old thing that popped into their heads. This certainly explained much of what I'd been watching down in archives.

I was keen to get Barry Humphries on as our first guest. Firstly, because I'd mentioned his name in my pitch meeting and felt obliged to follow through on at least one of the things I'd promised. Secondly, I just wanted to meet him and, as with Jerry Lewis, thought an interview the perfect cover for my fanboying. Thirdly, he'd be a great guest. As it was, he was in town – and, even better, in and around Channel 9. I happened to see him from a balcony when he was pacing the courtyard on his mobile dressed as Edna, after he'd flamed out on the celebrity version of *Who Wants To Be a Millionaire*.

'I proved myself to be quite the dunce,' he admitted in his own voice to someone.

I wrote a letter asking him to come on the show and arranged to have it hand-delivered to his dressing-room because I thought he'd appreciate the old-school nature of the gesture. Also, because I'd have felt a right noob just going up to him and asking. To my delight, he agreed and arrangements were to be made for us to talk about what he might like to do.

Meanwhile, someone at Nine suddenly realised that I'd never done an interview before and thought that perhaps I should learn how to do it before going on national television with a chat show. It seemed that up until then, the higher-ups at Nine had assumed the guests on *The Micallef P(r)ogram(me)* were real. A very accommodating stream of network personalities allowed me to practise on them, including, in what was probably his last recorded interview, Lou Richards. Among other things, I learned that he had once played football for a team called Collingwood.

When I got back to Daryl's office after interview practice, there was a message on my desk. Barry Humphries had called. Three times. I called back at once. Maybe he wanted Francis Greenslade's telephone number – but no, he was very concerned about the show. No one had called him to talk about what he was going to be doing. No pre-interview. No brief. Nothing. I apologised profusely, introduced myself and set out what I thought might be a number of avenues we could go down, including the more obscure Dada-esque escapades of his youth. As I'd demonstrated a knowledge of his oeuvre that went well beyond Edna and Sir Les, Barry, satisfied that he wasn't dealing with an idiot (he was wrong), rang off saying he looked forward to our meeting.

As I've mentioned, Barry was someone my mother and grandmother had taken me to see in Adelaide in the '70s. I'd taken Leandra to see him a few times in the '80s and '90s and had even seen one of his shows on the West End when a few of the people in the balcony, eager to catch the gladioli he was hurling into the audience, fell out and dangled. As I gasped, Edna continued dancing about: 'Wouldn't it be terrible if that happened every night,' she said. He was also in one of my favourite films: *Bedazzled* starring Peter Cook and Dudley Moore. How did he get there from here, I had often wondered. He plays Envy and has perhaps the best line in the movie. Looking over at another of the Seven Deadly Sins admiring itself in the full-length mirror it's wearing like a baby-harness, Envy-Barry hisses to Dudley Moore: 'Ooh, I wish I was Vanity.' Throughout what I'd seen of his career, Barry, endearingly, seemed to have the same disdain for the ocker persona as I had.

The first show went well. Our guests were not only Barry but Kath and Kim (Gina and Jane preferred it that way). We had to wait till next week for Shane Warne. I even got a nice joke in during Dannii Minogue's song, when a cutaway caught me watching Andrew Denton's *Enough Rope* instead of her. After the show, everybody congratulated each other in the green room and I had my picture taken with Barry. I was so happy that I didn't even mind that much when Jamie Durie, on the show for a quick gag, stood between us, ruining it.

The next day, the ratings came in: 1.3 million. Not bad for a 9.30 show – *and* we finished on time, which was good news for those who only had us on because they were waiting for *The Sopranos*. Later that morning, when we were trying to write the next show, the GTV9 Melbourne station manager dropped by to proudly show me the minute-by-minutes, a breakdown of the overall rating into sixty unhelpful slivers.

'You see here, your rating went up 12.7 per cent with women between eighteen and forty-five,' he cooed. 'You should check the tape, see what you were doing and maybe do something like that again next week.'

'Why?'

'Because that's when they switched over.'

'But how would they know what I was doing if they were watching another program?'

The station manager didn't look up from the minute-by-minutes, although he'd stopped nodding and smiling at them.

'Isn't it more likely an ad came on and they changed channels to see what else was on?' I reasoned.

'Anyway, congratulations,' he said, rolling up the papers. 'Great work.' His mobile phone rang and when he looked at the display, the blood drained from his face. 'It's Kerry Packer,' he said, as if a manticore was coming in through the ceiling. 'I must go.'

Next week's show did 1.1 million and I got Shane Warne to autograph a hockey stick. I looked for it afterwards, thinking it might be a nice memento, but someone had already stolen it.[*] Packer was reportedly baffled by the show but impressed with the ratings; and that was the important thing. The following week we were 1 million – still pretty good – *and* we had Gavin and Wazza on from *The Block*. The week after that, Amity Dry, also from *The Block*, sang her song 'The Lighthouse' and we dipped below the magic million, but we still won the night. A couple of episodes later, having run out of contestants from *The Block*, we were down to 850,000 and coming second to *White Collar Blue* on Channel 10. The Whitlams were our music act and McCaffrie almost wet himself laughing at the sight of Tim Freedman singing 'Royal in the Afternoon' while somebody behind him milked a cow. It wasn't Tim and the cow that made him laugh so much as the thought that somewhere in Sydney, Kerry Packer was sitting there watching the same thing.

The show was getting looser and would sometimes blow out from its scheduled hour to ninety minutes, enraging fans of *The Sopranos*, who would ring the switchboard to complain. On one episode, even I rang to give them a piece of my mind. The following week, minutes before the show went to air, I was taken aside by David Gyngell and asked whether we really needed to do any more jokes about Alan Jones, who also appeared on the network. I said that we only wanted to do

---

[*] Probably Eddie McGuire.

one more to complete the set of three we'd planned and to his credit he let us do it. By the time I tore the medial meniscus in my right knee a few weeks later while sliding down a pole for a fake ad promoting an equally fake Channel 9 show called *Undercover Fire Cops* and then spent the next episode miniaturising Robyn, Francis, Pete and Livinia (wearing a gorilla suit) and injecting them into my leg so they could operate on me, we were cooked. We hit 750,000, a rating that most shows would kill for today, but back then was a harbinger of certain doom.

I'd never been axed before and I suspect never will be again so nicely. Hilary made the call. I put my stuff in a box, said goodbye to everyone and went home. It was a pity. The episode we had planned for the next week had the Melbourne Symphony Orchestra playing 'Macho Man' while a chicken parmigiana rotated on a plinth. And they say we weren't connecting with the audience.

When things don't quite work as I expect, I always think, as I'm sure many of us do, of the old quote from avant-garde composer Cornelius Cardew:

*Often the wonderful configurations produced by failure reveal the pettiness of the goals.*

By the metrics of commercial broadcasting, sure, I failed; but by the conveniently arbitrary standards of my own whim and fancy, I had made something that was funny and worthwhile.

There had been attempts to get me to try and turn the ship around, but it was hard enough steering the thing in the direction we were going without having to redraw the maps and change course. Also, to push the metaphor to breaking point, I figured if I was going to go down with the ship, it should at least be *my* ship.

It was a curious time. While I didn't really feel like I'd failed, I was aware that everyone thought I had. The press rang wanting me to comment, a photographer took a picture of our house, I was even the subject of a cartoon in *The Australian*. My memory is that I was depicted as the Frankenstein monster strapped to a slab while a couple of Nine executives, who have just pulled the plug on me, look on morosely. 'I'm afraid we lost him,' one of them says.

My mother rang to commiserate. She'd being keeping a scrapbook and this most recent batch of clippings weren't in keeping with its hagiographic *leitmotif.* 'What happened?' she asked. I told her I wasn't sure, to which she replied: 'Well, you must have done *something* wrong.' As usual, she was right. I think it might have been that my need for approval always had to be on my own terms. The very thing that inured me to failure was, in this case, the cause of it.

| | | | / ⁀

My first movie, *The Honourable Wally Norman*, opened the Melbourne International Film Festival a few weeks later. Boy, was I in the mood for that opening night. The star-studded celebrity audience sat spellbound for four reels, never a good sign for a comedy. When the lights came up, no one made eye contact with me. Not even Greig Pickhaver – and *he* was in the movie.

The other movie I was in, *Bad Eggs*, premiered a month after that. While obviously a very different film and with a lot more going for it, my performance, hailed as 'decidedly unfunny' by *The Sydney Morning Herald*, did not see Paul Thomas Anderson or Terrence Malick beating a path to my door.

Returning home from Christmas holidays with Leandra and our by now *three* boys (Elias Joseph was the new addition*), I was dragging our bags off the carousel when I noticed former Victorian premier Jeff Kennett doing the same thing next to me. We'd never met each other but nodded hello in the way people do when they recognise each other from the TV. 'So, are you going back to the law?' he asked.

---

* We had by then run out of favourite names and so paired the second name of our second son, Gabriel Elias, with the first name of our first son, Joseph Gabriel – a permutation which meant all three boys were nominally joined together; an idea that seemed a good one at the time.

## CHAPTER THIRTEEN

# As the wakeful bird sings darkling

I'VE NEVER BEEN much interested in money. I considered myself lucky to have found my bliss and be paid to indulge it, but I hadn't become extravagant or more keen on material possessions. The ambition to possess something to the exclusion of others, to own a rare and valuable one-off of anything, has simply never been a part of my personality. Except that one time.

When I was still in high school, I used to hang around in the State Library and read old copies of *The New Yorker*. I was a pretty cool kid. Occasionally, there'd be a piece by Woody Allen, who was another of my comedy heroes back then, and I'd photocopy it for my collection. These pieces were different from the dialogue in his movies and the stand-up on his comedy albums, and I'd read somewhere that he wrote in the style of S.J. Perelman. That name rang a bell and I worked out that S.J. Perelman was the same S.J. Perelman who used to write for the Marx Brothers[*], of whom I was also a big fan.

Seeking out older copies of *The New Yorker*, I began to read and photocopy the pieces by S.J. Perelman that had so inspired Woody Allen. When I could afford it, I would also visit the Third World second-hand bookshop in Hindley Street and pick up the occasional anthology of his work. I really liked – and still do – the way he wrote. He had a way of mixing together the high-minded and the lowbrow that undercut pretension while it was sailing over your head. I liked that he called his *New Yorker* pieces *feuilletons* ('little leaves' to you, nudniks). Frank Muir called him the 'greatest comic writer in America', and as far as I was concerned, what was good enough for the co-writer of 'Balham, Gateway to the South' featuring Peter Sellers – yet another comedy hero – was good enough for me.

As I got older and started earning a pay packet, I began collecting his work in first editions. Foraging in second-hand bookshops was usually fruitful. If you're going to collect something, make sure it's not only old but unpopular. Very few people these days have even heard of S.J. Perelman, but people must have been more discerning back in the '40s and '50s because I always managed to find plenty of hardcovers, particularly in those little out-of-the-way country shops. 'Do you have any S.J. Perelman?' I would ask as I walked through the door, more often than not drawing a blank stare. *Perfect.*

---

[*]   Specifically, *Monkey Business* (1931) and *Horse Feathers* (1932).

*These suckers don't know they're about to be done over by an expert.* I'd sneak down the back and rifle through the humour section until I found something (usually *Listen to the Mocking Bird* with drawings by Al Hirschfeld). Towards the end of the '90s, I started going online every now and then to see what was available from around the world.

One day the usual antiquarian book search engines were getting me nowhere. I decided, just for the heck of it, to use the 'highest price' search option and – lo and behold! – up popped 'a travelling case owned by Jewish-American humourist, author and screenwriter Sidney Joseph Perelman'. It had his initials embossed in gold on the front and folded out into a portable writing desk. It also had a Compagnie Générale Transatlantique sticker on it indicating that Sid was sailing on 19 May from New York to Paris. My oesophagus was twerking. Surely this must have been the very case he used to carry his typewriter and notes; the same portable writing desk he would have used to write either, or perhaps both, *Eastward Ha!* and *Swiss Family Perelman*. His daughter, Abby, was selling it in a sort of cyberspace garage sale through James Pepper Rare Books. And it was a steal at only US$3000.

US$3000!!? *A steal?* What the hell was I thinking? I couldn't possibly justify forking out that much money for a dead man's briefcase. It wasn't as if it was a rare manuscript, or even that unfinished novel he was writing with his brother-in-law Nathanael West. This was something he put that sort of stuff *inside of*. It was a *receptacle*. Would anyone who hadn't taken leave of their senses pay that sort of cash for Molière's *filing cabinet* or Charles Dickens's *ring binder*? Of course not. And yet ...

It bugged me for days. I told myself that it would be a *practical* purchase. I could actually *use* the travelling case. My laptop would probably fit into it. The fact that it was once owned by S.J. Perelman would be a bonus. Why not? It looked like being a good year. A new contract with a commercial network, a sitcom coming out, a couple of film offers firming up; why, I deserved to reward myself a little. We could make savings elsewhere. We didn't need to *fly* to Adelaide this Christmas; the drive would do us good; it'd bring us closer together as a family. *And* I could bring the travelling case with us – and perhaps write the tales of our funny adventures on the fold-out writing desk.

It arrived a month later in a box stuffed with balled-up pages from *The South Coast Beacon*. I was so excited. It looked every bit as splendid as it had in the online picture. Soft tanned leather, gently weathered about the edges, the slightly crazy-like-a-foxed antiquity of the gold 'S.J.P.' I luxuriated in the decadent pleasure of my purchase a full forty-five seconds – at which point I noticed the latch was broken.

I've only used S.J. Perelman's travelling case once, as a bag for my toiletries when I went to hospital to have my varicose veins seen to. I had to hold it together with a belt. When the Egyptian orderly was shaving my legs he noticed the case on the chair next to my bed. 'Haven't seen one of them in a long time,' he said.

'It belonged to S.J. Perelman,' I told him.

There was no reply.

As the months passed, my guilt over such a colossal waste of money faded. Then, while internet-searching for the Holy Grail of Perelman books (*Dawn Ginsbergh's Revenge*, 1929), I came across a report on the AbeBooks website saying that my purchase of Perelmorabilia had ranked in the year's top ten most expensive sales in the world, just behind a first-edition six-volume set of Edward Gibbon's *Decline and Fall of the Roman Empire*, a letter from Mohandas Gandhi and an original essay by Erasmus.

Closer inspection of the baggage sticker reveals that Sid was in cabin 275 of the SS *Paris*. Another search tells me the SS *Paris* ceased its transatlantic service during the Great Depression. Sid married Nathaneal West's sister in 1929 and they honeymooned in France. Chances are he didn't write a damn thing on that trip.

| | | | / ⁄—

Regarding money as *maya* is all well and good but try telling that to the Department of Motor Vehicles when your registration is due. Following the axing of *Micallef Tonight* the obvious thing to do in my reduced circumstances was to raise some cash by selling S.J. Perelman's briefcase. For that, though, I'd need to find a simpleton willing to pay US$3000 for it, and I knew damn well he couldn't afford it.

Our three children had also inconveniently increased in size as they'd got older and the house we were in – particularly the room they shared – was fast growing too small. The youngest had started talking and almost from the beginning was asking questions about the cot we were still forcing him to sleep in. We had to move.

It's fair to say I was feeling a little gun-shy about work. For the first few months of 2004 I had been turning down most of what I was offered: mainly one-off appearances on panel shows (which I was never terribly good at) and a regular gig to be the hanging judge on some new talent show (the prospect of which depressed me). But I really didn't have the luxury of saying no to things anymore. In the back of my mind lurks a scenario where I'm outside Arthur Daley's in Swanston Street spruiking the latest bargains into a hand-held microphone. Hey, my darkest fear still has me working.

As I was unable to create my own work for the time being, my agent let it be known that I was back on the market and I got to do some fun things as a result. I interviewed Terry Jones for the Melbourne International Comedy Festival and Michael Palin live on stage about his *Sahara* book; I toured a show with my old friend Glynn Nicholas (well, we went to Perth, Adelaide and Burnie) and I had the chance to do some intentionally non-comic acting (*Through My Eyes: The Lindy Chamberlain Story*). Also, the telemovie I'd co-written

(*BlackJack,* whistle-blower cop, Colin Friels) finally got made; plus, I managed to get a role in a proper Hollywood movie just by auditioning over the phone. If only I'd rung the MTC instead of actually turning up all those times.

*Aquamarine* was a teenage mermaid flick starring Emma Roberts (Julia Roberts's niece). They were shooting it up on the Gold Coast and most of the supporting cast were Australians pretending to be American. My accent, according to anyone I have ever spoken to who has seen the film, was especially excruciating. I played a TV weatherman by the name of Storm Banks. Also in the cast were Claudia Karvan, Bruce Spence, Roy Billing and Julia Blake, none of whom I got to work with. I did, however, get to meet and eat with George Folsey Jnr, who was producing the movie.

George had produced and/or edited films like *Animal House, The Blues Brothers, An American Werewolf in London, Trading Places, Coming to America, The Three Amigos* and *Cheaper by the Dozen* and had just finished *The Pink Panther* remake with Steve Martin. The director had told me he was on set to oversee production for a few days; I expressed admiration for his work, she kindly mentioned this to him, and he sought me out in the catering tent one afternoon.

We spent a good hour and a half talking about all the great films he'd been involved with, including the more obscure ones I'd seen like *Schlock* and *The Kentucky Fried Movie*. We also talked about his dad, George J. Folsey, who had been a cinematographer during Hollywood's heyday (he'd even worked on the very first Marx Brothers film*). Mainly, though, he shared stories with me about Steve Martin, who it won't surprise you to know is also a comedy hero of mine. According to George, the moment in *Cheaper by the Dozen* where Steve is on the phone to his wife and says 'Whaaat?' was pulled out of the edit bin to cut together two different conversations. Steve is, in fact, responding to the director who, talking to him off-screen, said something he didn't quite hear before the take.

I'm afraid I have no stories about then soon-to-be Hollywood superstar Emma Roberts except that once, when I happened to be sitting alongside her mother between shots, she came over to announce that the wart on her knee had fallen off. No doubt when this book comes out, the tabloids will beat this charming little anecdote into some lurid headline. Jackals.

Back in Melbourne, things were looking up in terms of longer-term projects. I accepted a commission to co-write with McCaffrie a mock reality TV show called *23/7* about a failing talk-show host who stupidly agrees to have cameras follow him around twenty-four hours a day, with an hour off to go to the toilet and shower (although that could be seen in its entirety on *23/7 Up Late*). The idea was not mine but I was persuaded to attach my name to it as the lead and as we wrote and rewrote, it became more and more self-referential, meta and inaccessible. After a table-read before a phalanx of stupefied Channel 10 executives, the head programmer David Mott – who appeared in the show but was played by

---

* *The Cocoanuts* (1929).

an actor – politely passed on the project, saying he thought it was a bit 'in'.

Had I learned nothing?

McCaffrie convinced me that my television career might have a chance at resurrection if we returned to our roots and did another sketch comedy for the ABC. We approached them, explained our idea, told them Tony Martin would be involved, and they were good enough to pay us to write a pilot script. Fortunately, Tony agreed when we later asked him to write on the project with us.

The show was called *Mouse Patrol* and was, as you might suspect, a hybrid of *The Micallef P(r)ogram(me)* and *The Late Show*, with linking supplied by me driving around in a VW Beetle made up to resemble a giant mouse. When the script was delivered, the ABC, as usual in something of a Josephus problem with respect to its finances, executed all the projects in their circle of development except one: Chris Lilley's *We Will Be Heroes*, which went on to do astonishingly well.

Most of the sketches in *Mouse Patrol* did not go to waste, though. Many turned up a couple of years later on SBS in *Newstopiä* and one or two seven years later on the ABC in *Mad as Hell*. Tony's Eminem parody, Slim Shady Snr, even got a run on his Triple M radio show *Get This*. One sketch that never found a home was about an alien gynaecologist who spoke like Cesar Romero, but perhaps that's just as well.

Denied an office, we had been writing our pilot script in an area filled with abandoned furniture outside the now defunct

ABC comedy department where we had worked only a few years before. As well as storage, the area was being used as a handy shortcut for those working on a new music quiz show starring Adam Hills. The executive producer had fallen into the habit of giving us a cheery wave and calling us 'comrades' as he walked through, his arms full of tapes we uncharitably assumed to be illegal copies of *Never Mind the Buzzcocks*. As we packed up our things and stole some stationery on our last day, the EP happened past, called us 'comrades' and asked us what was happening. We told him we were leaving to spend more time with our families. He said he was leaving too but that he was helping set up a new FM radio station and had put together a breakfast team which included Steve Vizard; unfortunately, though, Steve had just dropped out and they happened to be looking for someone about his height.

Apart from some work at a community station and some $20-a-pop late-night comedy spots on Adelaide's SAFM back in the '80s, I hadn't really done radio. Perhaps my future lay not in my sketch comedy past but forward in time to meet fresh challenges. As the one remaining medium I hadn't yet failed at, radio proved an irresistible lure; I quickly succumbed to its siren song.

I would become a DJ (and Elias could move out of his cot).

## CHAPTER FOURTEEN

# Radio killed the video star

THE TEST SIGNAL had been rating quite well. Classic hits selected by an algorithm would one day become the way to run all FM stations but the dreamers about to launch Vega FM had bigger ideas. 'Radio National with music,' I had been told. Smart chat about what's in the news, some light-hearted banter, serious commentary when it was needed, pop and rock that people liked, and maybe some ads for the high-end products targeted at our older and more discerning audience. After a month on air we'd lost much of the test signal's loyal fan base.

I had been partnered with Denise Scott, whom I hadn't seen since *Full Frontal* almost ten years earlier, and newsreader Beverley O'Connor. I'm not sure the schizophrenic nature of the show played to our combined strengths. Pretty soon I was firing off the call sign and jingles for Radio Vladeracken 106.3 FM in the Netherlands instead of our own and doing time calls like 'It's sixty-nine minutes past half-past seven here on The Continental Breakfast ...' Our show wasn't even called The Continental Breakfast, so none of this exactly helped listeners.

Pretty soon we were ordered to play 'the best music from the '60s, '70s and '80s' and tell personal anecdotes along with our hot takes on the news. I was no good at personal anecdotes, and when I asked why the '90s had been left off our playlist, I was told that there weren't very many good songs during that decade. Also, the 'news' now included whatever had gone on in whichever reality TV show aired the night before.

Producers and program directors came and went, each pretty keen for me to let the audience know who I was deep down. I squirmed at the prospect because, unlike Denise, who was a stand-up and could talk about her life in a funny way, I had no idea how to do it. Nor did I want to. Mining my family for nuggets of relatable kookiness was anathema to me.* I was given a hand-held digital recorder and taped myself at home sorting out my sock drawer or talking with an eccentric fisherman on the beach (I did both voices) but that's not what they wanted. They wanted something real and personal. I recorded myself going to the toilet and played it on air. They took their equipment back.

Football and sport generally became increasingly dominant topics and, as I knew nothing about either, I'd either go quiet

---

* I mean, look at this book. There's virtually nothing about my children apart from their names.

or ask annoying questions like 'How many goals in a point?' or 'Why don't they play cricket with a superball so it's over quicker?' As for the reality TV shows, I couldn't bring myself to watch them, instead talking the others into recording our own version of the 1950s radio serial *Blue Hills* so we could discuss that.

Things came to an irresistible force/immovable object event horizon when one of the least sentient organisms I have ever come across – and I'm not a man given to hyperbole – was appointed program director at the station. He'd supposedly enjoyed success over in England putting together breakfast shows and had returned to Australia to weave his magic with us. He had his notebook full of sure-fire call-outs like 'What do you and your partner do to make sure the kids don't come into the bedroom while you're having sex?' It was all I could do not to vomit.

He was forever telling us 'your talk topics need to be compelling', which didn't really mean anything. I took to perversely posing the most mundane questions to our listeners like 'How far can you stray from the bathroom while still brushing your teeth?' and then, after we'd exhausted the few calls we'd receive, back-announcing how 'compelling' it had all been. Usually in his voice. Even the others started doing it. He told us prank calls were always funny and so I set out to show him how very wrong he was by ringing up the Amtrak lost property office in New York and claiming I'd left a valuable umbrella – one used by Burgess Meredith when he was the

Penguin in the TV series *Batman* – on a train to Weehawken back in 1972. Compelling, as we had taken to calling him, didn't feel that it was compelling enough.

I then rang him up pretending to be Alice Cooper, whose US radio show was syndicated and appeared on Vega, to complain about some half-arsed breakfast show, which, Alice explained, had made some jokes about him. Compelling was very apologetic and asked what these people had said. Alice lost his temper and said some guy had pretended to be him in a prank phone call to some half-arsed executive. There was a pause on the end of the line as several pennies clattered to the floor. I was forbidden to play the call on air and called into his office to have the Theatre of the Mind explained to me.

All this might sound vaguely amusing when reduced to a few pithy paragraphs but I'm afraid I wasn't a very nice person during this time. I wasn't happy and I was acting out and making everyone's working lives more miserable than they might otherwise have been. I'm not saying they *wouldn't* have been miserable if I'd behaved – it was commercial radio after all – but I could have been a bit cheerier about the whole thing and tried a bit harder to play ball. I'd arrogantly felt that breakfast radio was beneath me, when the truth was it was beyond me.

Though the hours were enervating, I still found the time and energy to do other things. *BlackJack* turned into a series of telemovies and I wrote the last one myself, even appearing in a Warwick Munro–ish role when Shane Bourne proved unavailable. In someone's idea of ironic casting, I appeared as the managing director of GTV9, the station that had fired me three years earlier, in a telemovie adaptation of Graham Blundell's book *King*, about the life of Graham Kennedy. Kennedy is quoted by Blundell as saying that I was 'too clever'. Mind you, he also said that Andrew Denton had 'too many teeth'.

As it happened, Andrew had turned up again, as he often does when my life gets a bit dull, to recommend me for something he didn't want to do. Russell Crowe was slated to host the AFI Awards and needed a writer. Three days' work, you're in, you're out, was Andrew's Danny Ocean–like pitch. Was I interested? Three days in a room with Russell Crowe? Sure. At the very least I'd get an anecdote out of it.

**DAY ONE:** I arrive and meet Russell's PA, a well-groomed epicene young man who barely looks at me when I introduce myself. He takes me through to Russell's dressing-room. Russell is lying on the floor picking at a bowl of macrobiotic something with his fingers. 'Here's the writer,' says the PA, like he's dropping off some dirty laundry. Russell is pleasant and charming to me and this will thereafter change the way the PA treats me. From now on the PA is solicitous and friendly and always smiling.

Russell and I spoke on the phone the night before our meeting and I was taken by his high-pitched infectious giggle, something I've never noticed in any of his movies, not even *Gladiator*. He told me he wanted the evening to be political and that I shouldn't shy away from having a few digs at the federal government's arts policy. News to me; I wasn't even aware the government had an arts policy. Russell laughed: yeah, that sort of stuff.

Apolitical by nature, I'd never much thought about politicians apart from surface things like voice and manner – stuff that I could use in sketches. McCaffrie would probably have been a better choice to write the sort of material Russell was after. Nonetheless, I went off, wrote some softball jokes about whoever the arts minister was and then pretty much ignored the brief I'd been given to concentrate on my stock in trade: parodying the closest genre to the one I'm working in.

**DAY TWO:** I arrive and Russell is on the floor working his way through a deep dish of what looks to be kale. He offers me some. It'd be bad manners to refuse. He likes what I've written but feels it's a bit wordy, so we sit down together to edit it. He also likes a joke I've suggested for the opening, where he threatens to throw a phone at anyone whose speech runs too long. In acting it out, he adds a line as he gestures with the receiver to the audience, 'Say hello to my little friend,' which makes it funnier. We get on well, but then I ruin things by getting Dylan Thomas mixed up with W.B. Yeats and Russell looks at me, disappointed, and I fear he'll never trust me again.

I notice that everyone wants a piece of Russell. On our way anywhere, he's constantly stopped and talked to, often for no good reason; people want to connect with him in some small way to feel important or have him appreciate them. I'd never been in this proximity to an A-lister before; Jerry Lewis was big, but the bloom was off the rose by the time I met him. I can see how Russell cutting a conversation short and moving on might be taken as a brush-off. I also see why he spends most of his time in his dressing-room. On our way to the theatre to rehearse, though, we pass a bunch of workers who are still building things for the night and he is happy to pose for photos and talk with them. He picks his moments.

**DAY THREE:** Russell is on the couch, leafing through a swatch of fabric when I arrive. Baz Luhrmann wants him to be in a film and has sent him a mood board of the material the costumes will be made of. Textures. Tones. I ask what the script is like and Russell tells me that Baz hasn't sent him one. It seems he must make his decision based on the fabrics alone.

Russell tested our material at the untelevised AFI Craft Awards he hosted the previous night and reports it went down well. The Craft Awards are the ones the TV execs don't care about because they go to people behind the camera with no name recognition. Russell tells me with a big grin he even ad-libbed a few jokes, and then gives me a few examples. He's so pleased I don't have the heart to tell him they were ones I'd written for him. Suddenly Jack Thompson is on the phone (he's presenting) and Nick Cave walks in (he's performing) and I pop out (I'm redundant). Everyone outside gathers around me, concerned. The EP says the material is too political and I need to talk Russell out of doing it. Russell will listen to me, he says. I can't think why. Someone else in a suit who has something to do with the network agrees with him. I *must* talk to Russell – and soon.

The downside of being an A-lister is that not only does everyone want to talk to you, but nobody wants to be the one to actually tell you anything. In the end, I compromise: I tell everyone I will definitely talk to Russell about the political stuff but then never raise it with him. I leave before the broadcast that evening because I'm keeping breakfast radio hours and must go to bed before my primary school–age children. I don't even get to watch a recording of it. It goes down well, though, and is generally regarded as one of the best AFI Awards nights. Even my sworn enemy Hedda Hopper, in his column some twelve months later, recommends that I write the next one. Russell sends me a nice bottle of wine which I still have in the cupboard because I don't drink. To this day, whenever I'm getting out the SodaStream cylinders and I see it, I am reminded of my three days with Rusty.

||||⁄—

My ABC comrade had told me that in radio there is no place to hide – and he was right. Despite early attempts to write everything I was going to say in the three-hour shift, I had ended up ad-libbing, improvising and eventually lowering my guard and being myself, though dialled up a bit. I'd always thought that it wasn't enough just to be myself; that it would be unprofessional. I'm still dubious about the value of it, but I began to see that comedy wasn't the only way of being comic and that laughs were to be had by discovering things along the way.

What was important was helping to create the right environment to find those things: something I had not been ready to do with the talk show. Despite our irreconcilable differences, radio had loosened me up and I was prepared to entertain the notion of guesting on a new improvisational show that Working Dog were putting together for Channel 10. Santo Cilauro very kindly repaid the opportunity I had given him to be a part of the turkey that was *Welcher & Welcher* by talking me into appearing in what would become the über-successful ratings juggernaut that was *Thank God You're Here.*

I ditched the air-check after the show one morning and popped around to Working Dog's secure compound off Chapel Street to watch a few scenes from the pilot, which featured Angus Sampson. Santo sat with me in case I stole anything. The show reminded me of the *Theatre Sports* game 'Endowments' but with costumes and set so the players didn't have to mime and therefore be annoying. I said yes straight away.

Suddenly a flash pot went off and Rob Sitch appeared. With a devilish smile, he likened getting laughs on the show to a tennis player getting a big response from the crowd when he does something vaguely amusing with a ball in between shots. I like Rob but he does talk shit sometimes. The show was nothing like that. It was a nerve-racking obstacle course of set-ups, and either you took the easy route and played the harried victim of it all (which I did the first few times I appeared) or you challenged it and forced it to become something else (which I did later and at which Frank Woodley and Hamish Blake were masters). Don't get me wrong, there was a lot of room to move if you did what was hoped for, but it was more fun if you played around. Either way, there was a risk that sometimes you might end up going nowhere. When this happened, they'd have to look after you in the edit, as it wasn't in anyone's interest if you ended up looking like a git.

The horn would sound once the Working Dogs felt they had enough material to cut the scene. Most of the time, I wouldn't be out there too long as I knew how to keep things moving, but on a couple of occasions I'd be out there for what seemed like forever and that meant that I wasn't giving them anything useful. It was always a bad sign when one of the permanent cast invited you to dance, because this was the last desperate card they would play in the hope of getting out on a laugh or what felt like one. We'd do it a bit on radio; something moderately amusing could seem like it was a punchline if you came in hard with the next song. Mercifully, this shameful indignity only happened to me once.

If radio had relaxed me in front of a microphone, then *Thank God You're Here* encouraged me to throw all caution to the wind in front of the camera. From then on, whenever I appeared on TV, I was much more reckless – or at least tried to give that impression.* It also had the effect of putting me back on TV as a comedian and I'm sure led to an offer from SBS to make a satirical news program for them. Five past ten at night wasn't exactly prime time and perhaps Wednesday wasn't the best day to present a digest of the week's events given only half of them had happened (let alone been digested), but it was a show into which I would have significant creative input as writer, script editor and host. McCaffrie was back on board, as was frequent collaborator Michael Ward. The off-Broadway timeslot and network would give us room to try things that might otherwise worry the programmers. I was over the moon.

We'd be making the show with the same people who had made *The King*, so I kind of knew them. Having worked for them as an actor, though, wasn't quite the same thing as working *with* them, so it was an education all round when, after a few weeks of writing, we were suddenly introduced to the company's non-narrative commediaturg. His previous show had been one I hadn't much cared for, so I was leery. McCaffrie had actually written for the show and knew this fellow's comic sensibility well.

He told us he had just come down from Sydney to say hi and that he'd read the scripts and was wondering how

---

* Sometimes this approach comes off looking as though I have contempt for the program I'm appearing on. My guest spot on Paul Henry's ill-fated breakfast news show on Channel 10 in 2012 is a case in point. I was told I could have fun on the show and play around a bit – which I did. I lay on the desk, wandered around the set, 'argued' with the hosts, read their lines off the autocue, pretended to get run over by a BMW on the video wall – you know, the usual stuff. At the end of my segment no one would even look at me. The publicist assigned to me could barely speak. I thought it had gone well and we'd all had fun. Man, did I misread the room on that one.

we intended to shoot them. We told him we were thinking of using cameras. There's an expression in this business — and he was wearing it: a wan smile while nodding with closed eyes. Yes, having worked with comedy-types before he knew what we were like. We added, trying not to sound too patronising, that given it was ostensibly a news show we'd be using the visual grammar of a news show. The reports would look like reports; the interviews would be cut like interviews; I'd look down the barrel of the camera and pretend to be a newsreader. It wasn't brain surgery (we didn't say this last bit).

He wondered whether the cutting patterns for the interviews shouldn't perhaps be different from a regular studio interview given we were shooting comedy and not actual news. We didn't see why; the camera should be a straight man, we said. He wondered if we might not miss some of the comedy in the reactions if we cut it straight; would it not, he wondered, be better to 'chase the comedy', particularly my reactions to some of the odd things my guests were saying. We explained that I would not be reacting to the odd things people were saying, nor would anyone at the desk react to the odd things I might say; that generally everyone would accept that the oddness was perfectly normal. He wondered whether that would be funny. I wondered whether he actually possessed a sense of humour (again, this was unsaid).

He recommended comic reactions like puzzlement and bewilderment, saying that they would help underline the comedy. He didn't specifically mention that we should theatrically scratch our heads, but perhaps that was a given. Also, in the switching, he went on, it'd be best if the director anticipated a lot of the reactions just in case we missed them. While McCaffrie stared at the man, perhaps in the hope that this might make him suddenly disappear, I said that we wouldn't be having any unmotivated cuts because it would, in fact, *ruin* the comedy rather than enhance it; nor would we be reacting to comic situations in the way he suggested because it was no longer 1910 (I didn't say the year bit). As there was nothing more to be said out loud, there followed a long uncomfortable pause and eventually he left, which I put down to McCaffrie's stare.

*Newstopiä* was less a satire of world news and more a parody of the way news was covered in Australia. The conceit was that because Australia didn't have a vested interest in the rest of the world, it was in the best position to judge it. Its overly editorial Sky News–like commentary was all arrogant swagger and the show, at least in its early days, owed more than a little to Chris Morris's excellent *The Day Today*. It also dealt with SBS's apparent obsession with Hitler documentaries, a foreign language crime drama called *Inspector Herring* (all cod-Russian gibberish and subtitles and a fish), a special Leni Riefenstahl version of *The Cabinet of Dr Caligari* starring Stan Laurel, and segments such as *Man in Time* (just an excuse for me to dress up and use accents). The show also had, for no good reason other than I wanted to show off, reports filed by Sir Alec Guinness, Sir John Gielgud, Christopher Walken and, of course, Cesar Romero as the Joker, all played by me.

Season 3 ended with us jettisoning the news entirely and running a full half-hour of *Inspector Herring*. SBS claimed we hadn't mentioned the switcheroo, but I'm almost positive I got permission from someone. The show featured Nicholas Bell, Peter Houghton, Kat Stewart, Julie Eckersley and Ben Anderson. They were all pretty damn good.

I'm not sure an all-white cast doing so much accent work and cultural appropriation would go down well today. In the pre-Twitter/Instagram/Facebook world no one ever complained, but the fact that no one was watching the show also may have helped. I certainly wouldn't think of doing that sort of thing today. Obviously, blackface, brownface and yellowface are unconscionable but even the soft racism of doing accents is problematic. That this realisation has come to me a little later than it might have has much to do with my age and influences growing up.

Aside from Peter Sellers, I greatly admired Alec Guinness and Laurence Olivier; I wanted to emulate their protean ability to disappear and become someone completely different. To transcend your own race, gender, age, body and life experience was what it was to be an actor. At least as far as I was concerned. Impressing people with this magic trick at school was a perfectly acceptable way of showing off, and becoming professional in a visual medium with access to costumes and make-up and eventually prosthetics was, it seemed, natural, organic and inevitable. I mean, accents and voices weren't all I could do but they were an important part of it. Racial stereotypes fell by the wayside pretty early on because they felt part of a bygone era, and cross-dressing for a laugh always seemed naff, so I rarely did that. Impersonations or impressions of actual people in public life, though, I thought justifiable, regardless of nationality or race, for a very long time. The rule then became that if I needed make-up to disguise my own skin colour or prosthetics to alter my ethnic features, then that was unacceptable. It just no longer felt right. Now, even with accents, I will tend to stay within my own European/Celtic milieu. But I make sure, because it's comedy, that the laughs aren't coming just from the accent, and that I am not plugging unthinkingly into marginalising tropes or prejudices. Regional accents within your own heritage and lived experience are a finer use of your talents if you have them anyway.

If I sound a bit guilty and uncomfortable, it's only because I am. Intention counts for very little when you're making a joke; what's important is how it lands. If your joke is reinforcing something ugly, then maybe the best thing is not to do the joke anymore, rather than die on a hill defending it. If you have to explain why something is funny, then it's probably not. I think a time will come, though, when either we don't do accents at all and actors will only play within their natural physical range, or it won't matter. I hope it's the latter. Of course, it will only happen when we all stop treating the white face like it's a blank canvas. Theatre as usual will lead the way and maybe when film and television get less literal it won't be an issue anymore. Things need to get to be how they are in *Hamilton*.

When Rove and Andrew Denton were the reigning talk-show champs on Channel 10 and the ABC in the early 2000s and Seven and Nine decided they wanted their own versions, the only people they could think of to host were Shaun Micallef and Shaun Micallef. When one of them proved unavailable, Channel 7 went for Mary Coustas as Effie hosting a show called *Greeks on the Roof*. These days, someone like Mary might be the first choice – and she might not be expected to do it as a character with an accent.

While I'm on the subject of causing offence: 'punching down' is an expression you often hear when someone is criticising harsher comedy, especially when it appears to be picking on what the comedian characterises as the particular shortcomings of someone or some group. I agree with the sentiment when the person or group targeted has no power or agency, but the expression assumes that the person using it is in the best position to judge where A and B are on the ladder. It also assumes that the person they regard as on the lower rung needs someone to speak on their behalf.

I've sometimes been accused of punching down on One Nation leader Pauline Hanson. I've often presented some of the garbled and reprehensible things she says as being excellent points that are well made. I'm clearly making light of her inability to articulate whatever she's thinking but I don't believe I'm punching down on what some regard as her lack of education relative to mine. I hold all our elected representatives to a higher standard than myself and I figure that if Senator Hanson wants to further her party's vile agenda, she should at least do so clearly. I wouldn't make fun of her malaprops if she was expressing her views in a vox pop segment in a news report like a regular idiot; it's that she does so on the floor of the Senate that's the problem.

| | | | / ⁄

By the end of the first season of *Newstopiä*, I had left breakfast radio for good and hitched my wagon back onto television's towbar. I committed myself 100 per cent to the show and found myself watching SBS news every night and taking notes. Something I still do today. I began to see patterns in the news cycles both here and abroad and got to know the tropes. Not only for those presenting but the devices they used to tell their stories and the people in the stories as well, particularly the politicians. Equal parts clueless and sly, they were simultaneously repulsive and fascinating. Mostly, it was bad theatre and I had fun being able to pinpoint the exact moment in certain interviews when whichever prominent person was being interviewed realised the jig was up. I also learned a lot more about what was happening in the world and how the people and countries fitted together. Unwittingly,

I was laying the groundwork for another show I would do five years hence.

*Newstopiä* slowly mutated from parody to satire without us realising. It was something that could only have happened because we were in a bubble. Free from network interference – we never got any notes – and with but a few night owls up to watch us, we only had ourselves to please. Doing jokes to the camera in an empty studio meant that I could play straight(er) and not have to sell the jokes as much, plus I would have to trust that they were working. It also allowed me to update my presenter character from the old *Micallef P(r)ogram(me)* days to something a bit more grown-up. Between this SBS show and the radio I'd been doing, though, I did miss the warmth and satisfaction of performing in front of a live audience. But I didn't have to wait long before we'd be together again.

## CHAPTER FIFTEEN

# Sawing the air

THERE'S A PLAQUE somewhere on the pathway around the Festival Centre in Adelaide, overlooking the River Torrens. It bears my name and sits between ones dedicated to Eric Clapton and Gary Sweet. The plaques are for artists who have appeared in productions in any of the three theatres comprising the Festival Centre. In truth, most of my theatrical appearances in Adelaide did not take place anywhere near the Festival Centre precinct, although I did once fall into the River Torrens after one.

I appeared onstage in the Festival Theatre for *Theatre Sports* but only ever did one actual play there. In 1991. For a week. My charity performance of Noël Coward's *Relative Values* earned me that plaque. It's not one of his best and my performance as the insouciant Peter Ingleton did not make it any better. Nor, in fairness, did the performance of anybody in the cast. Most were far too old for the roles they were playing. The eighty-year-old ingénue was the most believable one of the lot.

Peter Ingleton is the 'Noël Coward' character, something I completely ignored, playing it instead as if he were Eric Morecambe. During one performance, the old actor playing the butler, who in his younger days had worked closely with Terence Rattigan, fumbled for my character's name and I turned to someone in the audience and asked for their program so I could show him what it was: something that Groucho Marx had done in *Animal Crackers* on Broadway, so I figured it was acceptable. Another time, someone skipped about thirty pages in the first act, thus rendering the remainder of the play meaningless. At interval I suggested backstage that I go on after the curtain rose for the second act and improvise a phone call that filled in all the missing plot. The already bewildered cast nodded their assent and I went on, this time morphing into Kenneth Williams as I ad-libbed the necessary exposition into an antique telephone to my friend 'Derek', who was on holiday in Gibraltar and had, it turned out, just bought a small ape.

Towards the end of the run, I became very adept at 'covering' while the cast forgot lines or cues. One night – and it's hard to think of what could possibly have justified it – I took it upon myself to perform an elaborate mime while describing how I had caught a fish (not in the script). The former intimate of Terence Rattigan looked at me wearily at the end of it all and said, 'Yes – very good, sir.'

||||⁄‒

So while I hadn't exactly covered myself in theatrical glory in the past, when I got a phone call in 2008 asking if I'd be in a stage revival of *Boeing Boeing*, I couldn't say no. For those who haven't seen the play, *Boeing Boeing* is a French bedroom farce about a swinging bachelor with three airline stewardess girlfriends. Jerry Lewis had starred with Tony Curtis in the film version back in 1966 and, it being a Jerry Lewis film, I had of course seen it several times and relished the chance to do the same material onstage. Unfortunately, I was offered the Tony Curtis role.

The show had been a hit on both sides of the Atlantic in the 1960s, running in the West End for seven years – and a revival in 2007 had also been wildly successful, earning star Mark Rylance a Tony Award when it transferred to Broadway. Our success was assured.

I was miscast opposite the talented Mitchell Butel, a fine comic actor. We had different styles but managed to get them to mesh and worked well and effectively with each other, although I think I may have annoyed him occasionally by adding things that occurred to me, expecting him to roll with it. Mitchell had been doing theatre a long time and was far more disciplined; this was my first play since the Home Guard version of *Relative Values* sixteen years before and I was hopelessly out of my depth.

Used to autocue by then, I found it difficult to remember my lines. During rehearsals, Judi Farr, an accomplished actor who had played, among many other things, Thelma Bullpitt in *Kingswood Country* and was now playing the maid, would teach me the importance of having my lines exactly right by refusing to respond in any way to the approximations I was coming out with as we blocked our scenes. She would just stand there and look at me until I did them properly. Also in the cast were Helen Dallimore, Sibylla Budd and Rachel Gordon. They couldn't have been nicer to work with and nursed me through the lickety-split rehearsal period of only three weeks. As preview approached, however, I still didn't quite have my lines down and began to scope out a few places on the set where I could write them down in case I ran into trouble. The rolltop desk I sometimes had to sit at was ideal.

The negotiations for my fee had been dragging on and had not been sorted out by the time rehearsals started. Apparently, it's quite normal in theatrical contracts to have a clause excusing the producers from any ongoing financial responsibility to pay the actors if the play folds. I didn't know this. I was holding out for a pay-or-play clause; in other words, if any leg of the anticipated Melbourne-Sydney-Brisbane-Perth tour didn't go ahead for some reason, I would still be paid. It seemed only fair that if I was clearing my calendar for them, they should guarantee I wouldn't be left out of pocket. It was pretty standard for a season of TV.

So reluctant were the producers to even consider my argument that I grew suspicious. I rang the theatres we were supposed to be playing in the other cities, under the pretence of booking tickets, only to find that, apart from Sydney, tickets weren't available and that while the other theatres were on hold for the production, the seasons had not been confirmed. I dug in my heels and with opening night only a week away, the producers agreed to guarantee my fee whether the play went on or not.

The previews went well and though the play was undeniably hokey, the audience seemed to enjoy themselves enormously. I remembered most of my lines, was able to cover where I didn't and even found some extra bits of comic business on the way.

Opening night loomed. Like most opening nights, it was a papered house, meaning that the tickets are handed out to movers and shakers who will hopefully spread the word. I'd been warned that it wouldn't be like the previews; laughs and approval would be harder won because people in the industry are notoriously more difficult to win over than people who actually pay for their tickets and want to be there. I knew it would be a tough night; my parents were flying over from Adelaide to see it. This was the first time they would ever see me onstage. I'd always discouraged them from coming along to the university revues because I thought the language might be a little bit risqué for them; the expression 'shut up' was considered swearing at our house. The idea of me three-timing some over-sexed airline hostesses, though, was apparently perfectly okay.

It's understood that theatre critics don't review previews; that if they are going to disembowel you for a lousy performance, they'll at least have the decency to wait until opening night. Unbeknown to me, a writer for the Green Guide, the television section of *The Age*, had seen a preview and already written a scathing review of the play and my performance in it. My great crime, it seemed, was how different the play was to the now suddenly excellent-by-comparison *Newstopiä*. The Chaser, on the other hand, had done a live-on-stage show that was just like their TV show and better for the fans.

To have read that on the day we were opening would have probably taken the wind out of my sails before they were even up. The cast, the director, the producers and the crew kept it from me for a week, an act of kindness I will never forget. I eventually stumbled across it myself while looking for something positive about the show to compensate for the official scathing reviews which appeared the next week. I should say, the rest of the cast received deservedly favourable reviews for their efforts, but I couldn't help feeling I was letting the side down when I was getting paragraphs like this:

> *Shockingly miscast as Bernard,* [Micallef] *has about as much sex appeal as a jack-in-the-box doing a half-hearted Jim Carrey impersonation. You get the sense he knows he's not cut out for the role, too – his awkwardness is palpable, and excruciating to watch.*

It won't surprise you to learn that the producers did not put that one up on the theatre marquee.

I was disappointed for my fellow cast-mates and even the producers. I was also feeling more than a little uncomfortable. My insistence on a pay-or-play clause was looking like a masterstroke worthy of Bialystock and Bloom.[*] With notices like the ones I was getting, it was only a matter of time before the advance publicity killed ticket sales and the backers pulled the plug. Would everybody think my atrocious performance a deliberate ploy to get my payout? Would I end up in prison singing 'Prisoners of Love'?[**] No one would ever know as I would never be stupid enough to tell anyone.

||||/—

The play closed and I slunk back to late night on SBS with a third and what turned out to be final season of *Newstopiä*. We were all set to do a fourth, this time with a live studio audience, but there was a clash with the start date of a new show I was doing for Channel 10. Someone at SBS got their nose out of joint that I was seeing another network on the side and, rather than move the start date of *Newstopiä* back by a couple of weeks to avoid any problem, they decided to make the show without me and advised the production company I was not to be involved with it in any way. I assume this new version of *Newstopiä* is still in development and I'm very much looking forward to seeing it.

---

\* Mel Brooks' *The Producers*.
\*\* See above.

The new show that had caused all the trouble was called *Talkin' 'Bout Your Generation*. Hilary Innes, whose career I had ruined at Channel 9, had now moved to ITV and had helped develop a new celebrity panel show for Channel 10. It was a half-hour beat-the-buzzer type of thing like *Spicks and Specks* but with three teams representing the three demographics that watched TV advertising and bought things: baby boomers, gen X and the just-old-enough-to-appear-on-television generation Y. Hilary had approached me to host it; it looked like fun, I trusted Hilary and owed her big-time anyway. I said yes.

At that point (late 2008) I was doing the graveyard shift on the least-watched television network in Australia, had driven the ratings backward on a radio station and been responsible for the least-enjoyable night at the theatre since Lincoln was shot. It was a do-or-die chance to redeem myself. The show had been commissioned anyway so news of my involvement couldn't throw too much of a spanner in the works.

We went ahead with auditions for the team captains and eventually Amanda Keller, Charlie Pickering and Josh Thomas (all my favourites) were signed up. We did a few test shows and it became apparent that the real fun was in the ad hoc repartee, which was unfortunately getting lost when we cut the show down to its commercial half-hour (about twenty-three minutes). Management then decreed the show would run an hour and I helped pad it out with a few more segments and games that were a bit jokier than the rest of the show, though not in a way that would overwhelm it. Not yet anyway.

So successful had been the no-frills chair-and-table test shows that we were already in the programming schedule without the need for a pilot. A lot was riding on the show. Not only were we replacing the recently decamped *Thank God You're Here*, now over at Channel 7, but unfortunately, with my new Ten contract, I couldn't appear in that show anymore. With *Newstopiä* scuttled, all my eggs were now riding in the basket on the handlebars of this brand-new bike.

Because this wasn't a comedy show, no actual comedy writing was required. All I had to do was welcome everyone, explain the rules, start the games and throw to the breaks. Any fool could do it (and usually does). I had asked that Michael Ward be brought in to put the functional business of the show in my voice and he brought with him his frequent collaborator Stephen Hall to help. McCaffrie also contributed gags.

The night of our first record and I'm fretting in the dressing-room with Stephen as I go over what I have to do to keep the show moving and the games we'll be playing and who the guests are. In the test shows none of this mattered as I just improvised around some bullet points; now it's more serious, it's no fun anymore. I hate myself. This is my last chance and I'm not up to it and the whole thing is going to stink and I'm going to be humiliated. Again.

I'm pacing up and down, railing at everything, and catch sight of the open-mouthed expression on Stephen's face. I don't know Stephen that well at this stage and I see how I must look. 'Don't worry,' I reassure him. 'I'm always like this before

an opening night.' To try and still my nerves on *Boeing Boeing*
I used to re-read the entire script before every performance.
The problem with this show, though, is that there is no
script – not a real script anyway; just a running order with
some jokes weaved into the segues. Jesus Christ, I'm having
a heart attack. The door cracks open and I'm wanted on the
set. I check myself in the mirror and hate the way I look. I'm
ready. I give Stephen an eye roll and slump out, wishing it
would all go away.

For the first couple of segments, my eyebrows are crooked, a
sure sign that I am anxious. By the third ad break I've relaxed
and am improvising. For the rest of the season and the three
more after that it's a doddle and one of the most enjoyable
experiences of my professional life. The first show rates
1.7 million – again, a lot of people back then – and everyone
is happy. The show goes from strength to strength as I learn
how to present it on the job. Turns out I'm quite good at it.
Amanda, Charlie and Josh do the heavy lifting with the guests,
and working with them is like being in a family trapeze act,
where everyone trusts each other to catch them when they're
doing the double somersault. We get to know and like each
other over the episodes and the audience can see that. It's a
rare, precious one-off time that will never happen again.*

I make a decision very early on to not play the teacher
in some unruly classroom. Instead, I play it like one of the

---

\* Except when we did do it again on Channel 9 a few years later with Robyn Butler,
Andy Lee and Laurence Boxhall, with voice-overs by Pete Smith (my favourite).

students who's been put in charge while the teacher is out. I also watch a lot of Groucho Marx hosting *You Bet Your Life*. I even do his lope when I come on. The audience is young, so they don't notice I'm stealing. In fact, the studio audience is so young that my usual shtick doesn't quite connect with them and I have to make it more conversational. Fragments. Bits. Asking myself questions; providing my own answers. It serves me well and later becomes a standard device on *Mad as Hell*.

The show is busy, busy, busy and there's a welter of information and stuff for me to process: some I pretend comes in from off camera, other stuff is in front of me, some on autocue; then the phone rings, then a meerkat pops out of the desk with an envelope; there are horns, voice-overs, clips to roll, slides to show, organs to play, cymbals to hit, recorders to blow into, a bit of call and response with the audience, and of course there's Amanda, Charlie and Josh and their guests. It's mad, fast and stupid and it gives me a second lease on my TV life.

The show wins Logie awards in both the outstanding and popular categories. Incredibly I pick up one for me personally – a *popular* one – something that defies all logic and reason. I can do no wrong; I collect my award from Bert Newton and deliver Laurence Olivier's 1979 Honorary Oscar acceptance speech to hails of hearty laughter and rapturous applause. People love me. I am fêted by the great and near-great and also by Matt Preston. It's like a dream. I end the evening in a giddy whirl of flashbulbs and a press room of the nation's finest scribes wanting to know 'How does it feel to win a Logie?' and 'What's Josh Thomas *really* like?' I had always thought the Logies meaningless and rigged, the ceremony a night of stultifying tedium (even when *I* hosted it), and everybody who thought it important either vacuous or suffering from brain damage. I *still* think that, but I keep it to myself.

I was especially proud of the untelevised AFI Craft award I received a few months later. A technical award for Outstanding Achievement in Television Screen Craft, something they usually give out for production design and cinematography and musical composition – behind-the-scenes stuff. I got it for doing Groucho.

I wasn't the only one to reap rewards from the show's popularity. Amanda was doing fine as a radio host but she was able to parlay the success of *Your Generation* into another TV show and several more after that. Charlie quickly picked up a second job as host of a nightly news panel show and then onto the ABC after that to try and replace me. Josh was the breakout star and went on to have a spectacular stand-up career and two successful internationally funded sitcoms. We owe that show a lot.

Of course, I had to go and meddle with it. All I had to do was what I was told and not get in the way, but no, I wanted a little more creative control …

The first-season dynamic had been me trying to cope with the expectations of the show. It was funny to have me awkwardly throw to breaks or not know what the scores were or yell at the guests because I didn't know what was happening. I didn't think I could do this again in the second season; I thought the games themselves might need to look as though they were my ideas, and slowly they came to be more bizarre – giant Rube Goldberg machines to turn people into hot dogs; someone dressed as Gene Simmons from Kiss riding out on a minibike to hand me a card that said we were all going to play a game called Giant Jenga; Anagrams of Calista Flockhart. We made Todd Woodbridge wear a sombrero made of bird seed and put him in an aviary; we tied up Leo Sayer, poured gravy on him and released a puppy every time Amanda got a question wrong. If she got the questions right (which she didn't), I would give Leo a sausage through the mesh wiring. My favourite moment ever on television was during a family edition of the show, when the captains were partnered with their spouses, siblings, children, parents or other relatives and we got to douse Josh's grandmother in sour cream.

By the third season, the show had become twice as funny but half as popular and I thought it might be time to pull the pin. I had a new idea – in fact, I had a couple of new ideas – and I wanted to capitalise on my newfound bankability before my fortunes were wiped out again.

## CHAPTER SIXTEEN

# The thinking person's idiot

I'M GOING TO name-drop a bit here so brace yourself.

So there I was in Sydney doing a show at the Opera House with Stephen Curry that Barry Humphries came to when I popped into the ABC studios to plug my new novel, *Preincarnate*[*], on Phillip Adams's radio program, and while I was waiting who should I bump into but John Howard. I gave John an inscribed copy of *Preincarnate* and, wouldn't you know it, he left it in a hire car, only for it to be found later by Jennifer Byrne, who's married to Andrew Denton, and she told me about it on *The Project* with Waleed Aly, Carrie Bickmore and Peter Helliar.

Done.

Anyway, Phillip and I had a good chat and I even

---

[*] About a murdered man whose spirit reawakens in the body of someone who lived 400 years earlier and so puts his new body in suspended animation so it can be woken up in the present day and he can take steps to prevent his original self being killed. It did not win the Miles Franklin.

remembered to plug the book (*Preincarnate*) at one point. Among the many things we discussed on and off air (I can't remember which; Phillip doesn't have a performance mode, so it all blends together) was the idea that I should do a satirical news show for Auntie. This was Phillip's idea, not mine (I would never refer to the ABC as Auntie). I figured I was tapped out after *Newstopiä*. He said he'd speak to someone. I assumed he meant someone in charge like managing director Mark Scott, but he may have meant the guy at the security desk, as I had been hanging around the studio for a while after the interview and perhaps I wasn't picking up that he wanted me to leave.

Sometime later I rang Mark Scott and asked him who I should talk to about putting on a satirical news show. I don't know for sure whether Phillip ever spoke to Mark or indeed anybody at the ABC but I suspect he must have because things moved pretty quickly and, before I knew it, McCaffrie and I had a development deal to write a pilot script for a show called *Wazzup*. That's right – *Mad as Hell* was originally going to be called *Wazzup*, that is until somebody's senses came back from leave and made us change it. I'll be calling the show *Mad as Hell* throughout this book because the actual title of the program, *Shaun Micallef's Mad as Hell*, goes on a bit too long and makes me sound vain, the last things I'd want to do in an 80,000-word book about myself.

I'd been down this road before with *Mouse Patrol*, so I knew being paid to write a pilot didn't mean the show was a done deal, although part of me thought we'd sail through the commissioning process because Phillip Adams had already spoken to people at the top, much in the same way that Don Corleone arranged for Johnny Fontane to get that film role he wanted. My meeting with the ABC head of programming after the script was submitted went well and while there was no mention of any horse head, Phillip's message had obviously got through and the series was commissioned with no need to even shoot the pilot we'd written.

Given they seemed to know what they were doing and were used to me, I invited the same production team responsible for *Talkin' 'Bout Your Generation* to help put together this new show. McCaffrie and Michael Ward and now Stephen Hall signed on as writers, as did Roz Hammond and Francis Greenslade as part of the cast. We began to hold auditions for the rest of the cast between tapings of *Generation*.

We were after some fresh talent and, though we had twenty or so young people come in and read, only Tosh Greenslade was asked to join the cast. It was astonishing how many of the twenty-to-thirty-year-olds we saw had no idea how to perform sketch comedy. Most tried to be funny by putting on voices and overdoing things. Frankly that's my department and I can do without the competition. Others either didn't quite know where the joke was or knew where it was and sold it too hard. Tosh alone got it; he instinctively knew to play it for real, but not so real that the acting got in the way of the pace needed for the jokes to work. It's called sketch comedy for a reason and you only need a few strokes to create a character, not a full palette of colours.

Sketch characters are, to my mind, always funnier when they internalise their frustration, irritation, cluelessness or sense of failure; glimmers of what they are thinking or feeling are always much better than seeing them nakedly displayed. If that happens, the comedy gets shrill and arch and I have to turn away it's so awful. It's no different from regular acting in that regard and I never understand it – and am always slightly concerned – when a guest actor says to me, 'Oh, great. Comedy. I get to exercise a completely different set of muscles.' No. They're exactly the same set of muscles. If anything, you just have to use them less.

We hadn't had this trouble casting *Newstopiä* five years earlier. There were a few duds here and there, sure, but we were embarrassed with riches during that audition process. We picked the best combination from an A-grade crop. Maybe it was a generational thing, but this time around there just didn't seem to be anyone we saw apart from Tosh who had any idea how to do what we were after.

In ruminating on this afterwards with Roz and Francis, I was reminded of a very funny actor we had passed on for *Newstopiä* only because she was then already on air in another sketch comedy show. Her name was – and is – Emily Taheny and fortunately she was available. Completing the cast was Veronica Milsom, who had been recommended to me by Andrew Denton after he'd worked with her on *Hungry Beast*.

I'd also seen her on Ben Elton's *Live from Planet Earth* and agreed with Andrew she was excellent.

While all this was going on, I had thrown another show up the totem pole to see if the cat would salute. It's usual to have more than one project in development and even pitch several at a time because so few actually get up.

D-Gen alumnus Jason Stephens had produced *The King* and *Newstopiä* and we had come up with the idea of a crime-solving couple who happened to run a forensic cleaning business. We pitched the idea to Channel 10 and they said yes as soon as we walked into the office on the basis of a two-page precis we'd sent them before the meeting. I spent the rest of the hour desperately trying to avoid saying anything that would cause them to change their mind. That show was eventually titled *Mr & Mrs Murder*.

Things were going well. I had two shows to make that year and didn't have to shoot a pilot for either. Both went into the programming schedules in prime-time spots. Unfortunately, they overlapped with each other at the edges and neither network would move for the other.

Like the dog with two bones in the poem from ancient Rome made famous by Devo, I couldn't choose between the two. Rather than go from one to the other and eventually drop dead as the dog did in the song, I hatched an ingenious plan that I might have both and then some. It was a stratagem so daring that even Machiavelli himself would think it a bit much. I would offer Channel 10 a *fourth* season of *Generation* (ten episodes) in return for a later start date for production of *Mrs & Mrs Murder* (ten episodes) and in between I would do *Mad as Hell* (ten episodes). There might be some slight overlap with pre-production now and then but providing I divided my attention between the shows and ensured I didn't give each the full attention it deserved, I would be able to have not only both bones but a third to choke on as well.*

*Generation* came and went without a hitch. So far so good. The production team had some teething problems transitioning into pre-production for *Mad as Hell* but that was fair enough because they'd never made a sketch comedy in weekly turnaround before. Fortunately I was on hand to lend everybody the benefit of my experience; that is, when I wasn't on the other side of town at the *Mrs & Mrs Murder* office helping out with storylines. And when I say helping out, I mean sitting there and worrying that the writers were pitching funny murder scenarios when what I thought we needed were *straight* murder scenarios that the couple, now named Charlie and Nicola**, would make funny (like in *Manhattan Murder Mystery*, I kept suggesting). In the end, it was decided to limit my input to a dialogue pass for Charlie and the scripts were sensibly put under the aegis of a proper script producer.

---

* There was also a fourth bone, *The Cup*, a movie about Damien Oliver, starring Stephen Curry, Brendan Gleeson and Daniel MacPherson and directed by Simon Wincer. I played trainer Lee Freedman and when they asked me to dye my hair, I rang Lee and asked whether he would dye his hair to match mine instead. He declined.

** After Nick and Nora Charles of *The Thin Man* series based on Dashiell Hammett's novel. A reference I suspect anyone under the age of eighty may have missed.

Meanwhile, back at *Mad as Hell*, we were having trouble booking guests. I was a big fan of *The Colbert Report* and liked the idea of the last third of the show being an interview. Cat Stevens, whom I'd met and got along with when I was a guest on Adam Hills's ABC talk show, was in for a moment but then out, but we did have Masha Gessen, author of several books on Vladimir Putin. Rachel Perkins was also available in a few weeks to plug *Mabo*, which she'd just directed. Great, lock them both in. Ultimately, we would abandon the idea of interviews as they, while not approaching *Micallef Tonight* level of atrociousness, didn't fit tonally with the fake ones, which would become our bread and butter.

Casting was almost done on *Murder*. Kat Stewart, Lucy Honigman and Jonny Pasvolsky comprised the regular cast and some old friends like Stephen Curry, Roz Hammond and Bob Franklin were slated to appear as guest stars. Also, actors of the calibre of Steve Bastoni, Peter Phelps, Damon Gameau, Julia Blake and even Robert Taylor from the A&E series *Longmire* were being signed. The first couple of scripts were ready and we had a table-read for the network. It went much better than *23/7*.

I was particularly looking forward to working with Damon Gameau, who was McCaffrie's nephew and whose first job after graduating from NIDA had been to lie crushed under a cupboard on an episode of *The Micallef P(r)ogram(me)* (we also shot his bottom sticking out of the window of a stretch limo but this scene was sadly cut). The last time I'd worked with him was a few years earlier on a short film for which I couldn't remember my lines and so had the script sticky-taped to his tie so I could read it. I was hoping to show him how much more professional I had become since. He would later go on, with no help at all from me, to enjoy enormous success with *That Sugar Film* (2014) and *2040* (2019).

| | | / ⟋

*Mad as Hell* was made in weekly turnaround, by which I mean we'd start with a blank sheet of paper and have to make the whole thing in five working days. When we started, we were going to air on Friday nights but recording the show on a Wednesday, which didn't help the topicality. From the second season we were moved to Wednesday nights with a record night on Tuesday, which meant I would script-edit on the Sunday. With me eventually writing on Saturdays as well – usually in the stands when my sons were playing soccer, although I did look up when goals were scored – I was working seven days a week. Not that I'm complaining; I loved the show and it's proved to be the apotheosis of my working life.

*Murder*, though, almost killed me. As soon as we finished the first season of *Mad as Hell* – and I literally mean the next day – we were shooting. As I hadn't quite given myself enough time to get my head around who my character was, I just played Warwick Munro again, who gradually morphed into a thinly disguised version of me. This made my dialogue passes easier, as I didn't have to address my mind too seriously to things like backstory. My character would just say things that I would say. Problem solved.

The first shooting week went well but I was run-down after shooting *Generation* and *Mad as Hell* without a break and ended up with the flu. *Mad as Hell* had been a slog as it was a new show and we were still working out both what it was and what it wasn't. Of course, I know there are more tiring and, let's face it, important jobs in the world. Those Sherpas who carry all that luggage and equipment and the occasional unconscious climber up and down the Himalayas have more right to whine about their lot than me; but we only know what we know, and for a giant baby like me, getting up at five in the morning to go and pretend to be somebody else when not lounging about in my trailer was hard work. Plus, there were the rewrites.

No one, of course, had asked me to do rewrites but I did them anyway. I had unilaterally decided to expand my dialogue pass to other characters as well and even the BIG PRINT in the script, by which I mean the ACTION. The writers, as they were perfectly entitled to do, would write bits of business for Charlie and when I felt it could be improved, I would tinker with it or sometimes substitute something else entirely. The days were longer than I was used to, and I'd often be studying my script for the next day and rewriting dialogue and action for the next episode well into the night. The less sleep I had the more likely I'd be dissatisfied with what was in the next script and the more I would tinker and rewrite and sometimes even redraft. The more tinkering, rewriting and redrafting, the less time I had to sleep and so on and so on.

Eventually I turned into an ogre, unhappy with much in the scripts and now even having a go at altering the carefully plotted narratives that several departments were relying on not to change at the last minute. When I ran out of time to rewrite, I would word up the cast before a scene or improvise during a take. Kat Stewart, used to working with me in *Newstopiä*, rolled with it, but others who didn't know me as well were surprised when a scene finished up at the end of a take quite differently to how we'd rehearsed it only minutes before. It was, I see now, quite unprofessional and just made a tough job more difficult.

Meanwhile, the script producer, who was under the impression that she had been hired to produce the scripts, had to cope with having her work pulled apart and reassembled with no right of appeal. Sometimes, if there was time, she would reinstate things I'd removed so the heads of departments wouldn't have to draw a line through what they'd already spent weeks preparing. Turning up on set at the crack of dawn, bleary-eyed, to see my rewriting unwritten didn't improve my mood and the cast then had to deal with me fuming and, worse, fomenting against those back at the office. Jason did his best to placate me but usually I just did what I wanted.

As the weeks turned into months, I started bypassing the office completely with my rewrites, on one occasion, the night before a shooting day, sending the director an email entitled 'Secret Script', in which I rejigged several scenes, changed interiors to exteriors and even involved some new props which I made myself and brought in from home. Madness.

Another time, when an already filmed episode was running under, I decided I should direct some extra scenes to pad it out and fill in some much-needed exposition. During a hole in the schedule of the episode we were supposed to be shooting, I hopped in a production vehicle with Kat and Lucy and was driven to the unit base house, writing the extra material as we travelled. I shot them in the bathroom and the bedroom so I could use the mirrors in each and not have to shoot any singles or reverses. It wasn't quite as impressive as the ending of Orson Welles's *Lady from Shanghai*, but then I was no Orson Welles. He'd have been much easier to manage.

Obviously, none of this was going unnoticed. I thought we were doing good work, but I really wasn't in a fit state to judge a hot dog–eating contest let alone whatever the hell it was I thought I was doing. Whether it was good or whether it wasn't, what was being screened at the dailies increasingly bore little resemblance to the show the rest of the production team thought we were making.

Jason managed to keep the train on the tracks. Looming beyond the next tunnel, though, was something even he couldn't fix. We had slowly caught up with ourselves in terms of the scripts. Usually, we'd be filming one and midway through our ten-day shoot would have a table-read for the next. But for the last few episodes, the scripts were coming in later and later. This may have had something to do with me slowing down the process. Whatever the reason, it gave me less time to tamper with the material, which just made me more of a mess than I had been. I leaned on the cast more and more for support, which they generously gave.

The penultimate episode created a fresh challenge. We didn't have a script. Not one that was approved anyway. I don't know what happened, but that one definitely couldn't be sheeted home to me. Or maybe it could. We knew it would be about horses. Beyond that it was anyone's guess. The director was out scouting locations for scenes he imagined might be in the script, assuming one was ever written. Maybe there *was* a script and they were keeping it from me so I wouldn't try and rewrite it. Somehow it was shot. I'm a little hazy on the details.

Spent and ashamed of myself, I gave the wrap party a miss and went home.

|||/−

Home was somewhere I hadn't been in a while. Not really. I'd been there but I hadn't been present. Not as a husband and a father. I had some work to do on myself to make sure I fitted back in.

*Murder* did well enough for Channel 10 to ask for another season the next year, but I couldn't do it again and Jason was kind enough to let me off the contractual hook. *Mad as Hell* I could just handle, although I recall very little of it that next season. McCaffrie took over the lion's share of the scripting and retooled the show into the sleeker and more successful form that it still has today. Meanwhile, I lumbered along in a fugue; hardly writing anything; easily given to tears. I couldn't work it out. I'm not what you'd call an emotional person yet there was this cloud over me that I couldn't shift. Yes, I'd over-extended myself before, but this was different. And while I'd felt depressed now and then, as we all do, usually I could sense it coming on and just stand in a doorway until it passed. Winston Churchill used to talk about taking the black dog for a walk – all I'd ever done up until then was occasionally let a grey poodle off its leash for a bit of a run. This wasn't like that – and whatever was going on, it didn't seem to want to go away anytime soon.

I thought maybe I was going mad. And not in a fun way like my Nanna had when she sticky-taped pictures of the Toyota 'What a Feeling' chicken over all the family portraits on her mantlepiece or started drawing her eyebrows on with a blue biro or wearing dead moths in her hair. No, this was just miserable and depressing and there was no good reason to justify it. At least when we asked my grandmother why she was sticking pictures of a cartoon chicken around the room, her answer was, 'Because I like him.' A perfectly reasonable explanation.

Of course, me being miserable and depressed about something I couldn't quite put my finger on was the least of my problems. Marriage is a partnership and it would have been foolish of me to think that there weren't going to be serious consequences if one of us just decided to down tools for twelve months.

Leandra and I had always intended that the dynamics of our marriage be less about balance and more about harmony; in other words, we didn't sit down and carve up the running of our household along fifty-fifty lines, but instead tried to divide what needed to be done between us based on who was available. The thing was, I was *never* available. Even when I was home, I wasn't really there. I never turned down work. Even when I had too much, I would always say yes to more. Over time, Leandra had come to take on all my responsibilities outside of my work, as well as her own – plus the children, plus the business she ran – something she reminded me of now that I was back home and we had the time to talk. Doing everything was something she was prepared to do because we had a relationship, she said. If we didn't have a relationship, though, I could get off my arse and meet my own responsibilities myself.

We both worked at it. Occasionally I'd flit to an out-of-body perspective and see what I was going through for the sad-clown Pagliacci bullshit it was. Had I forgotten that I wasn't the centre of my own universe? This would irk me into feeling less sorry for myself and I'd get on with the day. Being miserable was bad enough without being a cliché as well. But it was Leandra who got me through it.

Hard truths, more talks and decent stretches of time together made things better. Even better than before. Life slowly filled back up with more important stuff. Yes, I did some soul-searching, but I looked out of myself as well. At the world. Nature. The night sky. Never especially spiritual, I wondered seriously for the first time about God and whether there was a purpose to my life or indeed Life in general.

Feeling insignificant is a helpful first step on the road to self-discovery. The world doesn't really need you to make sense of it. It'll keep turning regardless. What's important is that we make sense of our own life and give it some meaning, because it doesn't have one otherwise. At least that's how I saw it. But that's a hard reality to live in without a break, and there are some low times in your life when you find yourself hoping and praying that something bigger is looking after things because you know damn well you're not up to doing it. For the first time I found myself really wanting to believe that was true, even though I knew it couldn't possibly be. I envied people who had that certainty and I wanted to meet them.

## CHAPTER SEVENTEEN

# Learning to sit still

*STAIRWAY TO HEAVEN*, or *Shaun Micallef's Stairway to Heaven* as it had to be called because Led Zeppelin would sue us, was an SBS program that took me to India, by far the most popular place in the world for westerners to go and look for themselves, though this often proves difficult as there are a billion or so other people there already and it's easy to get lost in the crowd.

I started off in Puri, to the country's east, where I'd come to get some advice on the Self from the King of Puri, assuming I could hear him over the din. The Jagannatha festival was on and that meant that the already overcrowded streets were now teeming with almost a million extra people visiting from all over the country. Everyone was celebrating and dancing and the police did their best to keep order by yelling at people and half-heartedly hitting them with long sticks. Giant chariots, several stories high, trundled up and back through the city amid fireworks and horn blasts.

Of course, the King of Puri wasn't really a king as this hadn't been allowed since 1803 when the British moved in, but as the lineal descendant of the original maharaja he was in charge, as his forefathers had been, of the city's main temple and he lived across the road from it in a palace. While it was a palace in name only as well, compared to the rest of the homes in Puri it was quite grand, with many rooms and a walled-off courtyard. Next door was a restaurant which the king also ran, though he'd not been there the day I visited because he was busy hosing down some to-do with the priests. Apparently, the police had banned devotees from climbing the floats as too many were falling off and in response the priests had boycotted a planning meeting for a ceremony the next day in which the king would symbolically forgo his role as the representative of the Supreme Lord of the Universe on earth and become a lowly street-sweeper, following the chariots with a gold-handled broom. He told me all this when we met and I asked how lowly he could be when his broom handle was made of gold. 'It's only symbolic,' he reminded me.

According to my journal, the rest of our conversation went something like this:

HIS MAJESTY: Looking at the Self is about stripping away the *maya* to reveal the Soul.
ME: How do we do that?

244

HIS MAJESTY: To remove the *maya* you must remove the Ego.

ME: But I'm an actor. I need my Ego.

HIS MAJESTY: The Self less the Ego equals the Soul.

ME: Yes, but—

HIS MAJESTY: Action and thought with no Ego bypass our instinct for survival which, left unchecked, becomes Selfishness.

ME: [writing furiously] Hang on, let me get this down ...

HIS MAJESTY: Action and thought with no Ego are actions and thoughts for the General Good. Good takes root in others and will continue on.

ME: Uh-huh ...

HIS MAJESTY: Goodness is not giving people material things as this is just perpetuating *maya*.

ME: But wouldn't that rule out Charity?

HIS MAJESTY: Not all Charity.

ME: Most Charity, surely?

HIS MAJESTY: After we die, the change for Good we've left behind will be passed on to others ad infinitum. That is where the Soul goes.

ME: [pleased with myself] So, in other words, there is no point to Life because it is a circle.

HIS MAJESTY: [politely] Not quite—

He also recommended I find a guru to help guide me on my journey. He said everyone had a guru and mine was waiting for me somewhere in India. I asked if *he* was my guru as it would save me a lot of time looking and he chuckled warmly, saying no, it wasn't him and that I would have to go now as he had to have a meeting with some priests. I said I thought that meeting had been cancelled. He stood, pressed his palms together and I followed suit. 'Namaste,' he said. I mispronounced it back to him and took my leave.

I had always been envious of those who were certain about their faith and longed for if not a bolt of lightning then at least some milder epiphany. My early flirtation with the theatre of Catholicism had all but disappeared in my later school years, after a visiting Marist brother, fresh from building chapels in a leper colony, turned up in our classroom for religious ed., punched himself in the stomach and handed out small plastic bags containing, he claimed, fragments of the robe worn by the Blessed Marcellin Champagnat. The guy was clearly a loon and I couldn't help but be struck in that moment by what nonsense it all was. The following Sunday, I announced over breakfast that I would no longer be attending church. For the first time in his life, crossness furrowed my father's brow and he looked up slowly from his Rice Bubbles to fix me with a steely gaze.

'You *will* be attending church,' he said, in a manner reminiscent of Yul Brynner in *The King and I*.

'Oh, don't be ridiculous. We can't make him go,' countermanded my mother almost immediately.

And that was the end of that.

I'd thought about it since – as we all do from time to time, I suppose – and while I considered a life after this one where rights would be wronged unlikely, given there was no evidence at all of the natural world being especially fair, I felt there *should* be one in order for things to make sense. As I had thus far received no such revelation from above, perhaps self-realisation was the next best thing.

A sadhu took me under his wing in Haridwar and told me that Brahma, the Source of all things, had created us for his pleasure and that the meaning of Life was to experience the Source and become one with Brahma. The sadhus have renounced all material things and own nothing; they have even abandoned their families. Sadhus are done with *maya* and the material world and will not be reborn. I asked why, if Brahma put us on earth to be enjoyed, did He want us to ultimately escape it? I was told that because we are not Brahma we cannot understand His plan and must simply perform our role in it. Faith again.

Brahma does endorse reincarnation, though, for all except sadhus – the idea of samsara is that we are all reborn after death, in an endless cycle. Depending on how nice we've been, we might be reincarnated into something better than we were previously. I liked the idea of reincarnation because it meant we had a few takes to get things right. When I suggested to the sadhu that if we were to perform our role properly, we needed to at least know our lines, he took me to a beautiful waterfall and encouraged me to stand under it. I got wet but not much else.

If the purpose of Life is for the Source to experience Itself, I asked, how did we get to the Source? I was told I must search. Then a man came out of the small shop across the road, unfastened the litter bin from its pole, walked over to us and dumped the contents in the river.

| | | /—

In search of the Source (of the Ganges, at least) we travelled north to Gangotri in sheeting rain along treacherous roads. When we found stretches of the road washed away, we would stop and wait while illegal workers from across the Tibetan border – mainly women – rebuilt it by hand with stones. As we sat in the car together doing nothing, my sadhu guru traced his finger along the path of a rivulet running down the outside of the window and said that a droplet of water has all the properties of the ocean. Now we were getting somewhere.

Gangotri is the home of Gomukh, the glacier that feeds the Ganges. I was urged by the film crew to stand on the rocks atop another waterfall – from where the pristine meltwater crashed hundreds of feet below to begin its long journey to the sea. The rocks were wet with spray and the roar of the water was deafening, yet still my crew and our Sherpa guides below urged me forward. It seemed foolhardy but it was undeniably a great shot and I got as close to the edge as I dared. It was only when I climbed down that they rushed up to me to explain they'd been screaming and signalling for me to get *off* the rocks because it was very dangerous and I could have easily slipped and fallen to my death.

Over the years, the glacier has receded from Gangotri by several kilometres and one must trek there on foot. Our Sherpa guides, laden with our bags, ran it like a sprint while I had trouble walking more than fifty metres without having to sit down. My breathing grew shallow and I developed pins and needles up and down my arms. We were only in the foothills of the Himalayas but I assumed I was suffering from altitude sickness or perhaps having a heart attack and I had visions of being airlifted off the mountain on a stretcher attached by ropes to a helicopter. What a great shot for the end of the documentary, I remember thinking as I sat there pretending to the director that nothing was wrong. My guru had sensibly decided not to join us on this last leg of the trip but as I struggled over rocks and bridges on my own last legs, stopping occasionally to wheeze and slake my thirst with some of the glacial water snaking its way to the waterfall, I recalled one last thing he had told me. I had said to him that while I didn't expect to be able to understand *how* Brahma's plan worked, I should be able to get my head around *why*. According to my journal, Sadhu Maharaji responded:

*Imagine you are assembling a jigsaw puzzle which is facedown on a table. You can only fit the pieces together by trial and error and it is only when you have finished that you can turn the completed puzzle over to see the picture you have put together.*

As a metaphor for Life it wasn't bad.

I reached Gomukh and took in the enormity of the glacier and the fact it had been around since before human beings had even evolved. It occurred to me that it was a question of faith as to whether there was a picture on the other side of the puzzle at all. I hated myself for thinking it. It was like my father's sunset all over again. Why couldn't I just live in the moment?

In the end, perhaps it's the water analogy that gets me there. We are each of us droplets of water and we journey along the river with all the other droplets of water through history, smoothing the terrain in some small regard as we wend our way, making things a little easier for those coming after us. We make one trip or we make many trips depending on how you look at it. Personally, I don't think we evaporate over the sea and start again as snow on a mountain; I think we only get one shot at it. And I like that we are here to make things go more smoothly for others.

Impressive though the glacier had been, the most memorable moment of the trip for me was at Har Ki Pauri, the steps in Haridwar where the Ganges leaves the mountains and enters the plains. It was stinking hot and I was standing in line with a few million other people to get in the Ganges for an *aarti* when I noticed a little girl behind me feeding a banana to a cow. We both looked at each other and started laughing.

## CHAPTER EIGHTEEN

# Everything for a laugh

ONE OF THE benefits of emerging from a midlife crisis (which is what I assume that last chapter was about) is that you end up realising what is genuinely important in your life.

Sitting on a rock near the Kashmiri border waiting for the rain to stop, I was feeling homesick. Reception even in the foothills of the Himalayas is lousy and, as we'd been advised against using the satellite phone in case we were spotted by a sniper on the border and taken out, I couldn't ring home. It was my birthday. The producer came up to me and gave me a present Leandra had sent her to pass on. I ripped away the wrapping to reveal a packet of liquorice allsorts.

Normally I would have happily eaten them all by myself, but I had been living with sadhus for the last month and, imbued with their sense of selflessness, offered the open pack to my guru, who took, I thought, rather more than was necessary. No matter. There would be more lollies than I could ever dream of waiting for me in our plentifully stocked pantry should I ever manage to get home. On the high shelf too, so the children couldn't get at them.

One of the advantages of working in series television is that either side of the intense bursts when you're actually making a show, your time is pretty much your own to move about and do with as you please. When the boys were young I had oodles of idleness in which I could just play with them. When they were very little, I could fool them into thinking anything was fun. 'Who wants to go to Orange Juice Land?!!!' I'd ask, as if it was a thing. 'Me!!!!' they'd chorus back, and we'd all get dressed and walk down to the station to catch the train. Orange Juice Land was the stall at Flinders Street Station where I'd buy them each a small cup of orange juice. Once the juice was consumed, we would pile back onto the train before the ticket ran out and go home again. Of course, it was all about the journey – the stuff whizzing by, the people in the carriage, talking about nothing and everything. But our definitions of fun began to diverge as they got older. Pretty soon, Joe saw through my Orange Juice Land ruse and while I could still cast my spell on his younger brothers for a while, it wasn't long before they too wised up and I would be outvoted in favour of visits to comic book shops (which I didn't mind) and the local oval (where I was forced to kick a football).

Of course, all the things we enjoyed doing together when they were young were just extensions of my own childhood: Lego, toys, comics, dressing-up, drawing, building stuff out of cardboard, pretending. The old videos we watched together were usually Laurel and Hardy and Charlie Chaplin (*The Circus* was the one they always asked for) and it was reported back to me that no one at school knew what they were talking about when they described what they'd watched over the weekend. Eventually the children started calling the shots and Stan & Ollie and the Little Tramp went the way of those train journeys to nowhere.

Holidays became difficult to arrange. They were no longer happy just to go to Adelaide at Christmas time and hang around at the beach dressed as Harry Potter. Even northern Queensland, with its promise of bird parks, rainforest eco-huts and a boat trip to see something that may have been a crocodile, started to weary them. An all-expenses-paid trip to Phuket saw them on video games most evenings and even a trip to the zoo to see the cigar-smoking, bike-riding orangutan failed to delight them. So too the one-armed tiger keeper who insisted we pat his tigers as they were very tame got no takers (though this was probably fair enough). Our last big trip – a grand European Tour – had ended in the Uffizi Gallery in Florence with one of them dragging his feet behind us and farting every time we stopped to admire a painting or statue.

Mind you, I'd been just as difficult to please when I was their age. A trip to Mannum when I was eight, despite the irresistible lure of a mosquito-infested cabin and the half-submerged rowboat out the front, held little charm for me.

We left after only one night, probably at my insistence. My father was nothing if not accommodating.

I have always striven to be like my father. He is the nicest man I know. He always did his utmost to make sure my sisters and I had a better childhood than he'd had. Granted, two square meals a day and an education beyond Year 7 would have done it, but that he, as the family breadwinner during my formative years, was able to achieve this and so much more astonishes me to this day; and that he did so without a word of complaint or a roll of the eye at his son's Little Lord Fauntleroy ways is a testament to his character. His own father was often away at sea when he was growing up and died shortly after I was born, so Dad didn't have the advantage of a role model through his life like I did.

With our own boys now turning into men, Leandra and I decided on one last family holiday before they twigged they could get out of them by simply refusing to come along. What Mannum had been to my father, America was to me – a far-off El Dorado I'd only ever known from the movies and had forever dreamed of one day visiting. A middle-aged father, his wife and three teenage boys who would rather have been back home with their girlfriends: it was the stuff of S.J. Perelman; a *New Yorker feuilleton* come to life. Of course, reality is rarely as wry and riddled with bathos – you need some judicious editing to achieve that.

This was to be no by-the-numbers trip. I had pictured our American adventure as a combination of Jack Kerouac's *On the*

*Road* and *Easy Rider*, but with fewer murders. Hurtling along the Extraterrestrial Highway, the wind in our hair, pulling over at greasy-spoon diners and shootin' the breeze with simple folk in trucker hats. I wanted to see the real America that Steppenwolf sang of in *Born To Be Wild*, not some anodyne plastic version rolled off an assembly line for idiot tourists.

My dream of bisecting the USA in a fire-apple red Chevy, Hunter S. Thompson–style, though, was off the table very early during negotiations and instead we'd be making the journey by conventional passenger jet. Also, instead of Las Vegas to Stumpy Point, North Carolina, via Atlanta, we would be taking a direct flight from San Francisco to New York City. And sleeping under the stars eating peyote was out; we would stay in hotels and order room service.

I'd thought about buying all five volumes of Armistead Maupin's *Tales of the City*, one for each of us to read on the plane trip to Frisco so that we would arrive with an understanding of its people and a working knowledge of its history. Instead we just watched a YouTube clip of Max Zorin falling from the Golden Gate Bridge in *A View To a Kill*.

Alcatraz, trolley car rides and a day's hike through Yosemite were all arranged, but the boys were keen to visit the big Apple store in Union Square to purchase items that would enable them to spend more time on the internet. Frankly, I couldn't see how that was possible. As far I could tell, they'd spent every waking moment on their devices since we left for the airport. Presumably, some cutting-edge gizmo fresh out of Silicon Valley could now be plugged directly into the brain so their REM could swipe through whatever missives were pouring in from Australia while they slept.

The shop was fascinating: a two-storey glass cube and no furniture but for scrubbed wooden benches with nothing on them. Products appeared on HD digital wallpaper which read the metadata off your Fitbit as you walked through the door. Undercover staff pretended to be happening past as you made your selection. My sons purchased a variety of plugs and cables, paid for by pointing their screens at the sales assistant's belt. An Apple end-user myself, I thought I'd enter into the spirit of things and purchase a replacement case for my iPhone OS 2. The salesperson looked at me as if I'd asked him for a Morse-Vail telegraph key and my children beat a hasty exit lest I infect them with my lameness.

Our tour of Alcatraz was more successful. I was able to answer all the guard's questions to our group. I knew their most famous inmate was Burt Lancaster, the Birdman of Alcatraz, and that Nicolas Cage and Sean Connery had once foiled a biochemical terrorist plot from up in the guard tower in *The Rock*. As staff and visitors listened, spellbound, to my recounting of the plot of *Escape from Alcatraz* starring Clint Eastwood, my children snuck away, fashioned their own glider from bed linen stolen from the prison laundry and escaped back to the mainland.

Then it was on to Yosemite National Park for a spectacular view of what the children dismissed as exactly the same as the default Mac screensaver for OS Catalina, and a night at the theatre to see *A Christmas Carol*, where I glimpsed the back of what my wife assured me was Dan Aykroyd's head. Just as Scrooge learned the true meaning of Christmas after being taken on a journey by three ghosts, I hoped our three children would learn the same lesson on their journey with us. New York City – which Dan Aykroyd had helped to simultaneously save and almost destroy in *Ghostbusters* – lay ahead.

Tipping invariably causes me angst and I always tend to overdo it. After a porter helped us into the taxi with our bags I raced back into the hotel and pressed a handful of American dollars on him. He looked shocked and tried to give the money back but I insisted. Another man behind the desk in a similar shirt looked most put out and I then realised I had just given fifteen dollars to a guest checking into the hotel. Still, it was too late to explain so I handed over some more cash to the porter and another wad of bills to another man standing nearby so he didn't feel left out, bade everyone a merry Christmas and left as red-faced as old Saint Nick himself.

New York, New York was, as Gene Kelly, Frank Sinatra and Jules Munshin[*] once sang, a wonderful town. Unlike the three sailors on leave in *On the Town*, our three sons didn't so much run amok, singing and dancing, as dawdle along behind us as we visited places, mercifully only showing their disapproval by sighing this time.

---

[*] I admit it – I had to look him up.

Real Americans were on display everywhere. One enterprising fellow came up to me and asked if I'd like my shoes shined. As I'd bought them only an hour before from Henry Bucks I said no thank you and wished him well. Undeterred, he fell to his knee and grabbed my ankle, continuing his spiel with the can-do spirit of Horatio Alger. Didn't I know that a man of style such as myself deserved only the best and that he'd been shining the shoes of New Yorkers for fifteen years? Was I aware that he had once dubbined the oxfords of Mayor Bloomberg himself? I let him force my foot onto his crate.

My wife and children were keen to move on as they had made a booking for the back of the queue outside Carmine's for that evening, but this was a real moment of connection between two cultures, a bond forged in the melting pot of the New World. I nodded my approval and the man spat on my shoe and began rubbing it with his sleeve. When he tried to charge me sixteen dollars and I reached for my pocket, my wife stepped in and offered eight. The man, on both knees now, explained that he was married with three children. My wife replied that so was she. The man took the money and mumbled something about 'asshole tourists' as we ran down the street to join our children, who were almost a block ahead of us by then.

*'What a pity the kids are missing out on such a spactacular view …'*

Aside from Dan Aykroyd, our only other celebrity spotting was *Brooklyn Nine-Nine*'s Terry Crews at the Benjamin Steak House on East 40th Street on Christmas Day. He was there with his wife and children.

And God bless us, every one.

| | | /⟋

I had turned fifty and was about to embark on that part of my life where because there was nothing new left for me to try with my limited skill set, I would revisit past failures and have a crack at doing them properly this time around. It was like reincarnation except that I had to make do with my old body.

First cab off the rank was the sitcom. John Howard had been usurped as prime minister by Kevin Rudd back when we were doing *Newstopiä*. By the time *Mad as Hell* started, Kevin Rudd had been usurped by Julia Gillard. During our second season, Kevin was back again. By the end of our second season, he was back being an ex–prime minister again.

Between seasons I developed an idea for a series about a former PM – an amalgam of Kevin Rudd and John Howard – rattling around his big old home annoying his wife and daughter and ordering about the remains of his staff like a deposed king instead of writing his memoirs, for which he has already received and spent a handsome fee. The publishers assign a ghost writer to help him finish the book and it is through her eyes that we come to know his family.

I deliberately made the ex-PM of *The Ex-PM* a man of ambiguous political stripe, as Jim Hacker had been in *Yes Minister*. This was as much to avoid doing the more pointed party-political jokes we were already doing in *Mad as Hell* as it was to avoid alienating half our audience who statistically would be voting the other way from whatever choice we made. It wasn't a political sitcom; it was about a reluctant early retiree, albeit a high-profile one whom everybody recognised and had an opinion about.

I had heard a perhaps apocryphal story about John Howard after he'd recently left office which I used as the basis for the series. John and his wife Janette are out shopping and, chatting away as they walk back across the car park from the supermarket with their bags, they get into the back of their car, still chatting. It's only after a minute or so that they remember they no longer have a driver.

*The Ex-PM* was better written than *Welcher* and was shot entirely on location. The cast was top-notch, including Nicki Wendt, Nicholas Bell, Kate Jenkinson, Jackson Tozer, Ming-Zhu Hii, Lucy Honigman, Francis Greenslade (obviously) and another of my comedy heroes, John Clarke. The two seasons were well directed by Sian Davies and Shaun Wilson respectively, and I couldn't have been happier with it. I didn't even mind my own performance as the ex-PM.

My favourite episode was the one where the rights to the still unwritten book have been sold to a TV network to be made into a miniseries. Lachy Hulme is to play the ex-PM and spends the day with him so he can go all method with his performance. Lachy is hilarious playing a ridiculously pretentious version of himself, veering often into his impression of Adam West. He was the only guest actor comfortable enough to throw in ad-libs like our regular cast and he did so with great skill. It was the only time my character got bossed around by someone else and I think the episode was funnier for it. When I came to do the second season, I contrived storylines where this would happen far more often.

We were lucky to be able to do a second season given the show wasn't that well received. I think this may have had something to do with the not-unreasonable expectation that the show would be more political, like *Mad as Hell*, and the fact that a couple of weeks before we went to air, Tony Abbott had been usurped by Malcolm Turnbull as prime minister and we had a newly minted ex-PM wandering about ready for parody. The series was gentler than that; perhaps even old-fashioned with its use of physical comedy. It was more farce than satire.

I was over the moon that John Clarke was part of the series. He played a venal and corrupt version of Sir Humphrey Appleby, involved with laundered money and the Russian mafia. Eventually he gets kidnapped and winds up in the boot of his own car. John was up for anything and a better actor than people might give him credit for.

To have him perform material I'd written was without a doubt a career highlight. I'd had his 1979 LP, *The Fred Dagg*

*Tapes*, given to me as a birthday present when I was seventeen. It contained all the sketches he'd done on ABC radio from the previous year, including his appearance on *The Science Show* with Robyn Williams in a track called 'The Meaning of Life'. I can't begin to tell you how influential this track was on my writing. The density, pace and richness of John's writing and performance have not been bettered by anyone. It surpasses even the idiot-expertise of Peter Cook's E.L. Wisty and his various flights of fancy – Cook would take a point and slowly explore it; John is racing through twenty. It took me many listens over the years to catch it all, each yielding a new word or idea or ludicrous summation of a philosophical point. Consider this distillation of ennui:

> *Now, ennui is a terrible thing, and seems to have roughly the same effect as terminal boredom. Ennui actually is a French word meaning Henry. And the story goes that once you get a touch of the Henrys, it's all downhill and the only way to relieve the symptoms is to whip down the harbour and pull a wave over your bonce and call it a day.*

And even more incredibly, it's a seven-and-a-half-minute one-take performance. Not a stumble or a wrong inflection. Even when Robyn Williams interrupts to clarify who Bishop Berkeley and the solipsists are, John doesn't miss a beat. He agrees that Robyn has the right man and then ad-libs that the bishop's brother used to play for India.

262

I loved the guy. He was kind enough to appear on *The Micallef P(r)ogram(me)* when I had the audacity to ask him. Actually, McCaffrie was writing on *The Games*, so I had the audacity to get McCaffrie to ask him. John couldn't have been nicer, buying into the mean-spiritedness of the show as we sniped at each other throughout the interview. There was a script but we improvised around it. When we did another take to tighten it up it ended up two minutes longer.

We wrapped the second season of the *Ex-PM* with a cast party at a local pub. We were in a group and John came over to say goodbye, quite early in the evening. He looked a little tired. He walked off and I watched him, wondering whether I should go and say goodbye one on one. But no, we had made loose plans to catch up for lunch the next week and I let him go. He slipped into the next room and out the front door. He died the next day. It's not my story to tell, so I won't, but John was walking in nature, which he loved. He often had a camera with him, always on the lookout for birdlife.

The week after his death we started putting the show together in the edit suite and I wasn't looking forward to it. It didn't seem right to be trying to put together something funny in the circumstances. But it was like being with him all over again. John had a habit of talking right up until the director called 'Action'. As we edited the scenes with John and me together, there was John on the soundtrack as we took our positions, chatting to me about the things we always talked about: S.J. Perelman, Ruth Draper, Joyce Grenfell, Seamus

Heaney, Spike Milligan, a music hall sand-dance act called Wilson, Keppel and Betty. 'Wilson and Keppel kept changing the girl,' he says to me at one point, 'but they always called whoever it was Betty ...'

I don't think I was special in this regard. John was like that with everybody. He had this remarkable ability to quickly find what you and he had in common and he would flip that switch whenever he ran into you.

I regret not giving him a hug before he left. You want that last moment to be perfect, but it can never be. We'd have to make *every* moment perfect. Maybe he wouldn't have liked being hugged anyway. My last memory of John will have to be of him slipping away into the next room.

## CHAPTER NINETEEN

# Whatever became of me

THE OTHER THING I wanted to get right this time around was theatre. I wanted to do a professional job in a proper play. I was ready: my trip to India had stripped me of my Ego. There would be no ad-libbing, no mugging, no upstaging – and I wanted it to be a hit. And, yes, I even wanted a decent review. I didn't want 'Boeing Boeing ... Gone' to be my last ever headline in the arts section. Okay, so maybe my ego was still hanging around but I would definitely be keeping it in check. I would have my cake and eat it too and I wanted the cherry on top to be performing in an MTC production. I convinced the powers that be that I could pull a crowd and suggested Neil Simon's old comedy warhorse, *The Odd Couple*.

The play revolves around Oscar and Felix, two divorcee bachelors who live together and fulfil the old marital comedy trope of a long-suffering husband and his clueless 'wife'. It won't surprise you to learn that I asked Francis to join me as co-star. What might surprise you is that I had never read the play. I had just assumed it would be like the film, given that Neil Simon had written the screenplay – and indeed it is very faithful to its source material. What I missed was that Oscar has all the funny lines and Felix is the straight man, albeit one who is the butt of most of the jokes because he is … well, 'unmanly'. The play hasn't aged well in this regard. Having seen only the film, I wanted to play Felix because Jack Lemmon had somehow made Felix the funny one.

As it turned out, when Francis and I met up with our director*, Francis was under the impression that *he* would be playing Felix and, having actually read the play, assumed that I would want to play Oscar given that it was a bigger role and had most of the jokes. Our director suggested we read the script through twice, once one way and then the other to see which sounded best. I'd gone to all this trouble to avoid an audition for the MTC and here I was now doing two of them, and both up against Francis.

On the first run, I played Oscar and did okay. The character knew he was being funny most of the time (whereas Felix didn't) and while I felt it was against type to play a sports-loving slob, I knew how to do the jokes in a Borscht Belt–type way and had every confidence that I could sell the comedy so that it would actually be funny, instead of the sort of nerf-ball version of funny some theatre types mistakenly believe is the same thing. Francis too nailed Felix without any

---

* Peter Houghton, with whom I'd enjoyed working in *Newstopia*.

difficulty. We then swapped. Francis fell into the role of Oscar effortlessly and I did a pretty fair Jack Lemmon. By the end of our auditions, it seemed that Oscar might be a better fit for me after all, but our director decided the play would be better served if I was Felix because that's what the audience would be expecting.*

Because I wanted to avoid the worry I'd had learning my lines on *Boeing Boeing*, I decided to get them down before I even started rehearsals. I'd read somewhere that Laurence Olivier had done this once, although apparently it's a bit of a no-no because once you block the play, work out your moves and listen to the other actors, you might have to unlearn the version you've already got in your head and this can be difficult, if not impossible. Nonetheless, I thought I'd err on the side of caution as I didn't want to have to scribble Felix's lines down on pieces of the scenery.

On the first day with the other actors I was off-book but for a few lines in a group scene that involved a lot of yelling over each other, which I'd left to rehearse when we were all together. I'd also read Neil Simon's memoirs and the blow-by-blow account of writing and rehearsing and rewriting the play. I knew how lines had been changed and why and the genesis of certain scenes and gags and how laughs had been discovered on the way. I worked out an elaborate backstory for Felix and how he and Oscar had met. It was during the war,

---

* The rest of the cast were excellent: David Ross Paterson, Grant Piro, Hayden Spencer, Drew Tingwell, Michala Banas and Christie Whelan Browne.

probably armed forces radio given that he's a news writer and Oscar covers sports. They're both from New York. Felix went to NYU and studied journalism. After he was demobbed, he went to work in radio.

I wondered where he was born so I could get the accent right. I didn't want to do the all-purpose American accent I'd attempted in *Aquamarine*. That one was all over the shop: fine if we were doing *Flowers for Algernon*, but not this. Jack Lemmon has a Midwestern accent with an urban everyman anxiousness laid over the top but I didn't want to do the impression I'd done at the audition. I tried a Queens accent but that sounded too much like my Christopher Walken impression. Then I made him more working class and imagined he came from New Jersey. He'd flattened out the accent when he went to NYU, I reasoned, but it came out when he got hysterical. It was Jerry Lewis's Newark accent and I was very familiar with its cadence, though of course I would make it less yelpy. As a *pièce de résistance* I added a bit of Avenue J Woody Allen hesitation here and there to substitute for the naturalness I liked in Jack Lemmon's delivery.

During our family's recent Christmas in New York, I had also scoped out Riverside Drive where Oscar lives and looked out across the Hudson, taking in the view that Felix would have in the first scene when he looks out Oscar's window and his friends think he might jump. I took the walk down to NBC Studios, where I decided Felix worked, just to see a few of the things he might have seen on the way. He wouldn't have taken the subway; it's only a few stops. In short, I was as ready as I could be; in fact, I'd never been as over-prepared for anything in my life.

*The Odd Couple* is about two guys who end up hating each other. On one reading it's a very dark tale; Felix is suicidal for the first act and none of his friends can express their concern openly to him, particularly not Oscar. The inability to deal with it is played for laughs. When Felix's card-playing buddies do finally express their concern, they are comically emasculated and must leave. Oscar is left to cope with this weeping, catastrophising she-man.

I tried to play Felix for real (albeit with the occasional comic tic) and with only two exceptions kept it the right side of reality. There's a scene in the third act where Oscar leaves Felix alone with their dates, the Pigeon sisters (Christie Whelan Browne and Michala Banas). Small talk is awkward because this is Felix's first date since he broke up with his wife. He ends up reducing them to tears and Oscar's wolfish plans come unstuck when he returns from the kitchen to find them all howling like Sally Field. During the scene one night, when Christie went for the chip bowl, she knocked a chip onto the coffee table. I just stared at it and the audience laughed, knowing how much this would affect a neat-freak like Felix. Christie puts down her drink and returns the errant chip to the bowl but order has not been sufficiently restored for Felix. He places a coaster under her drink and adjusts it just so. Then he straightens the bowl and then everything else on the table. Then the table itself is realigned to some symmetry only Felix understands. Then his tie and the rest of his clothing is smoothed out. Imaginary lint is picked off his knee. He crosses and recrosses his legs until they are just right and then Christie goes for another chip. I confess to milking it a bit. And the scene did get longer and more elaborate as the season went on (except for the nights the director was in).

The other departure from reality was some comic business that Francis and I discovered during rehearsals as an angry Oscar chases a petrified Felix around the apartment, threatening to kill him. We're running in and out of doorways and at one point we thought it would be fun if Felix sits down for a rest while Oscar keeps on going; slamming one door, opening another, faster and faster in an impossibly small circle given he is racing into a bedroom and then coming in through the front door. Eventually Felix tries to make it easier for Oscar by opening the front door for him just as he runs in. Obeying Henri Bergson's principle that 'the attitudes, gestures and movements of the human body are laughable in exact proportion as that body reminds us of a mere machine', Oscar doesn't notice that the door has been opened for him. In again and Felix is more visible this time, having opened the door with great flourish. Oscar thanks Felix as he continues on and through the bedroom door. Pause. Biggest laugh so far – and these are the sweetest laughs; the ones where literally nothing is happening – then Oscar walks back in through the bedroom door to slow burn at Felix before the chase begins again in earnest. As Francis rightly observed at the time: 'This isn't Felix and Oscar; this is just Shaun and Francis playing silly buggers.'

Oddly enough, though, during the run I felt we both became versions of Felix and Oscar offstage. Despite our many shared experiences and excellent rapport, we have different ways of working but this seemed, to me at least, to be almost method acting. Felix drives Oscar to distraction as the play progresses and it seemed to me I was doing the same thing to Francis across the season.

Francis plays it very real when he's performing. During the massage scene, for example, he buried his knee in my ribs so hard I thought he was going to break a few of them and I had to ask him to pull back a little, which of course he was happy to do. I, on the other hand, don't disappear entirely when I play a character. I sit slightly outside it looking at the effect my performance is having on the audience – and I adjust my performance accordingly with extra bits of comic business or by shifting emphasis; in other words, it's not exactly the same performance every night. While I'd like to think I remained in character, there was a looseness in my approach which I could see might be taken as a lack of discipline, and I could feel myself irritating Francis. But, like Oscar in the first act, he wouldn't say anything to me about it, at least not directly.

Onstage every night, Felix would unknowingly annoy Oscar until Oscar could take it no more and would explode. This became a type of therapy for us, the yelling at each other particularly. At the end of every show, just before the curtain call, we would stand either side of the doorway in the back of the set, half in darkness, and Francis would always give me a thumbs up before we went on to take our bow. I think he knew that I knew it was just Oscar who was mad at me and I think I ended up using what I was feeling to help me play the abandonment that Felix was going through. Lee Strasberg would have been proud of me. Things returned to normal after the play finished and we've never really discussed what happened. Of course, it's entirely possible that it was all in my head and I was just projecting onto Francis. Maybe he wasn't irritated at all and I was unconsciously taking the frustration I was feeling over being less professional than I'd promised myself I'd be and attributing it to my friend who, after all, was standing onstage shouting angrily at me night after night. Complicated business, acting.

I love that there are still things I don't understand about comedy and that every new project leads to a new discovery. There was a laugh in the play that I've never been able to work out. It's not apparent in the lines, so during rehearsals I didn't even notice it was there. It's after Felix leaves Oscar and hooks up with the Pigeon sisters and then returns for his things. It goes like this:

GWENDOLYN: ... Felix Unger. That sweet, tortured man who's in my flat at this moment pouring his heart out to my sister.

OSCAR: [Turns to BOYS] You hear? I'm worried to death and he's up there getting tea and sympathy.

[CECILY rushes in dragging a reluctant FELIX with her.]

CECILY: Gwen, Felix doesn't want to stay. Please tell him to stay.

FELIX: Really, girls, this is very embarrassing. I can go to a hotel ... [To BOYS] Hello, fellas.

For some reason, the 'Hello, fellas' got a laugh on opening night. I think it had something to do with the way his buddies were looking enviously at him. He's got one girl on his arm and another in reserve – everything a red-blooded 1960s American man could want. Yet he's shrugging it off with such nonchalance. His friends all think he might have killed himself, and there he is noticing them *en passant* as if nothing has happened. Anyway, when I did the line the next night there was no laugh. Nothing the next night either. I wrote it off and didn't even think about it the night after and suddenly the laugh was back. *Great*, I thought. But the next night, when I was expecting it again, it wasn't there. Was it *because* I was expecting it? I tried to look as if I wasn't on the next night but got nothing. I gave up – then it was back again. Then I lost it at the matinee.

I started doing it differently; I played the 'Hello, fellas' as if I was rubbing their noses in it. There was a laugh but not as big and not the right shape; it also seemed a little out of character. It was the innocence that had been the key. I tried it as innocently as I could but the audience could tell I wanted it, so they didn't give it to me. I gave up again and it was back. Whatever I was doing – or not doing – to get the laugh, it had nothing to do with technique or timing; in fact, it had nothing to do with me. It was Neil Simon's laugh. I thought of emailing him and asking him why it was funny but didn't want to worry him so early in the production.

We played to packed houses, the crowd enjoyed it and it was the MTC's most successful show of the year. Oh, and we got nice reviews too. Even the critic who had so loathed me in *Boeing Boeing* wrote:

> *Micallef isn't as dry as Jack Lemmon as the (queerly domesticated) straight man, though if the performance is fruitier, there's also more range to it, from genuinely cringeworthy social awkwardness to barrelling physical comedy and outright farce.*

You hear that, folks? I have more range than Jack Lemmon.

| | | /~

Another good thing to come out of *The Odd Couple*, apart from me getting a decent review, was that Christie Whelan Browne ended up joining the cast for *Mad as Hell*. That she hit the ground running on a show that had already run eleven seasons is a testament to her skills at a whole bunch of things as well as being funny. She replaced Roz Hammond, who had been with the show since it started – even before if you treat it as an extension of *The Micallef P(r)ogram(me)* – and understandably wanted to move on to other things. Roz's most beloved character on the show, Jacqui Lambie's inarticulate boob of an adviser, Dolly Norman, is only a thousandth of what she can do.

Emily Taheny had also been in the show from the beginning: an extraordinarily gifted actor and singer as well as being a tremendously funny character comedian. Her chameleon-like ability to switch from LNP apologist Draymella Burt to ALP apologist Vaguary Bellchamber to Lois Price to Mary-Brett Punish to Concretia Doily to Sarah Ferguson to the expletive-ridden Zamilla and a dozen other regular and one-off characters is matched only by her almost uncanny ability to disappear so completely into those roles. Long-time fans of the show marvel at the string of actors appearing at the desk, not realising that often they're all Emily. She is truly phenomenal.

The roster of talent on the show is in my estimation equal to if not better than the best on offer anywhere in the world. I've already banged on far too much about how great Francis is, so I'll spare you any more gushing.

But I will tell you about the astonishing Stephen Hall, who moved from the writers' room to the main cast in the second season because of his remarkable ability as a mimic. It became clear pretty quickly that he was also one of the funniest character comedians in this country – in my view, the heir to Peter Sellers. Tosh Greenslade too is no slouch. He has given his youth to *Mad as Hell* and I have had the pleasure of seeing him grow from a novice actor with natural comic gifts and unlimited potential to a masterful comedian with a grotesquery of characters that can in turn both alarm and charm the viewer. The show has also benefited from wonderful work by Veronica Milsom (seasons 1–4), Ming-Zhu Hii and Molly Daniels (season 10), Michelle Brasier (season 11) and ongoing guest appearances by Mark Coles Smith and Zenya Carmellotti. As I write this, *Mad as Hell* has just finished its fifteenth season. That's even longer than *M\*A\*S\*H*.

I'm often asked whether any of the politicians we lampoon on the show ever get cross and complain. Truthfully, I'd be surprised if they even watched the show. Don't they have more important things to do? Having said that, when the current secretary-general of the OECD was just plain old Australian Finance Minister Mathias Cormann, I know he not only watched the show but was so taken with Stephen Hall's Schwarzenegger-like portrayal of his spokesborg, Darius Horsham, that he even agreed to appear on the show as himself to say goodbye to Darius when he (Cormann) was leaving politics for his new post. I also bumped into Bill Shorten a couple of times when he was Opposition leader and he was nice enough to pretend he didn't mind our Bill's Zingers segment where we openly mocked his inability to deliver his own terrible one-liners.

What anyone else thought of the show, I don't know, although I once had a Liberal senator actually ring me to take me to task over the way we'd referred to him. He asked me to keep the conversation between us and I wouldn't betray his confidence just to sell a few books. It was Bill Heffernan. Senator Heffernan was a pretty tough-nut Liberal and fans of political satire might remember him monstering Charles Firth when The Chaser tried to prank him in the National Tally Room after his party won the election back in 2007.

It was eight o'clock on a Sunday morning when I got a call from an unknown number. This had been happening a few times a day since we'd gone to air the previous Wednesday and, while I'd let the calls go through to voicemail, there was never any message. Eight am on a Sunday, though, might mean an emergency somewhere so I picked up and a voice tells me it's Bill Heffernan. The joke he objected to was so benign I had trouble remembering it. I'd been riffing on billionaire independent MP Clive Palmer's claim that in order to avoid any conflicts with his many business interests, he 'would leave the room if any government thing came up'. I mused on what exactly a 'government thing' might be and a picture of Bill Heffernan popped up on the screen next to me. That was it.

We'd picked Heffernan because he had a reputation as a head-kicker and wasn't the usual milquetoast nonentity we made fun of (like Ian Goodenough or Bert van Manen). It was very much a throwaway joke as we were really more interested in ridiculing Palmer's lack of understanding about what amounted to conflict of interest. A real crowd-pleaser, our show.

The senator was quite polite about it. He said he didn't think it was fair to call him a 'government thing' as he'd done a lot of good while in office, such as exposing High Court Justice Michael Kirby's improper Comcar use back in 2002. Remember, Heffernan was then prime minister John Howard's cabinet secretary at the time. Remember, also, that the Senate ruled he had breached standing orders by making a personal attack on a judicial officer without apparent cause and also that the records he was waving around in support of his allegations were bogus – and not in a good Bill & Ted way. Any allegations of impropriety against Justice Kirby ended up thoroughly discredited and Heffernan had to not only resign as parliamentary secretary but also apologise to Kirby. Yet here he was a decade later still banging on about it.

I didn't argue the point, instead explaining to him that our show wasn't a real news program and so we didn't tend to include pieces highlighting the positive contributions politicians had made to public life. The senator seemed to be under the impression that *Mad as Hell* was like *The Project*, which makes me think he'd heard about the joke rather than actually seen it. I apologised to him for hurting his feelings and he laughed it off as if it was nothing. The conversation ended pleasantly enough with him offering to have a beer with me next time he was in Melbourne. Mercifully, this was never followed up.

I regret not having the presence of mind to ask him where he got my phone number (presumably that snitch Firth handed it over), but the experience did make me think twice in future about having *ad hominem* slaps at politicians. Better to make observations about the atrocious things they've done or the ludicrous things they've said. Mind you, if we ever found photos or footage of Clive Palmer eating or trying to get out of a car, we'd always show them.

As in life, it's important to know when to get off. That twilight moment between the audience applauding you and them reaching for rotten fruit. I've usually grown tired of my work before the audience, so hopefully *Mad as Hell* can wrap up while it's still liked by those who watch it. Frankly, I've never thought there was anything startlingly original about the show. *The Roast* with Mark Humphries was on and The Chaser were still doing things when we started, and *Wednesday Night Fever* and *The Weekly* with Charlie Pickering and *Sammy J* have turned up since. News satire goes back as far as Juvenal, although as far as I know, he didn't have to deal with efficiency dividends and budget freezes or whatever the equivalent of Rupert Murdoch was back in first-century Rome. Mount Vesuvius, maybe.

As to what's next, who knows. Never the most astute of businessmen, I own nothing I've ever made, receive no ongoing royalties and so have to continue working – which is just as well as I'd go mad otherwise. I'd like to make more documentaries. Appearing in things by people I like and admire or helping young comics avoid the pitfalls in making TV also interests me. Books: both reading and writing them. A bit of gardening. Cleaning out my cupboard.

Regrets? Too many to mention. Unlike Old Blue Eyes, though, none involve destroying JFK's helipad with a sledgehammer or bricking up Swifty Lazar's walk-in wardrobe. I'm sometimes asked why I didn't try my luck overseas. To be honest, it never occurred to me. My regrets are less about opportunities I may have missed and more about the friendships I've loused up. I sometimes think about chasing up certain people from years ago and apologising, but then I realise I'd only be apologising to make myself feel better. You're only the main character of your own story; in everybody else's you're a bit player or a non-speaking extra. Most of the time we end up on the cutting-room floor.

| | | / ̲–

At the end of the day, my life is no different from any other: it's nowhere near as long as it needs to be to get done what you'd like but it'll just have to do. Given enough time, of course, you can accomplish anything. Look at the universe. In the billions of years since the very first cloud of gas collapsed in on itself, the universe as we know it (and don't) has come to be. The trouble with human beings, though, is that we don't have billions of years to get things done. We arrived at this party rather late and the way we've been carrying on, we're going to be asked to leave well before it's over.

As I've said, I've not been able to convince myself there's an afterlife to attend to everything I won't get around to in this one. But that's a blessing. If I had eternity to look forward to, I'd get blasé and waste it watching TV (and we all know what a worthless enterprise *that* is). Let's face it, we're more likely to make the most of something when there's not an endless supply of it.

Regrettably, I only twigged to all this when I hit middle age and so haven't really lived my life to the full. I've spent most of my almost sixty years in pursuit of the moment, with little if any regard for the responsibility I have to leave the world at least a little better than I found it. Other people devote their lives to others; I have squandered mine on myself, gobbling it down, like a block of chocolate in the car on the way home from the supermarket. Of course, I'm not dead yet and still have time to renounce my ways and dedicate what time I have left to helping those less fortunate – but who am I to presume I'm better off than someone else? And even if I am, should they have to put up with me imposing my values on them? No, my friends, no … it's best I see out my life as I am – a shallow, self-absorbed narcissist – rather than make some desperate, last-minute dash for redemption. If there is a God, then He or She would quickly see through such a ruse and rightly smite me for the sin of virtue-signalling.

I'm not sure my story needs a redemptive third act anyway. Thus far it's been an exciting climb to the top of the Australian entertainment step stool – and if I've bustled about in this world with any purpose at all, it's only ever been to try and lighten the mood a little.

I started in show business rather late and found I had a ravenous hunger for whatever it was out there. It made me in turns impulsive, arrogant, pathetic, protective, careless, ruthless, gullible and paranoid. My hunger eventually gave way to an appetite and I became more measured. I savoured the meal and grew more selective in my choices, graciously declining things that might not be good for me in my new and balanced diet. My appetite is gone now but I still have a taste for it.

Comedy, the comic, laughter and the joy of a funny moment will always be in my life. It's such a big part of whatever has become of me. The whole thing has been and remains an infinitely fascinating and ceaselessly challenging puzzle. If I ever finish it, I can assure you I'll be turning it over to see if there's a picture on the back.

# Afterword

Plato said an unexamined life is a life unlived, which is fine if you have the luxury to sit back and think about things, but most people are too busy surviving. I've been lucky. I've had the time to not only think about things but jot them down, the audacity to have them published, and now you've been good enough to read them. I'll leave it to you to judge whether it was worthwhile (as a life and as a book).

Of course, I've left a lot of stuff out. Most of it I've forgotten. Other bits were too long and dull even for me, too fleeting, too similar to something else, didn't fit or seemed like they'd be more at home in a Fellini film. Things like the burning heat of my father's steering wheel in the summer; that day I wet my pants in a phone booth; fracturing my skull after being dragged along the asphalt of a basketball court while hanging out the back of a trailer towed by our sports master; the tumour in my leg; the series of murders that took place while I was at university (no, I didn't commit them); the time I blew up a cake with detcord and covered an audience in frosting; the chats I had with Malcolm McDowell, Ben Elton and Donny Osmond (Vega was a very strange radio station). I've also left out my sigmoidectomy, faking my way through a conversation about Philip Larkin with Stephen Fry (I think he could tell I was paraphrasing Alan Bennett), the *Herald Sun* reporting I'd been hit by a car (I hadn't), the time I pissed off Jose Feliciano, Michael Crawford telling me about duct-taping tampons to his bloodied knees after falling down some stairs in *A Funny Thing Happened on the Way to the Forum*, the time I hosted *The Panel* and ballsed it up, the time I offended Paul McDermott, the *two* times I offended Dave Hughes, the time I got Judy Davis to wake up Colin Friels so I could talk to him on the phone, performing with Martin Short, arguing with John Laws (he said Peter Sellers wasn't in Kubrick's *Lolita*), me spending most of my life thinking 'ignomy' was a word, the time I played cricket with Don Bradman (I was drunk so it might just have been an old guy who lived in the same street), meeting George Harrison's coat, and other things I'll no doubt include in a follow-up memoir a decade or so from now.

I've also been sparing in my mentions of Leandra and the boys; not because they aren't important enough to write about, but because they are *too* important. Leandra is her own person and a million other things besides my partner in life and I hope I've done some justice to her in this book. Joe, Gabe and

Eli are all happy and healthy and seemingly none the worse for me being their father. Adults now, they are making their own way in the world. When they were little but old enough to walk to school on their own, I would stand at the gate and see how long before they looked back to see if I was still there. Eventually they didn't need to look back anymore. But I still waited.

If you picked up this book expecting *Angela's Ashes* you've hopefully been pleasantly disappointed, for it has been the comfortable ordinariness in my life that made me who I am; the stultifying tedium of my early years that drove me into comedy and my easy boredom which spurred me on to the many and varied projects chronicled herein. In short, my life has been an unceasing quest to relieve the bland monotony of being me.

I used to worry about growing up happy and comfortable. Maybe I wouldn't be funny enough to make it. Most of my comic heroes had it tough in their early years. Chaplin grew up in Dickensian poverty, Keaton with an alcoholic and violent father, Sellers a suffocating mother; Spike Milligan was even blown up by a mortar! All I had was my stupid loving family and a childhood where nothing horrible ever happened. Still, perhaps it was this perfectly ordinary life, free of psychological trauma of any kind, that made me doubt I'd ever amount to anything, or that there was even anything to achieve; that forced me to retreat into my head where things could be vastly more interesting.

I would like to be remembered – and I hope this doesn't sound pretentious – as the Jean-Paul Sartre of Australian comedy: challenging the spiritually destructive conformity of my bourgeois upbringing and ultimately finding a more authentic way of being as a light-entertainment television presenter. As Sartre and I always say: 'Consciousness is intentional and non-being is a nothingness quite distinct from the more abstract notion of not existing at all.'*

I wish I had some definitive Rules of Life to leave you with but I'm afraid I'm no Jordan Peterson (which is probably good news for both of us). Here instead are the answers to the twelve questions I'm most often asked. I hope they are of some help to you in the future:

---

* Sartre, of course, would have said it in French and this is where he and I must part company, for I cannot speak French. Not by choice but because through a caprice of nature and history, I was not born French – and yet deciding to not pay attention in Mrs Van Truck's French classes *was* a conscious choice from which derives my ongoing unconscious action of not being able to speak the language to this day. In attempting to transcend my nothingness I have, of course, from time to time, *pretended* I can speak French in my work – and while Sartre would argue that this is *false consciousness*, I would contend that if I can get a few laughs out of a bit of gibberish in a funny accent, then I have brought order to my nothingness and bridged the gap between purity and spontaneity by defining my Being as one who creates action-oriented constructs for a living.

1.  **FAVOURITE FILM:** Frank Capra's *It's a Wonderful Life* with Ridley Scott's *Blade Runner* a close second.

2.  **FAVOURITE PAINTING:** *The Accolade* by Edmund Blair Leighton. I'm also fond of Gustave Doré's *Andromeda* for some reason.

3.  **FAVOURITE SONG:** 'Ballad of Sir Frankie Crisp' by George Harrison.

4.  **FAVOURITE NOVEL:** *A Christmas Carol* by Charles Dickens.

5.  **FAVOURITE POEM:** T.S. Eliot's 'Burnt Norton'.

6.  **FAVOURITE COMEDY SCENE:** The room-shifting scene in the Marx Brothers' *A Night at the Opera*.

7.  **FAVOURITE ROMANTIC SCENE:** Cary Grant doing a highland reel with Ingrid Bergman in *Indiscreet*.

8.  **FAVOURITE SIGHT GAG:** Archie driving off with his briefcase on the roof of his car in *A Fish Called Wanda*.

9.  **FAVOURITE DOUBLE TAKE:** Bruce Willis noticing the gun case is empty in *Death Becomes Her*.

10. **FAVOURITE DOG:** Wire-haired fox terrier.

11. **FAVOURITE FOOD:** Lemon cheesecake.

12. **FAVOURITE MAD KING:** Ludwig II of Bavaria.

# Acknowledgements

When she was about the age I am now, my grandmother's ability to recollect things and remember people started to fade. I don't mind being forgotten but I dread forgetting myself, so I'm glad I got some things down just in case. Not the events so much but the people who were such an important part of them.

I've referred to Hilary Innes in the book a few times but I haven't told you about Peter Beck, who has played almost as big a role in my professional life as Hilary. Peter was the co-creator and executive producer of *Talkin' 'Bout Your Generation* and is the executive producer of *Mad as Hell*. He is an indispensable part of my life and a good friend. I owe them both so much.

I've mentioned Ted Emery but not his talented protégé Jon Olb, who has helmed *Newstopiä, Talkin' 'Bout Your Generation* and *Mad as Hell* as director and without whom I would be lost.

I also haven't mentioned my three wonderful sisters, Tracee, Tammy and Mandy, because I think they deserve their privacy. Also, their names sound like I've made them up. Tracee is a lawyer, Tammy the operations manager at an aviation company and Mandy is a nurse. They're all a lot smarter than me and I love them dearly.

My mother and father I have mentioned in this book but not by name. That's because I've presented them almost as cartoon characters. In real life they are fully rounded three-dimensional human beings without whom I'd be somebody else or not at all. Their names are Judy and Fred.

I also want to take this opportunity to thank (and apologise for otherwise leaving out of the book) the following people who have done their best to help me avoid tripping over myself: Miss Brooks, Miss Flaharty, Mark O'Loughlin, Kevin Ward, Steve Walsh QC, Deslie Billich, Michael Steele, Michael Davis, Peter Jones, John Connolly, John Toole, Kate Jordan-Moore, Tim Potter, Mark Thomas, Peter Goers, Tony Roberts, Maree Tomasetti, Jack Higham, Denis Watkins, Geoff Portmann, Rory Callaghan, Michael Healy, Paul Clarke, Mark Fennessy, Matt Campbell, Matt Saville, Brendan Dahill, Leonie Lowe, Karchi Magyar, Yuri Worontschak, Gail Mayes, Ken Hardie, Scott Findlay, Olivia Hiddlestone, Tarni James, Adrian Swift, David Mott, Andy Matthews, Pat McCaffrie, David M. Green, and Anita Punton.

Also, for helping me make sure I didn't avoid *Tripping Over Myself*: Arwen Summers, Emily Hart, Sonja Heijn, Brent Lukey, Reg Abos, Graeme Jones and Emma Schwarcz.

And finally— oh, that's enough.

# Appendix A

It's not every day you meet an icon. For me it was last Thursday. The icon? Jerry Lewis.

Jerry Lewis has been a rather large comedy icon for fifty years. From the early days as half of one of the most successful comedy teams of all time to maturity as a solo act which saw him become the most popular film comedian in the English-speaking world, Jerry Lewis casts a giant shadow. More than one critic has observed that love him or hate him (and for most it's a case of one or the other), he's impossible to ignore.

At seventy-four he's enjoying what he calls his 'chevalier' years, performing to his fourth generation of fans. 'It's phenomenal,' he says, citing a recent experience in Las Vegas. 'I had a grandmother who saw me when she was a kid who brought her daughter, who brought her daughter, who brought her daughter of fourteen years. It's very stirring.' The show he puts on for this new legion of fans reaches across his whole career. Way back to the 'record act' (lip-synching to Mario Lanza) which he did as a struggling stand-up in the Catskills in the early '40s, through tap dancing, cane routines, a magic act, to conducting the orchestra (a perennial Martin and Lewis bit). He sings too. 'That Old Black Magic' from *The Nutty Professor* (1963); a Jolson medley which is as much a tribute to Lewis's father, Danny, as to Jolson himself; and 'Rock-a-bye Your Baby', which was a number one hit for Lewis in 1957. 'That was a fluke. That was weird,' he says of the record's success (it in fact outsold Al Jolson's original). He recreates some classic moments from his films ('The Typewriter' song from *Who's Minding the Store*, 1963) and shows clips of others. Of course he mugs, tells jokes and does shtick. And of course the crowd love it.

Tellingly, the film clips he shows are only from those movies he wrote, directed and produced himself. He's especially proud of them. Not, one suspects, just for the comedy they contain but for the film-making processes that created them. Looking at a photo-spread of the huge open dolls house set he had built over two sound stages for *The Ladies Man* (1961), Lewis pointed out to me the monitors he used as part of a video-assist system he developed to enable him to direct a scene he was appearing in. Essentially it is the video-split system de rigueur on all film sets today but back in the late '50s, when Lewis decided he wanted to direct himself, no such thing existed.

Ironically though, despite being such an innovator himself, Lewis is not a great fan of the way film comedy is made today. 'There's too much technology now,' he says. 'The film-maker doesn't need to know anything anymore. He sits with an electrician … there's no more sitting at the moviola with the film in your hands, marking it with a white crayon: "cut it on that frame", "God damn it that's wrong", "it's gotta be two frames later". That's gone.' Nor does Lewis like the trend in modern comedy films to allow the stuntman to take the fall, or for the physical comedy to be helped in any way by computer graphics. Part of his chevalier years involves putting together deals to remake his films. *The Nutty Professor* with Eddie Murphy was heavy with special effects and Lewis is keen to avoid this happening again. Of the proposed remakes now on the drawing board – *The Bellboy* (1960), *Cinderfella* (1960), *The Errand Boy* (1961) and *The Family Jewels* (1965) – Lewis vows, 'There will no special effects.' He warms to the topic.

I show a clip in the show which taught me a great deal. We did the barbells in *The Nutty Professor* (where the professor's arms are stretched to the floor by the weight) and when it was over I said, 'I think I would be remiss if I didn't tell you, ladies and gentlemen, that there were no special effects in those arms. We did that.' And they cheered. And I said, 'Holy shit they're smarter than we thought.' I worked my heart out eleven hours to get that joke to work.

Even assuming Lewis can convince the studios to avoid the CGI work in these remakes, who would he get to play the Jerry Lewis role? Jim Carrey would seem to many to be an obvious choice, but not as far as Lewis himself is concerned. While conceding that Carrey is a fine physical comedian, there is something he doesn't connect with in the younger comic. He prefers Mike Myers. And in fact is talking to him at the moment about doing *The Errand Boy*. I rather suspect that Jim Carrey would be able to do any number of the remakes extraordinarily well – *Liar Liar* (1997) was basically a Jerry Lewis film – but the big risk would be that the public would view them as simple re-enactments of the original films rather than re-interpretations. It would be as pointless as Gus Van Sant's shot-by-shot remake of *Psycho*. And despite the surface similarities between Lewis and Carrey, it is Mike Myers who is closer in spirit to Lewis when it comes to screen performance. Carrey is certainly very funny but there's a slight menace about him when he's playing his overtly comic roles. Something which makes it hard to warm to him or care about what happens to the character. Myers might not necessarily be as manic as Carrey, or as good an actor, or even as funny – but one can see in *Austin Powers: International Man of Mystery* (1997) something of the throwaway quality and spontaneity of Lewis's self-directed work. Plus he shares Lewis's penchant for multiple roles. Says Lewis, 'Most of the people that wrote (about *Austin Powers*) accused him of being influenced by my work, and he gave an interview to *The New York Times* and he said, "I don't have to apologise for being influenced by Jerry Lewis. I wish the hell I had more of it." He was very nice about it.' Older comics like Steve Martin, Chevy Chase, Martin Short and Robin Williams also happily admit being influenced.

Williams is another comic Lewis says he is keen to work with. Certainly his recent crop of film roles fit into the clown-with-a-heart range of Lewis's work. But this isn't the first time Lewis has looked for someone to take on the chore of playing the Jerry Lewis role in his films. As far back as 1966 he told *Cahiers du Cinéma* that he was looking forward to moving behind the camera – 'My ass is sore from years of taking pratfalls' – and finding a new kid to put in front of it.

In fact Woody Allen came to him in 1965 and asked him to direct a film script he'd just written. Allen considered Lewis to be the 'greatest comedian's director around'. Whether Lewis could have adapted his approach to suit the Woody Allen persona is another thing. In *One More Time* (1970), Lewis's only directorial effort in which he doesn't star, the film's lead, Sammy Davis Jnr, appears, at certain times, to be doing a Jerry Lewis impression. In any event Lewis advised Allen to direct it himself (and indeed later, Allen would have to contend with his actors doing impressions of him).

Lewis has always been generous with comedy advice and encouraging of younger performers. At Paramount in the '60s he ran comedy workshops for potential comedians, comedy writers and 'anyone who was interested in comedy'.

He lectured at the University of Southern California's film school about his films and film-making in general. He recalls showing a young student's film to his class and saying, 'That's what film-making is all about.' The film was *Amblin'* and the young student was Steven Spielberg. He had an open set policy on his own films. A young Francis Ford Coppola would come down and sit in the studio bleachers day after day and watch Lewis shooting *The Ladies Man*. A generation of new comedians have directly and indirectly benefited from his work. It's unlikely that Woody Allen and Mel Brooks would have been as easily able to produce and direct their own work had Lewis not paved the way. Lewis was the first American comic in the sound era to do it. And only the second in the history of film-making after Charlie Chaplin.

As a younger man Lewis himself received advice from an older film comedian which he says was invaluable.

Stan Laurel says to me one day, 'Never ever ever fool with the rule of three.' I said, 'I know what you're talking about.' He said, 'No you don't. Listen to my three. (1) Tell the audience you're going to do something. (2) Then do it. (3) Then let them know it's been done.' The most brilliant information I ever got.

It's significant that Laurel's advice was more about the audience than it was about the gag itself, for at the end of the day it is ultimately all about the audience, according to Lewis. It's about the laughs. The veteran comic says he no longer cares what the critics have to say. He doesn't even have too much time for what film scholars might read into his work either – even if it's positive.

> If you're getting into the work I've done you're getting into low-brow. The critic is obsessed with snobbery. He'd like to go to the theatre and critique John Gielgud because look at the assignment he's got – John Gielgud! But you take this fop who now has to write about Jerry Lewis and he's demeaned by that. Therefore he can't like it.

He prefers the critic who simply reports that the crowd is laughing. 'They (the audience) give me all the information I need,' he says.

Probably the most important audience Jerry Lewis ever played to was at the Olympia in Paris in about 1970. Jean-Luc Godard was there. Francois Truffaut was there. Maria Callas, Catherine Deneuve. 'The first 400 seats was the cream of show business, theatre music, film,' says Lewis. But these people weren't as important to him as the small white-haired man watching him from the lighting box. Charlie Chaplin. Lewis wasn't even aware he was up there at the time. He found out later. 'And it was the most glorious triumph of my life,' says Lewis.

Later, when the two men met, the older comic asked the younger one to name a gift. Lewis demurred but Chaplin insisted. And after thinking long and hard Lewis asked for a mint condition copy of his favourite Chaplin film, *Modern Times*. Chaplin agreed, but only on the condition that Lewis send him a copy of *The Bellboy*. He shakes his head at the memory of it all. 'Jesus, I couldn't catch my breath.' Over thirty years later he still can't quite believe it. 'First of all I now know I'm getting *Modern Times*, right? But, he wants mine? The gooseflesh on my body ...'

We get the wind up and I realise that the Chaplin story is the last one I'll hear. I also realise that I've been speaking to a very happy man, rather than an icon.

As we rise to say goodbye I also notice that I'm actually about four inches taller than Jerry Lewis. I don't know why but I always thought we'd be the same height. I shake hands with the man and say goodbye. Of course as soon as he's out of the room he becomes an icon again. And taller. Go figure.

Published in *The Sunday Age*, July 2000

# Appendix B

## THINLY SLICED CLEESE

John Cleese is on the phone from Boston, Massachusetts. He's explaining the reason he's a bit late (it's only five minutes) was because the fire alarm went off and everyone in the hotel had to evacuate. He's back in his room now. 'Hang on, Shaun, I must listen to this announcement.' I listen with Cleese to the pre-recorded message being piped into his room explaining that it was a drill and that the hotel is not actually on fire. 'American panic,' he decides. I am seized with a nerdish instinct to bring up the fire drill scene in 'The Germans' episode of *Fawlty Towers* (series 1, episode 6) but mercifully contain it. 'Now, is this interview about *Spamalot*?' asks Cleese.

Cleese does have a bit on at the moment. He's in Boston to meet with Steve Martin, with whom he is co-starring in the sequel to last year's *Pink Panther*. He's taking over the role of

Chief Inspector Dreyfus from Kevin Kline. Cleese is due to start shooting the day after next 'and I've got to go off and figure out whether or not I'm going to do it in a French accent'.

I confirm that we are indeed talking about *Spamalot*. Like *Pink Panther*, *Spamalot* is what the Americans call a 're-imagining' of an original work; it's a stage musical version of the original cult film success, *Monty Python and the Holy Grail*. The Australian production of the Broadway hit starts in a few weeks but must seem a million miles away for Cleese, who co-wrote the script with fellow Pythons Graham Chapman, Michael Palin, Terry Jones, Eric Idle and Terry Gilliam way back in 1973. The film was done on a shoestring; a contrast to the spectacular budget for the lavish stage version he saw premiere at the Shubert Theatre on March 17, 2005. We guess at how much money *Spamalot* cost to mount; I'm way off, suggesting a mere ten to fifteen times the cost of the film.

'Well, I think the film was made on a budget of £240,000 and I don't know what the *Spamalot* one was but I think a lot more than twenty times more than that,' says Cleese, cheerily but with a pang of envy.

I mean, we had so little money that we only had about four or five umbrellas and it was raining all the time so we all got wet every day. Then we were staying in a hotel where only half the crew got hot water, because there wasn't enough, so there was this terrible scramble. The first assistant said, 'It's a wrap', everybody was sprinting for the cars trying to get back to the hotel. And just before we went up there the producer rang me up and said, 'Do you mind sharing a hotel room?' I said, 'I thought I was supposed to be a film star. I don't think film stars share hotel rooms.'

Of course, since that film, Cleese has become a very famous film star. But suppose *Monty Python and the Holy Grail* had not been a low-budget film and had been a musical in the first place. If he'd auditioned for the roles he wrote for himself – Lancelot, Tim the Enchanter, the French Taunter – would he have got them?

'Nope, not at all because I am so terrible at anything musical,' he admits.

I mean this is how terrible I am; I was asked in 1965 when I was in New York to audition for a musical called *Half a Sixpence* with Tommy Steele. And I went along and I read the script and made them laugh, you know, but then they asked me to sing and I said, 'I can't sing.' And they said, 'Well, you know, sing something.' I said, 'I don't know anything.' They said, 'Well can you sing your national anthem?' and I said, 'Probably – how does it go?' which got a laugh. Then I sang it and went off thinking how hilarious it was and the next I got a call saying 'you've got the part'. And I called my agent and he said, 'Well you'll only be on stage for the chorus numbers, it won't matter.' So I went there and learned the dance movements, you know, which weren't difficult, thank God, because I have no talent for that either. And I was just galloping around on stage and mouthing. And after about six weeks I joined in one evening just for fun because I was loosening up a bit and that night the musical director was waiting for me outside my dressing room when I came out and he said, 'John, are you singing?'

His appalling singing was what eventually led to Cleese being sacked from *Half a Sixpence*, which was ultimately a good thing because he went back to England, worked on *The Frost Report*, met Idle, Palin and Jones, reunited with Chapman, called up Gilliam who he'd met in the United States and a few years later they all gave birth to *Monty Python's Flying Circus*.

Like a lot of Python output, *Spamalot* was born of conflict. Terry Jones told me in 2003 that Eric Idle's nose was out of joint with them all because they'd sort of agreed to put on a Python reunion show in Las Vegas but then Jones and Michael Palin and then Terry Gilliam decided they didn't want to do it and pulled out. Idle didn't participate in the BBC 35th anniversary reunion show in 2004 (apart from a pre-recorded piece) and went off by himself across the United States doing a Python show on his own. It was quite successful for him and in his downtime he conceived of *Spamalot*, a musical stage version of *Monty Python and the Holy Grail* – which was itself in the first place a bit of a nod to the musical *Camelot*. He downloaded the script from the net and began tinkering, contacting the others in the team by email and getting their views. Cleese had his doubts. 'I mean, I wasn't sure if it was going to work but when I discovered that Eric had got Mike (*The Graduate*) Nichols directing it, that was the moment that I thought okay, because you know, I knew Eric was going to write good songs and funny lines but you need someone who knows how to shape it.'

Unlike the first screening of *Monty Python and the Holy Grail* to investors – which was greeted with very few laughs and required a re-edit – *Spamalot* was greeted very warmly by the audience. But what did Cleese think of seeing other people perform Python material? 'I was very pleasantly surprised by how much I enjoyed it,' he says.

I was surprised at times that the longer dialogue scenes seemed to work on stage. It surprised me because the audience was laughing a lot at them and I would have cut them myself because I would have assumed they wouldn't have worked at the original length. I thought the songs were excellent. I'd heard them before on a tape that Eric had sent us, but it was the atmosphere that I loved. It was a really fun, silly, sort of pantomime evening with everyone having a wonderful time and I think it was something about being in New York at that time, with everyone being so depressed about George Bush – you suddenly thought 'My God, silliness is still viable.'

Silliness was and is the chief ingredient of Python but the thing about 're-imaginings' is that sometimes, as might be argued in the case of the 2006 *Pink Panther*, it's like taking the ingredients for the recipe of a cake you like and using them to make a risotto. The flavour might be there but it's all rather odd.

And *Spamalot* is an odd musical. Most of the audience are going to walk into the theatre knowing the dialogue, but not the songs. Usually it's the other way around with musicals. Stephen Hall, a talented young comedian who plays Cleese's roles in the Australian version (Hank Azaria did them on Broadway), says he had his lines down twenty years before the audition. Cleese laughs:

> Yes, well it was like that when we used to do the stage show. I mean, there was a time once when Michael Palin broke me up – he ad-libbed something – and by the time I had recovered from laughing I'd forgot where we were and I just said to the audience, 'What's the next line?' and about sixty people shouted it out.

All of the film's famous set pieces are in the stage version and the dialogue is mostly left alone. But there is added dialogue and some of these new bits may rankle Python purists. As they've been added by Eric Idle, one can't be heard to complain too loudly, but I do so with Cleese anyway about a new line added to Cleese's own Tim the Enchanter scene. It's where, after Tim has been exploding things and being eerie in an eccentric Scottish accent, he introduces himself as 'Tim'. Idle has Sir Robin (his character in the original film) turn around and say, sarcastically,

'Ooh, what a scary name.' It's a line that just seems wrong to me and I ask if Cleese could please get Idle to remove it. There's a moment's pause on the end of the line and then:

> Well I think you're right actually. That's very smart of you if I may say so – if it doesn't sound condescending – because you're right. I did notice that line at the time and I remember thinking it sounded strange because it's sort of explaining the joke. Tim is not a very scary name, and I think because it makes you think of timid and timorous, you see what I mean? Very good point, I'll have a word with Eric about it.

I leave off recommending any further revisions. The show has been doing perfectly well without me, let's face it. Without Cleese and the others too. 'We don't have to do anything at all. We just can sit here and count the money,' says Cleese. Although, in a way, Cleese will be casting a watchful eye from above during the Australian production. He plays the Voice of God (albeit in pre-recorded form). *New Yorker* critic John Lahr wrote that it was a part Cleese was born to play. And Cleese is particularly pleased with the casting of Bille (*The Judas Kiss, Exit the King*) Brown as Arthur.

> Well, Bille's a terrific actor you see. Bill was in Fierce Creatures with me and I just thought he was marvellous and then when I did a little stage show in New Zealand, which was about fifteen months ago, Bill directed it, so

he's an old friend. I wrote a note and I recommended him because I think he is a terrific performer.

Just as Steve Martin took over Peter Sellers's Clouseau in the re-imagining of *The Pink Panther* and made it into something else again, the Australian cast of *Spamalot* will no doubt make the characters of *Monty Python and the Holy Grail* their own.

And while this is happening, Cleese will be making Chief Inspector Dreyfus his own too. 'I'm looking forward to it because I love those old movies,' says Cleese, 'and I knew Sellers when he was doing them.'

I nerdishly gabble on about *The Magic Christian*, a film he made with Sellers in the late '60s; it's the only time the two comedians worked on screen together and it's one of my favourite films. Cleese is a snooty Sotheby's art expert selling a Renoir to Sellers, only to watch in horror as the latter instructs his son (Ringo Starr) to cut out the nose because 'he only likes the noses'. 'Yeah, but I watched it the other day and I played it much too slowly,' says Cleese. He agrees there's a special way of performing revue material that isn't like real acting. 'Oh yes,' says Cleese, 'it's got to be much more energetic.'

Still, I hope he plays Dreyfus in an English accent.*

**Published in *The Saturday Age*, October 2007**

---

* He did. When I met him a few years later (he made a guest appearance on *Talkin' 'Bout Your Generation*), I reminded him of the interview. 'Oh, did you see that film?' he asked, half amused/half appalled. 'It was *terrible*.'

# Appendix C

## THE RICKY ROAD TO FAME*

*In his first Australian interview since* The Office, *Ricky Gervais speaks to Shaun Micallef about the new ABC comedy* Extras.

I'm keen for Ricky Gervais not to think me an idiot. So far my plan is not working. I've arranged through various intermediaries that he ring me at the studios at Vega so I can record the interview professionally. Unfortunately I have no idea what I'm doing. He's rung three times in the last five minutes and obviously can't hear me when I press various buttons and try and talk to him. On the last call he says 'Hullo?' with what sounds like at least a small measure of irritation and then hangs up with what I fear might perhaps have been a large measure of finality. With mounting panic I

---

* This is most definitely *not* my pun. I think I titled the piece 'Prized Gervais', which is marginally better.

press another unlikely combination of buttons and hope like hell he rings again. This is the only Australian interview Ricky Gervais is giving about his much anticipated follow-up series to *The Office* and I suspect that most people are going to want to hear more about it than 'Hullo?'

Fortunately Ricky does try again and gets through. Even more fortunately for me, he's perfectly nice about it all, claiming that he too is terrible with machines. In fact he's just left one, an Avid, in order to talk with me. An Avid is an edit suite and Gervais is in the middle of putting together the *second* series of *Extras*. As with the first series, which airs on the ABC Wednesdays at 9.00 pm (from August 16th), he is not only the star but also, with Stephen Merchant, the co-writer and co-director.

But I'm confused – in the first series of *Extras*, which follows the set-to-set travails of a couple of background actors, Gervais plays Andy, an extra who gave up his job in a bank to become a star and who, in order to become that star, connives and hustles and eventually writes a sitcom script that sounds remarkably like *The Office*. By the end of the series Andy looks well on his way to becoming as successful as Ricky Gervais. How does he end up as an extra again in the second series?

'Well, [the second series] starts with me on the day that I'm going to record my sitcom for the BBC,' says Gervais, 'and he fails miserably because everybody interferes so now he's doing this very broad camp comedy that's been designed by committee and interfered with. It's everything he didn't want it to be – it's on BBC1, it's filmed in front of a live studio audience, it's just banal and watered down and begging for ratings and aimed at, you know, thickos and their kids.' Needless to say it doesn't work and Andy ends up back where he started.

Obviously this wasn't the fate of the real version of *The Office* but given that so much of the uncomfortable humour of *The Office* is based in truth I wonder whether Gervais had to dodge this type of interference in order to bring the appalling David Brent to life. The answer surprises me, as it might anyone who has worked in, or perhaps even just watched, television. 'Well, we didn't, because I just went in there and said we're doing it this way or not at all. And miraculously they went, "Yeah, all right, whatever." I think because we were low risk, you know, it was very cheap to make, they put it out in the summer.'

This sort of chutzpah has stood Gervais in good stead. Making *The Office* on his terms and having it be a success has enabled him to make *Extras* exactly the way he wants to and because that success also extended to the United States (he picked up a Golden Globe and the American version of the show starring Steve Carell is now in its third season) he has been able to lure stars like Ben Stiller, Kate Winslet, Samuel L. Jackson and Patrick Stewart to act alongside him. And though it is because of David Brent that Gervais gets to do what he wants, Gervais has decided not to play David Brent in *Extras*. Mind you, he's almost the only one in the series who isn't. Ben

Stiller, in particular, seems very Brentish in the first episode. 'In a way the David Brent character is sort of anyone who is sort of pompous and desperate,' explains Gervais, 'you know, we inject a little bit of that into all the other players.' There is a pause and then Gervais momentarily turns into David Brent for me: 'Wherever there's pomposity mixed with pretension and neediness – there's a little bit of Brent Dust.'

Gervais's new character, Andy, has a lot more self-awareness than David Brent ever had. He's also better looking, more talented, and actually has a decent sense of humour. Andy makes jokes that are actually funny. They're often nasty jokes about other people which reveal his own shortcomings as a human being, but they're good jokes nonetheless. We're laughing a lot more *with* Gervais's new character than we ever did with David Brent. 'And that was a conscious decision,' says Gervais. 'We thought it would be best for me not to be the lead funny-man so it moved it away from Brent, you know. So we tried to make it as different as we could without losing our style of comedy.' In fact, Gervais is almost the straight man in this series. He's the one who suffers the fools – all close relations of the fool he played previously – and he does so with a mix of eye-rolling, muttering under his breath and outright rudeness. 'But strangely,' says Gervais, 'you don't laugh as much *with* Andy as you laugh *at* David Brent … I still think the heartier laugh is probably from laughing *at* someone – their delusion, or their misunderstanding or their mistake.' That's not to say Andy doesn't regularly humiliate himself for our amusement. Usually it's in front of a large group of his peers or a big Hollywood star or someone else who can end his career. For an extra who craves the limelight he seems pathologically incapable of doing anything other than embarrass himself when he becomes the centre of attention. Or perhaps that's why he becomes the centre of attention. Either way, it's funny.

Ditching David Brent for a whole new character is a risky thing for Gervais to do. Any comedian who hits pay-dirt with a comic creation could be forgiven for mining that seam for as long as the audience wants him to. Yet this is not Gervais's way. David Brent was all over after two series and a couple of Christmas specials (and one slightly ill-fitting *Simpsons* episode). He uses his cachet in Hollywood and his considerable clout back home in the UK to simply do projects that interest him, like stand-up comedy (*Ricky Gervais Live: Animals* and *Ricky Gervais Live 2: Politics*), being the voice of a fat pigeon (*Valiant*), or a role in a Christopher Guest film (*For Your Consideration*). 'One of my comedy heroes,' says Gervais of Guest. '*Spinal Tap*. The biggest influence on me, you know. Straightforward influence on *The Office*.' It proved to be something of a mutual admiration society. 'He was a fan of *The Office*,' continues Gervais. 'Him and his wife, Jamie Lee Curtis, gave *The Office* DVDs as presents to all their friends a few years ago and then he contacted me and we just sort of became friends. So when he said he was writing a part for me it was like I'd won a competition.' Gervais interviews

Guest in another of his projects, *Ricky Gervais Meets ...* It's a five-part series where Gervais interviews his comedy heroes, who also include Garry Shandling, Larry David, 'the *Simpsons* guys' and John Cleese. A five-part series is unusual. Networks usually want a block of at least six or eight, preferably ten. 'It's five because I can't think of a sixth I want to do. It's as simple as that,' says Gervais. 'These are five people in the world in comedy who I really, really want to sit down and talk to.'

John Cleese has been the biggest influence on Gervais growing up and since he's been doing his comedy but his earliest influence was Laurel and Hardy. And it's an influence that is still felt. In fact, you can see quite a bit of Oliver Hardy in Gervais's long-suffering Andy of *Extras*. 'That's exactly right!' enthuses Gervais. 'I think of everything in terms of Laurel and Hardy, really. Because, you know, if you look at Tim and Gareth (in *The Office*), that was Stan and Ollie ... And this [Andy in *Extras*] is much more Ollie than Stan ... it's fun to play Stan, but it's nice to play Ollie as well now and again.'

This seems pretty much the key to Ricky Gervais. He's at the point in his career where he has the freedom to do whatever he wants and he chooses to do things that he thinks will be fun. Usually these are projects that he writes and over which he has the greater level of creative control, but not always. For example, he wrote and starred in a recent episode of *The Simpsons*. 'Now that wasn't my thing but it's the greatest comedy show on TV and I thought that'd be fun,' he says, 'and the fun for me was doing it, not particularly the results or whether it upped my profile.'

Gervais speaks about his work and his abilities with a refreshing lack of false modesty, but this should not be misinterpreted as a lack of genuine modesty. He told me about having turned down a number of film roles (*Mission: Impossible III* and *The Da Vinci Code*, for example), plus several others which required him to play the leading man, which he says is ridiculous. I ask why. 'Because I wouldn't pay ten dollars to see me in a film,' he says. I point out that Peter Sellers played a leading man and he wasn't exactly a leading man type (and if I'd thought about it some more I could have listed almost every other film comedian star since movies began). Gervais says that Sellers did what he was good at and 'I know what I'm good at and what I'm good at is acting in something I've written for me – and then I make sure it's directed how I want it to be directed.'

Gervais may have chutzpah and a certainty about where his talents lie but he remains a little gob-smacked at his success. 'I've been incredibly lucky. I don't know why it's gone so well. I really don't understand it. I think it's because I've never bluffed. I've always said, "Do it like that or I'm not interested" – I do it graciously, but I really can walk away. I don't want to make it at any cost.' Is it because he's not actually hungry for success that he has achieved?

Well, I'm not hungry for fame – and I think that's what sometimes makes people make bad decisions. They just think 'well, if I just get on telly and do this then someone will see me and I'll get that' and it just doesn't work. Go straight to what you want to do ... Why would I do a panel show to get recognised so they let me write my own sitcom? Just write your own sitcom. If they don't take it, then someone will. Do you know what I mean? I've never understood this.

But Gervais does understand this. Whether he knows it or not he's describing the plight of his own character Andy in *Extras*, who is prepared to debase himself to any depth to get just a single line in a movie. He'll undergo any humiliation and every compromise imaginable to become a proper actor, even if it means selling his own sitcom down the toilet.

Fortunately for us this is not something Ricky Gervais will have to do anytime soon.

**Published in *The Age*, August 2006**